THE VOID, THE GRID & THE SIGN

THE VOID, THE GRID & THE SIGN

Traversing the Great Basin   William L. Fox

UNIVERSITY OF NEVADA PRESS ▲▲ RENO & LAS VEGAS

The Void, the Grid, & the Sign: Traversing the Great Basin
was first published by The University of Utah Press in the
United States in 2000. The University of Nevada Press
edition is published by agreement with William L. Fox.

University of Nevada Press, Reno, Nevada 89557 USA
Manufactured in the United States of America
Cover design by Carrie House
Library of Congress Cataloging-in-Publication Data
Fox, William L., 1949–
The void, the grid & the sign : traversing the Great Basin /
William L. Fox.
p. cm.
Originally published: Salt Lake City : University of
Utah Press, © 2000
Includes bibliographical references.
ISBN 0-87417-618-2 (pbk. : alk. paper)
1. Great Basin—Description and travel. 2. Great Basin—
Geography. 3. Great Basin—Discovery and exploration.
4. Human geography—Great Basin. 5. Natural history—
Great Basin. 6. Fox, William L., 1949—Travel—Great
Basin. 7. Cartography—Great Basin—History.
I. Title: Void, the grid, and the sign. II. Title.
F789.F69   2005
917.9'04—dc22   2004025918
The paper used in this book meets the requirements
of American National Standard for Information Sciences
—Permanence of Paper for Printed Library Materials,
ANSI/NISO Z39.48-1992 (R2002). Binding materials were
selected for strength and durability.

University of Nevada Press Paperback Edition, 2003

ISBN-13: 978-0-87417-618-6

for Beth
  and the Boys

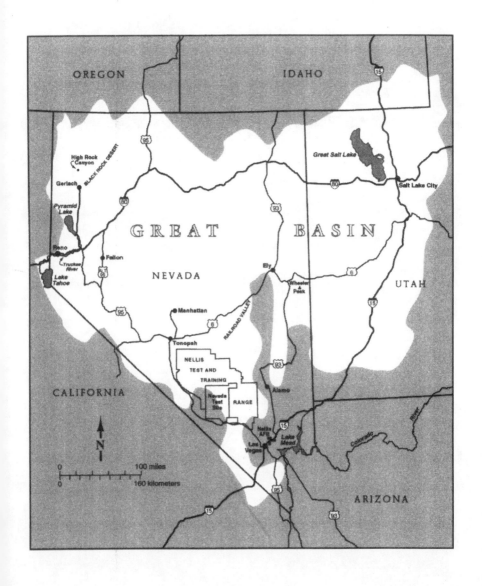

CONTENTS

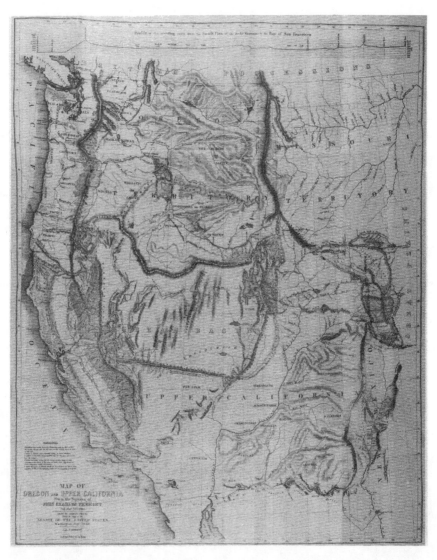

Map, dated 1848, drawn by Charles Pruess, cartographer for John Charles Frémont's second expedition of 1843, showing the nonexistant range of mountains in the lower Great Basin.

Of Parallax and Privacy

T HE DESERT MORE often appears to us as space, not place. Uninhabited land is what we take to be the former, while the latter is invested with our presence. Another way of saying it is that we think of the desert as undifferentiated land, an area without landmarks, hence not a landscape. Land is a state of matter, landscape a state of mind, and the desert is notoriously resistant to colonization.

Comparatively few Americans live in the desert, hence our culture has only a relatively small body of art and literature to guide our expectations and perceptions in the drylands. We have trouble, therefore, perceiving its physical and cultural boundaries, contours, and contrasts. The desert has few easily discernible landmarks and is thus a topography where few if any memories accumulate. Time seems to pass without much perceptible effect. We label desert the "void" and move over its surface, looking at it from different angles in an attempt to establish the sight lines and degrees of parallax necessary to measure it. We map the void with a grid of intersecting lines and travel along them, erecting signs to guide us.

The Great Basin is only one of America's four deserts, but, though it shares this designation with its hotter cousins to the south, the Mojave and Chihuahuan Deserts, and the almost perversely lush Sonoran, the Basin is the largest and least inhabited of them. The heart of the Great Basin lies within Nevada, where this book "takes place." It's a high and dry region where all waters flow inward, a land that Native Americans, ranchers, miners, and others have inhabited successfully for centuries—but it's also one that most people find visually intolerable. We drive as fast as we can across its immense salt flats on improbably straight roads, and from the air-conditioned cockpits of our vehicles erect the illusion that it looks more like the surface of Mars than of Earth. We treat it as if it were science fiction and in our minds populate it with alien spacecraft.

It is often said of deserts that they are where the Prime Mover was practicing before making the rest of the world. Such definitions imply that the desert is where we are closest to the creative spirit of the universe, and it's not coincidental that several of the world's great monotheisms were born and raised in the desert. Salt Lake City, the home of Mormonism, is the largest city within the Great Basin; the other large city nearest the region is Las Vegas, which has more churches per capita than any other city in America. Interstate freeway signs heading into the Basin from Los Angeles display the mileage to one atop the other. We call the desert a wilderness, the closest synonym in the dictionary for which is "wasteland," and can't decide which it is. We turn wilderness into parks and wastelands into nuclear dumps. The Great Basin hosts both, like other deserts a home to the anomalies of the divine.

I am preoccupied with our opposing needs to preserve this void for the sake of our national imagination, versus attempting to colonize it with overlayers of maps, roads, and signs. We seek to neutralize our fear of the void, yet court its essence. The influence of these contradictions on how we both view and actually inhabit the Great Basin is the subject of this book.

The first section, "The Void," describes how the Great Basin appears to us, and examines how the artist Michael Heizer articulates a specific subset of the void in his immense and mysterious sculpture *City*, which he has been working on since 1970. Heizer's work, which has provoked reactions ranging from awe to dismay over the scale of his earthmoving, offers us an opportunity to examine how our perceptions attempt to cope with large empty places. The next section traces how the evolution of cartography intersected with the exploration of the region so that we could "grid" the void—and shows how that grid, the map, is read and misread. The third and final section examines the language we place around the void, how we extract metaphor from everything in the Great Basin from ancient petroglyphs to the neon of Las Vegas, and explores further how Heizer's work relates to research done by his father, Dr. Robert F. Heizer, the preeminent archeologist.

The people in this book with whom I've been privileged to travel through the Great Basin know how much of it is surprisingly fragile, dangerous, on

Of Parallax and Privacy

private property, or simply off-limits. Although the sites of some petroglyphs on public land are well known, others are held in as much deliberate isolation by the Bureau of Land Management and other agencies as it is possible to achieve. The only hope for survival of the rock art is obscurity, and I have been deliberately vague about the locations. Michael Heizer's sculpture is on private land somewhere in central-eastern Nevada. Because it is an active construction site, that's all he will acknowledge for now. If a lack of precise directions seems at times odd to the reader, it's because I've tried to not provide clues as to the whereabouts of certain cultural resources, an admittedly precarious stance from which to write a book.

NUMEROUS PEOPLE throughout the years have helped me explore the Great Basin and our ideas about it, and without them this book would not have been possible. Alvin McLane has shared with me for more than twenty-five years his extensive collection of nineteenth- and twentieth-century maps, journals, expedition reports, and rock art records. Michael Heizer is an extremely private man, who, despite his disabilities and the enormous tasks facing him in completing *City*, has lent me his time and archives. Jennifer Mackiewicz and Mary Shanahan, Michael's assistants, have been gracious and knowledgeable hosts. Craig Schriber and Stephanie Kruse have generously allowed me to camp out in their guest room in the years since I moved from Reno, and without such a base I would never have been able to return as often as I have.

Dan Welch of Santa Fe, formerly of the Zen Center in San Francisco, introduced me to the Buddhist concepts of void in the kitchen of Deborah Madison and Patrick McFarland, while Steve Glotfelty at the Sierra Mountaineer in Reno helped me comb topographical maps for evidence of it.

Friends and colleagues at the University of Nevada, Reno, who have provided advice and support include Cheryll Glotfelty and Scott Slovic of the Center for Environmental Arts and Humanities, Bob Blesse at Special Collections, and Paul Starrs in the Geography Department. The Hilliard Fellowship Committee kindly provided me a chance to try out some of these ideas as a visiting scholar in the spring of 1998. In addition, the brilliant independent scholar Rebecca Solnit and the writer/editor Greg McNamee prodded me to think more deeply about a variety of cognitive issues.

Babette McCormick, who has generously funded a number of art projects in Nevada, provided a grant that enabled me to do the fieldwork, as well as to write a substantial portion of the manuscript.

Most sincere thanks go to Dawn Marano, my editor at the University of Utah Press, who has been sympathetic and sensitive while rummaging deep in the innards of the manuscript to tune it for publication.

The Void, the Grid, & the Sign is a creative nonfiction by a certified nonspecialist, and I assume all responsibility for its speculations, none of which can be laid at the feet of the above, nor at those of the sources quoted.

Of Parallax and Privacy

THE VOID

I have nothing to say, and I am saying it.
    —John Cage

Those who hasten toward it dare not enter, fearing to hurtle down through the void with nothing to cling to or to stay their fall. So they look to the brink and retreat. This refers to all those who seek such a goal through cognition.
    —Huang Po

THE GREAT BASIN: diameter 11° of latitude, 10° of longitude: elevation above the sea between 4 and 5000 feet: surrounded by mountains: contents almost unknown, but believed to be filled with rivers and lakes which have no communication with the sea, deserts and oases which have never been explored, and savage tribes, which no traveller has seen or described.
    —John C. Frémont

❧

ONE
୧

THE WHITE Dodge Ram pickup flies over a hump in the dirt road then thumps down decisively on the other side, just in time to take the shallow curve at fifty miles an hour, startling a pronghorn a hundred yards ahead and to our left. The antelope-like buck springs gracefully off southward into the sagebrush, our tires bite deeply into the dirt, and we careen around the bend. Mike Heizer drives with his right hand, the fingers of his left paralyzed from a neural condition that now severely limits his physical activities. In his early fifties and weathered to a crisp, Heizer is pensive this afternoon. I'm visiting from Los Angeles, here to get a desert fix for my addiction that stems from having lived for thirty-three years in Nevada. Between us sits Mary Shanahan, one of his assistants.

"No such things as flying saucers," Heizer growls. A world-renowned sculptor who makes the largest earthworks on the planet, he has bulldozed hundreds of thousands of cubic yards of dirt and gravel during the last quarter century to carve out elegant and mysterious negative spaces on the valley floors of the Great Basin. The sculptures are said to evoke the monuments of Mesoamerica and Egypt, hardly an unnatural comparison, though an incomplete one. His father, Dr. Robert F. Heizer, was one of the world's leading authorities on the archeological conundrums of how early civilizations displaced monolithic stones weighing far more than any rocks moved since, even with the largest hydraulic equipment available. It is true that his son, the sculptor, spent time roaming around and working at various archeological sites throughout the world while he was growing up, but to overidentify his work with archaic megaliths is to miss the point, which is an altogether more complicated cognitive geometry.

3

The Void

The truck crests another rise in the road. We go light in the springs and get as close to becoming an unidentified flying object as anything Heizer's seen since he moved to Nevada in 1970. "The military flies all sorts of stuff through here all the time," he continues, and it's true. When the United States Department of Defense hosts Red Flag weeks for international combat simulations, there's a regular *Jane's Year Book* of military aircraft parading through the desert skies, some of which don't look at all like what the Air Force flies; some of which, in fact, don't look like they should fly at all. We're only a couple of mountain ranges and valleys from Area 51 at Groom Dry Lake, that much touted corner of the Nevada Test Site shrouded from public view by massive withdrawals of public lands, fences, warning signs, motion detectors, and armed helicopter and ground patrols. Both the real and the imagined activities in the Groom Range area, from the development of Stealth technology to the supposed warehousing of captured alien spacecraft, are the subject of ongoing stories in the press, several television and movie productions, and speculations by every science-fiction quaffing paranoiac in Western civilization.

Behind us the green windbreak of cottonwood, elm, and Russian olive surrounding Heizer's property is growing more minuscule by the minute. The sculpture-in-progress, *City,* his largest project, is virtually invisible. The valley we're in is not large by Nevada standards, roughly twelve by forty-five miles, but it easily reduces his property to a singularity within one of the ninety empty basins that, taken altogether, constitute the major void in our continental imagination. The Great Basin, that highest and driest of the American deserts, that last empty tract on the nineteenth-century maps of our continent, is the only geophysical province in North America where all waters drain inward either to sink into the ground or to dissipate upward into the thin dry winds that constantly scour the region for stray moisture. The waters, confounding our expectations that all rivers flow to the sea, instead disappear as if absconding our expectations of how to measure space and time. No wonder both Heizer and the legions worshiping the otherworldly gather therein. Only in the void, a disorienting space we conceive of as being vacant and thus a landscape of open possibilities, can we imagine ourselves to step outside the boundaries of what we know and receive intelligence from some other place, somewhere alien to the egocentric pivot of our bodies.

Heizer traces lines in the dirt and displaces huge volumes with bulldozers, defining negative space and evoking the past. The UFO watchers also draw lines in time and space, insisting, "This is when the Other came from up There to visit down Here." Of course, the two occasionally collide, much to their mutual disgust. Heizer just wants to keep people off his property and away from the ongoing work. The UFOers are convinced he's a tool of the aliens, building landing strips for the invasion and refusing to let them in on the secret. This conflation between the ancient and the alien is one that the artist's father coped with in his professional life as well, noting in one of his reports on the petroglyphs of Nevada that the prehistoric rock art of the West would always attract practitioners of pseudoscience. He was never able to assign a reason for it, but acknowledged that there always seemed to be "two worlds—the real and the imaginary, and this duality is for some reason necessary."

Topping a small pass out of the valley we find what we're looking for, a stand of large juniper trees. We pull off to the right and into a short wash. While Heizer gauges how deep the sand is in the gully, I get out to lock the hubs into four-wheel drive. It's not that Heizer doesn't like trees—although any desert dweller has an ambivalent view of them. On the one hand, they're good for shade from sun and wind, and welcome visual relief from the relentless horizontals that predominate the landscape. On the other hand, they block what would otherwise be a fine and unobstructed view of the void, which is one of the primary reasons people who live here choose to do so. And they make good fence posts.

Heizer takes the long view inculcated in him as a lad following his father around on digs in South America and Africa. "Junipers," he states flatly, "are late Pleistocene invaders. Not native here at all." By this he means, geologically speaking, that they arrived only yesterday, part of the piñon-juniper woodland that now covers 17 million acres of the Basin. The juniper colonized the Basin range-by-range from between forty thousand to only forty-five hundred years ago, and now covers more acreage than any other tree in Nevada. By comparison, what we define as the contemporary basin-and-range structure of the Great Basin was formed by an uplifting and stretching of the earth's crust that raised mountains and dropped valleys starting more than 17 million years ago. It is a long and ongoing process that includes the regional uplifting of the entire West from the Sierra to the Rockies between 10 and 5 million years ago to its present-day base elevation. What used to be a shallow seabed is now a series of basins, which usually meet the ranges at somewhere around five thousand feet. Going back even further, the most ancient rocks in the region are schists on the Nevada-Idaho border that are more than 2.5 billion years old. That's the thing about the void of the Great Basin: big space means big time, the two being somewhat synonymous in our understanding of the universe. Despite their status as latecomers, though, Heizer admires the beauty and toughness of the juniper, and is rankled by the massive chaining of them up north near Ely by a chipboard company.

Mary and I hop out of the truck, Heizer stepping down slowly and gingerly. While Mary fires up the saw and goes to work on the trunk as close to the ground as she can maneuver the chain, Heizer pries a small rodent nest out of one of the crotches in the branches. I move in to take a look, and he cautions sharply: "Stay away from this and don't breathe in any of the dust. This is hantavirus territory." He pitches the nest into some sagebrush, then squats down next to Mary to advise on the angle of the cut, preferring her to lay down the tree somewhere other than on top of the truck. After moving aside the branches trimmed off the lower part of the trunk, and there being nothing else for me to do at the moment but watch, I mosey up the wash to its head, then turn and climb up the small knoll to my left.

The top of the hill is orange and flat, a barren hump that has been blasted by wind and lightning. The rocks are all shattered, many patined with a delicate black desert varnish as their iron and manganese contents have oxidized in the ferociously alternating conditions of the great open empty of the Basin. Picking up several fragments, I weight them gently in my hand. They're as thin and light as fragments of Anasazi pottery.

Covering virtually all of Nevada, western Utah, and parts of southern Oregon and Idaho, as well as most of the Mojave Desert in California, the Great Basin is the driest part of the continent, yet has torrential downpours during the late summer monsoons. Nevada's average annual rainfall is only nine inches, the least of any state in the Union, and temperatures can fluctuate 150 degrees over the course of a year. The Basin can run 130 degrees during daytime and then, because there's no humidity to hold in the warmth, drop easily more than fifty degrees when the sun goes down. The subsequent day-after-day expansion and contraction of rocks on this hill has blown them slowly apart, the alternating currents of wet and dry, hot and cold eventually shaking loose everything out here. The sharp whine of the saw below is just a sped-up, higher-pitched version of the entropy that occurs in the junipers as seasons go by, branches splitting with age and sun. Up here it looks as if the elements have been at war with each other for every day of the Great Basin's existence.

To the north and east is a random collage of shadow and sunlight as late-afternoon thunderstorms coalesce off the slopes of the nearest mountain range. At eleven-thousand-plus feet the cool and relatively moist peaks are virtual islands above the desert floor, each of the ranges in the Basin separated from its neighbors by hot, dry valleys on all sides. The biotic community on each range is unique, the genes of everything from ants to the junipers to chipmunks drifting away from the baseline of evolution established during the Pleistocene. The climate then was cooler and wetter, allowing animals to migrate from range to range. Now they are marooned by the desiccated valleys, a barrier they cannot cross, and stay within the self-contained meadows and cirques of the high mountains.

To my right and southeast is another range, its highest peak supposedly a spot from which one can spy into the Groom Dry Lake. Not far away the immensely long Railroad Valley joins up with Sand Springs Valley in that familiar pattern of the basin and range, the valleys running from north to south, hemmed in on the west and east by the ranges. Driving Nevada lengthwise is to follow the seemingly endless valleys, the grain of the land formed as it faulted during the ancient uplifting. Traveling across that pattern you rise and fall and rise from block to fault to block, from mountain pass to valley floor to mountain pass. Although only twenty or so miles wide, Railroad Valley is well over a hundred miles long; one story has it that the valley got its name because the only way in the nineteenth century that you could imagine getting through it was on a train, the two ends obscured from each other by the curvature of the earth.

Mary is about finished when I get back down the hill, and the fifteen-foot-high juniper comes down with a prolonged crack, falling only when sawed almost all the way through from both sides. It's a tough tree, and it has our respect. Mary and I buck it into the bed of the truck with a come-along, as Heizer climbs carefully with his good hand into the cab. We get out of the wash just as the first raindrops fall. Back over the rise Heizer thumbs on the radio in the cab of the truck. Even with a clear line of sight to the trees in his yard, so small from here that they're just a minuscule patch of nearly imaginary color on the desert floor, it's hard to get a clear signal. He wants to tell Jennifer Mankiewicz, his other assistant, that we're running a little late for dinner, but not to worry. It's a wise habit, staying in touch. Too much can go wrong out here, from a flat tire to a breakdown, and the nearest organized assistance is at best an hour away, probably more like two.

Heizer is quiet, and even Mary and I are subdued after the effort of load-ing the tree, heavy with its survivalist store of sap. "So, Mike, you never see unidentified flying things out here . . . ever?" I'm teasing, knowing the answer. Heizer repeats sternly: "No such things as flying saucers."

IT WAS SUPPOSED to be like this. In the late 1830s, when that avant-garde of the government, the U.S. Army Corps of Topographical Engineers, sal-lied forth in the latest thrust of the forty-five hundred years of the feint-parry-counterthrust of westward expansion, they would march from the Mississippi to the Rockies, cross the mountains and locate the source of the legendary Rio San Buenaventura, then float downstream across what would someday be called Utah and Nevada, eventually reaching California and the Pacific Ocean. Even as early as 1607, it by then being known that a conti-nent stood between the Atlantic and Asia, the Jamestown colonists had been urged to seek a navigable river leading to the Pacific. The river the topographical engineers were to map would provide the final leg in a route between the Atlantic and Pacific Oceans, provide easy access to the interi-or West for settlers, and remove the last geographical trade barrier in what was already a centuries-old dream of linking together all the continents for the unimpeded circulation of capital around the globe. That particular des-tiny, which most American leaders thought manifest in the Bible's dictum to "go forth and conquer all before you," would be fulfilled.

The only problem was that no one could find the Buenaventura—a not surprising development since no such river exists. What kept the hope alive, and what to this day still leads astray some writers describing the region, was an inability to visualize how the western United States is constructed. Even the noteworthy French intellectual Jean Baudrillard, in his frenetic 1986 tract *America,* confuses the western slopes with those of the Rockies, a seven-hundred-mile geographical blunder that has him describe water flowing off the mountains in Colorado and into San Francisco Bay. The collective wisdom of eighteenth-century European cartography assigned only one very large mountain range to western North America, the Rockies, and then a blank space to the remaining left-hand portion of the continent, which they showed terminating at the Spanish colonial outposts on the coast of California. Although the high desert region had been crossed and recrossed by fur trappers and explorers in the early part of the 1800s, the error wasn't corrected until John C. Frémont in 1843–1844, himself in search of the Buenaventura, circumnavigated the region and confirmed with survey data that it had no outlet to the sea. He was the first person to call it "that Great Interior Basin" and to note that sterility was its most prominent characteristic.

The history of western expansion across America is filled with what we now consider comical presumptions about its geography, given our cumulative hindsight, but early explorers were following the most accurate, if sometimes scanty, information available, as well as falling into the preconceptions of European-trained mapmakers. Before Frémont, the maps they used were derived from a secondhand cartography based not on the newly deployed mathematics of surveying, but on verbal accounts and firsthand sketches that were, at best, approximations reported by the travelers of where they thought they had been. Thus, the maps often displayed more of humankind's desire for geophysical symmetry and aesthetic balance than reality. And because Europe was crossed by rivers that arose in the Alps and emptied into salt waters, it was assumed that North America was structured the same way. Even after the discovery of the Sierra Nevada, a range that for all intents and purposes isolates California from the rest of the lands to the east, it was still assumed that all of the rivers in America drained oceanward. It remains a miracle that more explorers didn't die from such a refusal to acknowledge the reality of the Great Basin: that all its modest rivers run inward to arid sinks, and none to the reputed salvation of an Edenic California.

It's an understandable mistake, though. The only other lakes of much magnitude formed by interior drainage that were known to the Europeans, and even then through, once again, second- or thirdhand information, were on the Anatolian plateau of Turkey and in central Asia. It's not as if the explorers of North America had had much experience with interior basins—and certainly none as large, as extensive, and as forbidding as the Great Basin of America. Frémont acknowledged in his report from the 1843–1844 expedition that "[t]he whole idea of such a desert . . . is a novelty in our country, and excites Asiatic, not American ideas. Interior basins, with their own systems of lakes and rivers, and often sterile, are common enough in Asia . . . but in America such things are new and strange, unknown and unsuspected, and discredited when related."

The Basin remains anomalous and contradictory. It contains the lowest and hottest places in the country, but is home to more mountain ranges per square mile than anywhere else on earth, save Afghanistan. Nevada alone has at least 316 separate mountain ranges, most of which average fifteen miles wide by fifty miles long. The valley floors are sometimes as high as sixty-eight hundred feet, the peaks topping out at thirteen thousand. It is a geological maze no one has yet fully deciphered, a region existing almost solely within the rain shadow of the two-mile-high Sierra Nevada. Geographers today still find themselves disagreeing about its most basic fact, the size of the region. They politely allow each other differing parameters based sometimes upon hydrology (the direction of drainage), biotic community (the spread of various species of plants and animals living in the Basin), physiography (how the Basin relates to continental tectonics), and ethnography (the distribution of culturally similar tribespeople). The hydrological definition, the one most commonly used, stubbornly produces varying estimates of the Great Basin's size ranging from 165,000 to more than 220,000 square miles. Two contemporary authors actually go so far as to claim it is twice that size and that it extends over one-fifteenth of the more than 3 million square miles of the lower forty-eight states.

If a maze, it remains a relatively empty one. Fifteen of the seventeen counties in Nevada, for instance, hold fewer than two people per square mile, the minimum level used by the U.S. Census Bureau in the 1890s to

The Void

define the frontier, which supposedly closed in 1891. In 1890 the population density of the United States was roughly 17.8 people per square mile; a hundred years later it stood at 70.5 people. Although Nevada has been the fastest-growing state in America for the last quarter of a century, it has also been the most highly urbanized: 86 percent of its 1.6 million residents have settled in and around Reno and Las Vegas.

The latter is a city that technically only borders the Basin, being part of the Colorado River drainage that ends in the Gulf of California. But, it is also Nevada's largest city and, along with Salt Lake City, one of the major urban centers defining the void, if for no other reason than the contrast its proximity offers. Adding more than six thousand people a month to its population, and developing land at the incredible rate of two acres an hour, its 350 percent population explosion during the last twenty-five years pushed it over a million people in the 1990s—a figure expected to double early in the twenty-first century. However, even if we add it to the demographic equation, the Great Basin in Nevada and most of Utah is, in aggregate, the same now as it was 150 years ago: a relatively vacant territory surrounded by widely spaced settlements.

All of this makes the Great Basin the American frontier of cognitive dissonance, which is a state of confusion defined as trying to hold two contradictory ideas or perceptions in mind at the same time. The Great Basin is a place where our eyes have trouble getting a grip, no matter how many numbers we throw around trying to quantify it. Seeing that as much as 80 percent of the information we take in daily comes through our vision, this is another aspect of the problem we have when deciphering the Basin. We can't fully see it, thus fail to perceive it correctly, and end up fatally misunderstanding its nature, often as much a problem for residents as well as for visitors to the region.

To start with, the pattern of mountains and valleys is on a scale so large that we can't get our minds around it by just looking at it, Railroad Valley being a good example. You have to travel through it to gauge for yourself what its size is in relation to your body, the oldest and most genuine way we have of relating to and measuring the land. The physical structure of the Basin and its paucity of tall vegetation mean you can see long, long distances, sometimes more than a hundred miles if you're up on one of the peaks. But the air is so dry and clear on most days—the clearest in the lower forty-eight, in fact—that where you expect landforms to be softened by atmospheric haze, they're instead standing sharply defined at thirty and forty miles away. All our experience with distance is confounded by the difficulties we undergo in adjusting our sight values to the Basin. The cognitive dissonance is caused by our visual expectations being wildly out of synch with these perceptual realities.

From another standpoint, we expect a certain level of contrast in the landscape, colors and shades helping us differentiate shape and form. The predominance of unrelieved sunlight at relatively high altitudes and the subtlety of color in the Great Basin lead the untrained eye to fall off its subject matter. Early pioneers sometimes wrote about the Great Basin as if it had no vegetation whatsoever; the spectrum of color was so narrow that they just couldn't see the sagebrush, shadscale, and dry grasses stretching out before them. In 1876 the famous author Washington Irving borrowed their accounts to describe the desert, which he had never seen in person, as "undulating and treeless plains, and desolate sandy wastes, wearisome to the eye from their extent and monotony." He reinforced the perceptual failures of those crossing the region with a loop of self-reinforcing misinformation.

In addition, where we expect distance to be signaled by the colors in the landscape fading from nearby warm browns to faraway cool blues, what vegetation we do manage to see lacks any familiar shades of green, but tends to muted browns and silver-grays, which slow that shift in the spectrum and further confuse our vision. And the lack of verticals on the desert floor—the absence of buildings or people or simply anything at all we can use to calibrate our sense of scale—is dizzying. Mary Ann Bonjorni, an artist who has traveled over much of and worked in the Great Basin, says that the only way she can keep pace while driving through it is if there are telephone poles running alongside the road, predictable verticals raised at unvarying intervals to which she can count cadence.

Apart from the minority of people who have found ways to adapt to the severities of life in the Basin, the Native Americans who have been here for millennia, and the much more recently arrived ranchers, miners, and assorted desert rats, we have three common responses to such overwhelming dissonance. We can leave it behind us, which is what most people have done in the Great Basin, crossing it as quickly as possible with eyes averted as we seek the green solace of California or the Midwest. Or, we can break it down into pieces small enough to analyze. We isolate one peak at a time in the distance and imagine ourselves climbing up its steep alluvial fans; we ruminate on the nearest sagebrush, obtaining comfort from the small sliver of the spectrum it delivers to our color-starved eyes. Or, we can assign it a symbolic value in order to file it safely away where we can ignore it: we define it as the Big Empty, as a wilderness—or as the nearest synonym to that word in the dictionary, a wasteland. We relegate it to the toxic ministrations of the armed forces in the largest military preserves in the hemisphere, which is why the Environmental Protection Agency has placed solar-powered radiation monitors throughout this part of Nevada that they check monthly. It's an odd kind of sunflower, but exactly the mutant sort of vegetation we allow ourselves to accept in a place as far outside our expectations as the Great Basin.

We have, more or less, conquered our physical ignorance of the region, but we're still having trouble coping with it in our imaginations. We maintain expectations of it that are at odds with the reality of the desert. We still see aliens just off the edge of the map, those invisible inhabitants of terra incognita we call the Other, and with whom we collaborate to define ourselves.

THE NEXT MORNING I'm up just after daybreak, everyone else still asleep, the sun hidden behind the gray remnants of last night's storm that pounded the valley. It's unusual to have moisture this early in the summer, but an El Niño current has been setting up in the eastern Pacific, already warming the waters off the Baja California coast by five degrees above normal, which in turn creates and intensifies more storms from Peru to California. We're far enough south here to pick up the increased moisture, which is sneaking up from Mexico almost two months early in the annual monsoon schedule.

To accept the fact that deserts of the American Southwest receive monsoonal rain requires a mental gymnastic: the rest of the year is so dry that the total annual precipitation remains under ten inches. The rainfall throughout this specific part of the Great Basin actually averages from four to nine inches, depending on where you put your rain gauge in any particular year. It's not only a low rate of precipitation that makes this a desert, but also the power of evaporation, which in the southern part of the Basin easily exceeds seventy inches a year. The winds do their part, too, as in all of the world's arid regions. A powerful evaporative factor, here they also push the Pacific storms so hard and fast up the western slope of the Sierra that they sail overhead without dropping their moisture until they hit Utah's Wasatch Mountains on the eastern edge of the Basin.

At any rate, it's cool enough this morning for a sweater as I head out across the yard and climb the fence marking off Heizer's house and work area from the unbounded desert. Five hundred yards ahead of me stretches one of the long berms of *City,* the legendary and remote sculpture that the artist has been working on since 1970. Planned as part of an aggregate of interrelated sculptures, the first element that was built sits on the desert floor as a 110-foot-long earthen ramp that culminates in a steep 140-foot-long-by-23¼-foot-high slope facing west. *Complex One* is covered in a rough rusty-chocolate-colored cement invented specifically for the sculpture by Heizer, who had his crew add volcanic cinder to the mix. Its frontal visage is framed by a series of steel-reinforced gray concrete forms, angular beams that from a straight-on perspective form a drawing on the face, but from the side or oblique views compose a geometrically transparent sculpture. The ramp itself is slated for removal in the near future, which will leave just the mound with its two horizontal elements of thirty tons each cantilevered out in front of the sculpture, a clear demonstration of Heizer's engineering skills.

When it first appeared in magazine and book photographs, the only way most people have ever seen it, *Complex One* was as startling as any artwork could be. Compared to other sculptures of the time, its dimensions and imaginative scale were immense, a fact only heightened by its surroundings of low sagebrush and lack of other structures in view. It was as if Heizer had uncovered the site of a very old and unfamiliar civilization, and then re-created its mathematics, its art, and its religion all in a single structure. The bunker shape outlined by its projecting and rectilinear arms evoked for some readers entire architectural mythologies, from the thousand-year-old ball courts of Chichén Itzá in the Yucatán and the temples of Teotihuacán outside Mexico City to the military-industrial sublime of the Nevada Test Site.

This was not exactly a common response to the cognitive dissonance of the desert, and for those of us who grew up in and around the Great Basin, it was hard to resist tacking up the photographs and worshiping the image nightly on our knees.

Two earlier sculptures had set us up for such an epiphany, and as I walk through the sagebrush, sharply pungent after the downpour last night, the sun still screened by clouds, I remember how Heizer's *Double Negative* affected me in 1970, and then the next year, Robert Smithson's *Spiral Jetty.* First, almost no one had seen them in person, certainly no one I knew, and the only evidence viewers had was in photographs. Smithson's 1,500-by-15-foot rock jetty curled out into the Great Salt Lake just a few miles south of Promontory, where the golden spike was driven to celebrate completion of the first transcontinental railroad. Jeff Kelley, an art critic who grew up in Las Vegas, is fond of pointing out the irony from our vantage point of a century later. The first trains run in from east and west faced each other headfirst at the ceremony, the officials realizing only afterward that they had no way to turn around the engines with their carloads of dignitaries. Everyone had to backtrack to sidings many miles away, a dead-end confrontation that added a touch of the absurd to the occasion.

Spiral Jetty had a bit of that self-enclosed gesture about it and embodied a classical symbol of entropy at just above lake level, a rocky pathway the eye wandered out onto—only to have to unwind itself, to retrace its way out by going backward. It was a symbol derived equally from the shape of spiral galaxies and the petroglyphs of the Anasazi, and all the more intriguing because it existed for us only as an image in a photograph, a remoteness of representation that respected the vast distances of the space it inhabited. It was, however, a gesture that could only capitalize upon the much more resonant sculpture built by Heizer a year earlier.

Double Negative was nowhere as easy to read, its two huge downsloping trenches carved out in the sides of a mesa that folded around a valley to face each other. Compared to the 10,000 tons of rock dumped out to form the Smithson work, *Double Negative* displaced 240,000 tons of dirt and rhyolite from its trenches and remains the largest single volumetric form Heizer has constructed. It provoked in us a sort of dumb amazement at the scale of the gesture, and it took a while for the more serious implications to sink in. It was obvious that the sculpture was a "double" negative in that there were two trenches, and also in that the space between the two cuts—the visible emptiness over the valley linking the trenches—was another negative element defining the object. Two sets of negatives made a sculpture.

Double Negative was an empty *space* articulated in an empty *place,* the void of the Basin, so it became an identifiable mark directly addressing both its own nature and that of its surroundings. That much we got right away, but it was only over time we realized that there was yet another aspect to the sculpture. The displaced material fanning out below the two trenches in light-colored contrast to the valley ground showed us a reversal of figure and ground. The absence of the ground in the two cuts and the space in between, the "negative" elements, formed the figure; the pushed-over remains literally became the ground, another doubling back on our expectations for how what was absent could be seen as an object.

Although *Spiral Jetty* was a handsome piece complete with a train of art-historical allusions, *Double Negative* was rooted in a stronger intellectual gravity and primal geometry. That is, *Spiral Jetty* could have decorated the shoreline of any lake in the world, but Heizer's sculpture was exactly specific to its place—the art was the displacement of the place itself. And what a place! The Great Salt Lake has appeared on every map of the United States printed since the late 1800s, but Mormon Mesa, the site of *Double Negative,* not only was a geographical enigma but remains to this day difficult enough to find that visitors still get lost, even while clutching their maps furnished by the Museum of Contemporary Art in Los Angeles, which owns the sculpture.

Immediately following the completion of *Double Negative,* Heizer started conceptual work on *Complex One.* After conducting a two-year, two-person ground and aerial reconnaissance over five western states, as well as perusing selected county records, he purchased land in Nevada where he could build the sculpture. "Material is place and place is material," Heizer states emphatically. "I'm not here because the mountains are pretty, but because it has the materials I need, the rock and gravel and sand." Heizer is irritated by the basic misunderstanding of his work by people who insist on mistaking it for landscape art, or thinking that he chose the desert as a theatrical backdrop. As I walk up the west end of the prism-shaped northern berm above *City* that's identified as *Complex Two,* it's easy enough to see how those mistakes get made: what's proposed here is not only physically embedded in the earth but also massively more complicated than *Double Negative.*

Just as previous generations had preconceptions about the nature of the Great Basin, so twentieth-century audiences seem to have preformed ideas about how Heizer's *City* resides in its physical context. If this sculpture is planted prominently in the middle of an otherwise empty landscape, then surely that's what it must be about; its meaning must flow outward to the mountains around it—right?

Wrong. The meaning flows inward, just as water does in the Great Basin. What Heizer is building, he notes, is sculpture as rigorously geometrical as the internal structure of a crystal. His forms are related to those found in nature, to be sure, but once his ideas have been developed here, his work could be installed on a civic plaza or in the confines of a museum—and has been. Heizer is a sculptor investigating the fundamental ways we shape the world, in all literal senses of the phrase. Personally, I think the work is better done here, in the cognitive dissonance of the void, but not because it's an attractive setting. Being forced to experience *City* in a place where our visual expectations are already upset allows us to experience the sculpture with eyes freed from convention.

ON THE CREST, now, of *Complex Two,* it is possible to see the entire sweep of the slowly evolving site for *City.* Forming a trapezoidal enclosure open to the west, the three enormous berms of *Complex One, Two,* and *Three* define the east, north, and south elements of what was at first a twenty-eight-acre site, but in the latest drawings may eventually total forty-six acres or more. I'm standing atop the longest of the three mounds, which runs for 1,036 feet, almost a quarter of a mile; across from me *Complex Three* stretches 680 feet. The valley floor underneath the sculpture slopes slightly downhill to the west, but the berms are engineered to match elevations and form a consistently level rim. In the middle of this arena the floor has been excavated to form a pit sixteen and one-half feet below grade, so I'm perched forty feet above the bottom of the negative space. An access ramp enters from the west, sloping down from the airstrip/road that runs diagonally between the work done so far and the site of what will be additional forms carved out of the dirt.

If the first component, *Complex One,* was a positive counterpart to *Double Negative,* as Heizer once stated, then *City* as a whole is an admixture. It registers the void through both negative space and positive shape. The top edge of the sculpture where I'm standing is rimmed with a concrete curb, which functions as both a line drawn on the earth and as part of the erosion-control elements. It outlines the face of the berm against which rest three of the nineteen "stelae" planned to rest eventually all along the second complex. The three enormous rebar-reinforced concrete elements, looking like blank, irregular megalithic tablets, are propped up on two earthen forms projecting out from the berm, triangular and rectangular faces that form a bay between them. "There's a lot of chaos in the stelae," Heizer commented, their rough concrete surfaces standing in opposition to the straight-edged geometry of the berm and the smooth recurving curbs.

City has the odd effect of turning the void back upon itself. First and foremost, it is a set of sculptures investigating size. Sheer, unadulterated brute size—just how heavy a rock can we move, how large a hole can we dig, how massive a concrete slab can we pour? Size preoccupied Robert F. Heizer as he pondered how ancient monuments were constructed, and Mike Heizer takes pride in confounding movers with the sculptures that he fabricates here for shipping all over the world. They're heavy enough that Heizer's blue hydro-crane, rated to lift up to twenty tons, has trouble lifting them. Yet, these sculptures, if placed within *City,* would virtually disappear. That brings up the second issue: scale.

If size is a set of objective dimensions, then scale is the relative measurement, how things compare in size to each other, ourselves, and to the rest of the world. Making *City* isn't just about creating something large, but also about changing how we see ourselves in relation to space. By constructing a sculpture that is scaled more like architecture than what we normally call art, Heizer is upsetting what we expect to be our normal experience around artworks. *City* may not be about landscape, but placing it within the Great Basin, a region that likewise turns inside out our notions of scale, certainly magnifies our perception of the sculpture.

The third issue continues Heizer's thirty-year investigation of negative space. *City* removes, displaces, returns, and otherwise reverses the ground upon itself. It lifts up one portion and drops another to create an emptiness.

Most remarkably, it does this with a sculptural vocabulary that is not European, but one derived from the sunken courtyards, massive stoneworks, and curbings of the ancient Olmec culture of Mexico and the funerary complex of Saqqâra in Egypt.

The Olmecs were the progenitors of civilization in Mesoamerica. They built its first empire, and during their reign from the thirteenth through the first centuries B.C. set the imperialistic template for every other Mexican culture until the Aztecs fell to the Spanish conquistador Cortés in 1519. They also understood and used negative space in their architecture and zero in their calendars. The Olmec site most influential in Heizer's thoughts is La Venta, an extensive assemblage of ceremonial mounds and stelae located on the coastal swamps of Tabasco. Originally an important archeological site, excavated, mapped, and analyzed by Dr. Heizer and his colleagues in the 1950s, it's now mostly obscured by an oil field and petrochemical refinery with only a small park near the Hyatt Hotel reserved for selected artifacts. Prior to local industrial development the two-mile-square site, with its Complexes A, B, and C and leaning stelae marked on the maps, and with its immense basalt and serpentine stones floated on rivers and hauled overland from distances of up to a hundred miles away, was reportedly one of the most impressive archeological locations in the Western Hemisphere. Individual stelae carved by the Olmecs range from just three feet to more than seventeen feet in height; the foreboding, deeply carved colossal heads for which they are famous run up to twelve feet tall and twelve tons.

Saqqâra, roughly eleven miles south of the Giza suburb of Cairo, was the necropolis built to serve the ancient Egyptian capital of Memphis, and was initially excavated by the British starting in 1801. As Mike explains it, while he and his father were working in Egypt during 1970 on the Colossi of Memnon at Luxor, they took a trip to Saqqâra. There they met the French anthropologist Henri Lauer, who explained to them his restoration-in-progress of the funereal complex. Designed circa 2650 B.C. for King Djoser of the Third Dynasty by his high priest, Impohet (who is credited with being the inventor of early Egyptian architecture), Saqqâra probably owes its construction techniques to the Mesopotamians, who used similar methods for the temples of Uruk built slightly earlier. Heizer acknowledges that *Complex One* is actually a squared-off variation of the mastaba form underlying the

Djoser Step Pyramid. The mastaba, in Arabic meaning "bench," was initially a very stable mud-brick form built with sloping sides, which archeologists speculate may have evolved from the earliest mud-covered reed-wall architecture of Mesopotamia. The Step Pyramid, the world's earliest known example of such a monument, is also its first large architecture executed in stone. The curvilinear curbing that traces the baseline of the pit in *City* stems from Heizer's memory of the curved walls shown him by Lauer in the burial chambers deep beneath the pyramid.

In pondering the earliest forms of monumental architecture from both civilizations, Heizer went back to the world's first formal organizational principles of articulated space and then worked forward in a line entirely new to sculpture. He was not satisfied to adopt or adapt the language of sculpture handed down by European history, which is why to this day his forms do not resemble those of artists who later inherited earthworks as an art movement, such as Christo in his pop gestures with fabric, or Walter de Maria in the modernist severity of Lightning Field.

These ancient precedents inform how Heizer demands we deal with space. Instead of limiting himself to what were then the accepted venues for art, the galleries and museums, he turned in the late 1960s to the real and open spaces of his upbringing, which offered cheap and, for all practical purposes, unlimited materials. He made huge dirt and dye drawings on dry lake beds in the Mojave, incised tunnels underneath alkali flats, and displaced dirt in the desert with granite boulders from the mountains, all methods of invoking the megalithic gestures of previous civilizations. He was forging a new vocabulary for sculpture, that medium in which we address the nature of space itself, and in so doing made visible a new branch of the socially constructed calculus we call "place." He became so accustomed to working in the void that now, when he participates in museum or gallery exhibitions, he installs works that literally and figuratively strain at the walls and floors of their enclosure, just as they do the lifting limitations of his crane.

City is itself a closed system. We're meant to go into it and be visually enclosed. This morning, a thin sheen of water stands trapped in the pit after the rainstorm—just as surely as it does when it rains anywhere within those ninety sinks of the Great Basin. It will disappear within an hour of the sun coming out from behind the clouds, though, just as standing moisture will evaporate from those intermittently wet lake beds, the playas. Heizer has plans to install a dry well in the bottom of the pit to ensure that the footings of the stelae will remain safe from excess water accumulating in the sculptural basin.

The people who once inhabited this region, their material traces the tools and shaman pouches that Robert F. Heizer so carefully cataloged throughout his life, would have marveled at yet probably understood what Michael Heizer is doing. The organization of his sculpture must be understood through our haptic sense, a full-body sensory involvement of space that people who live outdoors tend to retain. Sensing space haptically is to be in it, not simply looking at it. If *City* is material is place, then evoking the haptic sense should be effective as a way of experiencing it. To see if my point is valid, I walk down off the berm, where I have been pacing next to the projecting tops of the stelae, and go out onto the floor of the sculpture.

What I first notice is that the shapes of the land disappear. Heizer has replaced the sculptural elements by lowering me beneath the horizon of the berms, partially why the meaning of *City* flows inward as a formal sculpture, not outward as a piece of landscape art. All around me is sculpture under its dome of sky, and that's all. Despite being enclosed, the space of the sculpture feels limitless, the tops of the complexes just far enough away to compel the arc of my vision into the unbounded sky. It's disconcerting, standing down here in the damp sand. *City* is much stranger than anything the UFOers could come up with; the best they can imagine is Michael Heizer as a Martian collaborator, which ironically doesn't begin to even approach how genuinely alien *City* feels upon first inspection. Because of its illusion of the limitless, it makes my body feel larger than it otherwise would. My sense this morning that I can reach out and touch the sky is a perceptual shift well documented by cognitive psychologists.

When I get back to the house coffee is on and Heizer is sitting at the end of the kitchen table.

"So, if material is place and place is material," I quote, "does that mean that negative space is a material you find in this place to work with?"

Heizer considers me patiently. "No," he replies in a tone close to that of dismissing flying saucers. "Space is just space. It's just a matter of physics."

"Is space monolithic?" I ask, pressing my luck. Another long look. "No," he again replies, this time getting up and walking toward the living room. Heizer has spent too many years calculating the specifications necessary to move some of the largest monoliths in modern history to worry about the purely verbal leverage of philosophy. I realize that this visit will end without my yet being able to satisfactorily define either Heizer's use of negative space or the nature of the surrounding void.

THAT NIGHT AFTER DINNER, followed by another thunderstorm, I walk outside and am momentarily stunned by the sharp and poignant air. Ozone, I think. No, it's something that's growing, something familiar. It takes almost a minute of concentration to get it: sagebrush.

I'm embarrassed. When people talk about missing the Great Basin, they talk about space and the smell of sagebrush. How could I misplace one of the primary sensory memories I have from living in Nevada most of my life? Is it another variation on cognitive displacement? When I was walking through the sagebrush this morning, I had no difficulty associating the smell with the appearance of the shrub. Now, in the dark with the sage out of sight, the smell has been uncoupled from my dominant sensory apparatus, my vision. I am disquieted, realizing that I could misplace so easily what I thought was a hardwired olfactory definition of the desert and an important memory of a specific place.

Before going in to pack and then to bed, I take in several deep breaths so deep that they make me lightheaded, storing up the scent. That I am now aware of having come so close to losing track of a key piece of localized knowledge is reassuring. I'll keep better hold of it. Knowing that I will return soon, and have other chances to renew the sensory data underlying the memory, is what carries me to sleep.

T W O
☙

It's a month later, the first day of August, and this time my wife has driven back out with me from Los Angeles to the site of *City*. Beth hasn't been out here in almost a year, and she's been looking forward to the trip all summer, glad to have a chance both to be back in sagebrush country and to visit with Mike, Mary, and Jennifer. We arrived just after lunch to find two more juniper tree trunks propped in the front yard. After catching up for a bit, I've left the four of them so I can spend some more time with *City* and the imponderables of a negative universe.

It has continued to be a wet summer, a third of an inch of rain falling in each of the last two days. The halogeton brushing against my bare legs is plump, prickly, almost sticky it's so full of water, the green leaves and purple stalks as waxy as if it were a succulent. First found in the far northeastern corner of the state in 1935, it's a prodigious weed native to, appropriately enough, the high alkaline drylands of Asia, and is considered by ranchers to be a different kind of, and much more threatening, alien invader from either flying saucers or artists. By the early 1970s it had infested more than 2 million acres, finding as its ideal niche the soils disturbed by livestock. Maybe that wouldn't be so bad if it were decent forage, but once there's a freeze in the Basin halogeton becomes highly toxic to cattle, sheep, and horses. Eating it, they bloat and die. Eradicating the stuff from just a single given acre can take from five to ten years of assiduous chemical warfare, an expensive and perhaps even more disastrous alternative.

Then there's the harvester ant problem, which becomes apparent as I cut through the sagebrush toward *City*. Dotted every few yards are circular wastelands of cleared sand about ten or twelve feet in diameter, areas devoid of sage, halogeton, or anything else except for ant sentries on patrol. Heizer estimates that the large red ants have taken over about a quarter of the pasturage maintained just outside the windbreak for Jennifer's and Mary's sheep. The only way known to drive away the ants involves tactics more akin to Vietnam than modern-day ranching, which he is loathe to implement. It's apparent, though, that Heizer's been mulling over the problem of both the halogeton and the harvester ants. For one thing, he says, if you could squeeze the water out of all the halogeton in the Great Basin, you could probably reduce substantially the pumping of precious groundwater throughout the region.

As I walk eastward down the ramp leading to the bottom of the pit, both the weed and the anthills disappear along with the rest of my view of the land, until once again I am physically and visually surrounded by the sculpture, which is slowly becoming a familiar place. The body of geometric contemplations constantly reorganizes itself in front of me, a process akin to our perception of nature itself, but not an attempt to simply reproduce or represent it. Nor is there much evidence of Heizer himself in *City*, no overt and competitive flourish of the hand to assign ego or authorship.

Almost all of the artist's work since the mid-1960s is about the movement of mass from one state of our awareness to another, from his initial "negative paintings" composed of empty geometric figures in 1966, to the depressions, trenches, slits, slots, and other absences carved into dry lake beds across the Basin in the 1960s and '70s, many of which have long since been literally reabsorbed into the land. It is a corpus that is as consistently devoid of gesture as are articles about Heizer's life devoid of personal details, both examples of Heizer's concentration upon the contemplation of sculptural form. Although he does apply surface to his work by hand, the subsequent marks are more like traces of a natural process, as if gesture were weather and erosion. Likewise, he insists that writers focus on his work and avoid discussing his personal life, including his location, which he considers a private matter mostly irrelevant to an examination of what is important, the work.

It's appropriate that, as I pause at the bottom of the pit and look around, all that's apparent is form. From the eight trapezoidal faces making up the face of *Complex Two* on my left and to the north, to the curvilinear curbing sweeping from behind me on my right to underscore the preliminary berm of *Complex Three*, a concrete line that then bends sharply to cross in front of me, underneath and then around the far side of *Complex One,* it's an array of earthen mathematics. And if the projecting beams fronting *Complex One* sometimes recall the Aztec iconography of Chichén Itzá in the Yucatán, this afternoon they instead conjure up for me the functional geometry of the Bauhaus.

The concrete curbing is a linear allure I can't resist, and like a little kid I jump up onto it, elevated off the ground by all of maybe six inches, and begin walking the southern slope of the pit, which is unified by the continuous line of cement. I know I'm going to have a hard time describing the shape inscribed by this line, which runs out to two slender and acute angles to its east and west ends, and can think, as I strive to maintain my balance, only that it is an almost symmetrical pair of steer horns pointing first across, then down and out from the brow of the berm, a hopeless analogy. It's an aggravating habit, trying to shoehorn an abstract form into a representational figure the reader can recognize from some other experience, but one to which writers often fall prey. I fall off the curbing, losing both my balance and my train of thought, then step back on and continue tracing its path.

I give up on trying to organize my notes and concentrate on my footing. Coarse gravel that has been spread over the entire area enclosed by the curbing still bears traces of how it was spread, faint horizontal lines stacked up like the receding shorelines of the Pleistocene Lake Lahontan, which at its maximum was a shallow body of water covering 8,665 square miles of the Great Basin. Ever since its retreat, which started well over ten thousand years ago and left behind remnants such as Pyramid and Walker Lakes, gravel benches have marked the high water levels. A drop in only a foot or two would uncover hundreds of square miles of land, and some of the valleys bear more than a dozen distinct terraces marking successive droughts. The prehistoric mega-lake didn't reach into this particular basin, but Heizer sometimes accompanied his father along its ancient shorelines to the north where he was excavating caves. What is below me is not a representation of geology down which I could take a rough tumble, but an abstract form that is inevitably related to nature. If you spread gravel across a slope, this is how the angle of repose will organize itself through friction and gravity, whether it's from the wave action of an ancient lake or the blade of a bulldozer.

The law of landslide is everywhere evident here; though small grains of sand come to rest at 36 degrees, and chunks of coal heaped up outside mines can stabilize at up to 47 degrees, dirt starts to slide at anything steeper than 45 degrees, one reason all of the interior faces in *City* will eventually be covered, like *Complex One,* in eight inches of cinder cement poured over metal mesh and rebar. *City* is designed, like its ancient counterparts, to last a long time. Erosion and slippage on the outside slopes will be controlled through the planting of hybrid crested wheat.

I finish my traverse out to the west and descend once more back into the pit. Across the floor of the pit are three of the nineteen stelae planned for *Complex Two.* Each of them is roughly thirty-five feet high and weighs up to 750 tons, thick slabs rising from the bottom of the pit to just over the top of the berm. Poured over rebar forms, vaguely rectangular in proportion but varying greatly in width, the concrete is a mixture of cement and cinder with a subsequent coloration similar to that of *Complex One.* "Stelae" are defined in the dictionary as engraved upright markers serving as monuments. Although they lean back (as do the ones at La Venta) and bear no inscriptions, they look like immense blank tablets. *Stela* is a descriptive term Heizer appropriated from archeology, a volumetric solid added to the sculptural repertory of cube, cone, and polyhedron.

Walking westward to the left-hand and most narrow stela, I run my hand over its rough surface, then clamber up the projecting ends of the rebar. I'm slightly winded at the top by the moderately thin air at this altitude, which reminds me how frustrating it is to live in Los Angeles, at sea level for the first time since I was nine years old. The top of the stela to my immediate right is appealingly wide, and I walk over to it, pulling out my notepad to sit down.

It's windy up here—as it is almost every summer afternoon in the Basin, part of its evaporative cycle—and I wish I had a Chapstick. I peer down into the pit, then north and east to the mountains, then back down again. The color and shapes of the stelae are very similar to the western-facing ramparts of the nearby slopes, which are just now beginning to pick up that late-afternoon glow so beloved by photographers of the desert. I'm gazing distractedly through a low pass into the next basin eastward, and struggling with this collision of allusions—abstract volumes, archeology, and organic or natural geometry—when a jet bomber lumbers majestically down-valley, just on the other side of the pass. It's below my eye level, absolutely silent, a huge gray ghost of an airship that disappears behind the other half of the range south of the pass.

I am still shaking my head ten or twelve seconds later when the bomber vaults slowly over the far southern end of the valley, tilted acutely over to starboard as it makes its turn over the ridge. Maybe two hundred feet off the deck and less than a couple miles away, there is still no sound of its engines. The jet has made it about halfway across the valley before two fighters pop up over the range, following almost exactly the trajectory of the bomber. Now there's a muffled roar, that familiar and almost reassuring annoyance of high-octane jet fuel being consumed under pressure as the pursuers scramble after their prey. Two more fighters bank steeply over the ridge, joining the chase and turning up the volume. Within only a few seconds they're all running out of room in the twelve-mile width of the valley, and the bomber breaks away south toward the Test Site, flying over the wash where we collected the juniper tree. The fighters peel off in the opposite direction, pulling up in a loose formation before they disappear.

The roar of the aerial minuet fades quickly, and the only movement in the valley is a pair of dust devils that have arisen in the disturbed air at its southern end. About as high as the altitude of the bomber's flight path, they course slowly up toward me, highly organized conical vortices of air made visible by the dirt they assemble, a sort of geometric performance piece. For nearly twenty minutes they continue up the western side of the valley, keeping pace with each other until they, too, disappear in the distance, the far northern reach of the valley that is my horizon.

Heizer once said about *City:* "The work is not put in a place, it is that place." As I step off the stela and walk down to the eastern end of *Complex Two,* I consider that in addition to "Material is place is material and place is material." It's a simple equation with outreaching implications: *City* is place is material.

I had recently had a discussion with an archeologist about Heizer's work, and her contention was that *City* was a travesty upon the land because it did not serve as a dwelling place. Her complaint is one that has been voiced over the years by numerous critics, not just about Heizer's work since *Double*

Negative, but about large earthworks as a class of objects. For her, because *City* was not inhabitable it had no utility to society, and was thus merely an egotistical desecration of the environment. It didn't matter that Teotihuacán outside Mexico City, a place she venerates, was only a ceremonial space and much larger, to boot. The forty-five-acre site for *City* pales in comparison to Teotihuacán's eight square miles of pyramids and plazas, a solar-oriented, highly geometrical earthwork constructed from A.D. 150 to 750 out of much suffering and literal human sacrifice. Teotihuacán is justified for her because it served a purpose in organized society, the observance of the agrarian calendar. To the archeologist, *City* was simply the will of one person imposed upon the land for his own pleasure.

But doesn't our imagination need places of habitation? I wonder to myself, wishing I had been able to come back with such a reply then to her vehement rejection of the sculpture. Don't we need to create opportunities to contemplate space in both positive and negative manifestations as part of our understanding the universe, which is, after all, more void than not? And isn't art, along with religion and science, a legitimate mode of consideration? Isn't this, too, a legitimate ceremonial space? Eventually, *City* will be the province of a nonprofit organization devoted to maintaining it for public contemplation. And, just as *Double Negative* is visited by thousands of people annually, especially by those from overseas who are fascinated by both Heizer's work and the openness of the American desert, the void of the Great Basin, a space they do not have available at home, so, too, *City* may become a destination where the void is still visible on the face of the planet.

I'm still working on my set of rhetorical questions as I wander down off *Complex Two* and over to the easternmost edge of the cleared site for *City.* A few weeds and grasses have established themselves on the site during the rains, a green fuzz that will be bladed off in the next few weeks, but the perimeter is still quite distinct, a low rim of dirt bulldozed along the edge separating the piece from the sagebrush and halogeton. I bend to pick up a stray piece of concrete from *Complex One* that has been pushed up to the boundary. Almost exactly the size of my hand, and nearly as light and porous as a piece of pumice, the solidified cinder mix is lightly coated with pale dust. It looks like a natural piece of the valley, and I am unsure if I'm picking up a fragment of sculpture or of place. Both, I surmise, carrying it back to the house, a sonic boom rattling faintly over the desert at my back.

THE NEXT MORNING I get out of bed an hour before sunrise, leaving Beth still asleep. I close the bedroom door and turn on a desk light over my scattered papers, and there rests the fragment of *Complex One* that Heizer assured me over dinner was mine to keep. Evidence, I think to myself as I heft it, something I can carry with me to evoke the memories, which in turn will make it possible to write about *City* and, by extension, the Great Basin. I don't have any specific plan this morning, but am definitely restless from being back in the Basin. Moving from Nevada to Santa Fe several years ago, and then to Los Angeles, has left me feeling as if I'm geographically unanchored. Sitting at the desk with the granular chunk of concrete in hand, I realize that I'm investigating how we use memory to transform land into landscape, or space into place, in order to reaffirm my own placement.

The Basin is, though not exactly empty, after all a desert, and as such is much less filled up with artifacts than other kinds of places. It's been civilized much less by us than the forests of the mid-Atlantic, which have been harvested several times over in some places, or the Great Plains, which have been plowed and replowed hundreds of times. Memory is therefore more precarious here, won and maintained by late-twentieth-century Americans with more difficulty than elsewhere. Walking or driving through a cultivated or built environment, assuming it has any longevity during our lives, means we can collect stories about what happened in those places. It has landmarks to which we anchor those stories. We construct a narrative of the larger world that contains and reinforces our lives. "Here's the street corner where I got into my first accident," or "There's the house where my wife lived before we met." Without such markers in what we perceive to be an empty landscape (that is, egocentrically, a land empty of visible human gesture), it is harder for us to build such a context for our lives. The lack of human-derived visuals and our inability to remember specifics about the desert is directly related to my disconcerting sagebrush dislocation the last time I was here. Out of sight, out of memory.

Just as we experience a cognitive dissonance when we try to acquire an accurate spatial perception of the Great Basin, so we suffer from a contemporary inability to stratify time in it. Without constant practice, it all looks much the same, and without markers in space we lose track of time. Memory in the Great Basin wouldn't be so difficult to acquire for a people used to living, as we say, closer to the land, whether they be natives of the Australian outback with their songlines, which recapitulate and mentally re-create the features of the land, or Western Apaches with their numerous and richly endowed place-names, each of which refers to specific stories rooted to place. Even most ranchers working in the Great Basin, as improbable an activity as that can be in the drylands, have built up enough sensitivity over intimate local conditions to retain a fully realized set of memories in the desert. "Here's where I lost a calf to heat that one summer when there was no snow on the peaks since June" is a memory that can carry with it an entire family history and the meteorological record of more than a century. Contemplating the rock art they find on the rangelands that was made by Paleo-Indians, they easily identify their own struggles with the economics and operating ethics of animal husbandry during the last several millennia.

But for a boy raised in a two-story brick house in Reno, even though I spent as much time outside as I could as a kid, keeping hold of the desert means staying in it, or at least visiting frequently, making afresh the old memories and constantly creating new ones.

Shrugging on a pullover, I step outside. The stars are gone, and there is a hint of light on the horizon. My shorts are sufficient cover for my legs in the cool air as long as I keep moving, so I walk briskly along the quarter mile from the house to *City*. To the right, three or four coyotes softly yowl, pacing me a few yards off in the sagebrush. The one farthest behind calls to the one or two next to me, who then call to the leader a few yards ahead, or so it seems to me. The melodic, minor-key yowling has no echo—the space here is too large—but, instead, sounds as if it is an echo in and of itself, exactly the kind of sound you would expect in a void. Its eerie self-referentiality is another way of measuring the space and my response to it.

This isn't a threatening situation, though I'm definitely more awake than I was when I first walked outside. Solo coyotes don't bother me, and are welcome when I'm out camping. Coyotes in packs, however, are cause for watchfulness. We've been enforcing a lopsided program of selective breeding upon them for more than a hundred years, the federal government alone since 1990 killing more than 638,000 of them. Nonetheless, during the twentieth century coyotes have vastly extended their range and population from their original habitat in the Great Plains to the entire continent. They can now be found from the Arctic Circle to Costa Rica, and they're not exactly getting more shy. What the species was in the mid-1800s is no more, having been forcibly evolved into an animal with a very different and perhaps more intelligent agenda. It gives one pause to think, but when I turn to trudge up the west ramp of *Complex Two*, they fall silent. I have the advantage of height, which makes them nervous about being spotted, and I can turn my attention to the approaching sunrise and its effects on the site.

In the just-before-dawn light, the absence framed by *City* is much more palpable than in the strong unfiltered daylight of the high desert. Last year Heizer made two new "negative paintings," empty square and circular steel frames. They need to be watched for a while before it becomes apparent that the frames are not the art. They are devices to focus our attention on what's not there, the spaces enclosed by the steel. That's also one aspect of *City*. The geometrical lines and solids of the complexes are more than just a frame, are indeed objects to be looked at and considered, but they also define and articulate an empty space, an absence, that is an essential component of the sculpture.

I say "watched" instead of "looked at" because the active elapsing of time in the process of consideration is important. We don't just look at, or even into, a void, though that's how we usually "frame" the activity with words. We actively engage it. We first look at it, then into, then all around it to see if we can find its edges, not least of all so we don't fall into it! Our vision penetrates the empty space, and our eyes attempt to focus, an automatic and uncontrollable reaction of the nervous system that is doomed to failure, there being nothing our binocular gaze can coordinate upon in space. All of this takes a few seconds before either we begin to move away from what has become an unsettling experience, or we settle down to see what happens.

Often our responses are those mental and perceptual shifts into what we define as meditation and/or hallucination; the longer we watch, the stronger becomes the dislocation out of our everyday train of thought. Just as the disturbed soils of the desert floor provide a ready habitat for plant species alien to the native flora, so does the dissonance in our perceptions allow us to drift from reality and into extended speculations over matters spiritual. Desert voids have spawned the world's great monotheisms, are fertile ground for Ghost Dancers and peyote worshipers, the shamans of the Anasazi, and the frankly mystical Art Bell broadcasting from Pahrump on the other side of the Test Site.

The sun is coming up through the same low pass through which I first saw the bomber yesterday afternoon, and it throws my shadow from the top of the long berm out across the desert floor for a quarter mile, breaking the otherwise clean sweep of slanting lines cast out from *Complex One* and *Two*. I'm disconcerted to see myself in the world after being lost to it for a few peaceful moments. More accurately, it is a negative image of myself, and I move to the far side of the berm to erase it, a playful "double negative" of my own. Within seconds the sun hits the valley floors, a thermal shift that starts the air moving. By the time I've finished my notes fifteen minutes later, the breeze is enough to flutter the tops of the weeds on the sculpture.

IT'S OBVIOUS THAT Jennifer and Mary have determined that Heizer needs a break today, a Saturday, and that they have chores to attend. Breakfast is finished, and they suggest that perhaps Beth and I would like to drive up into the mountains. Jennifer has been up there recently and says the wild-flowers are spectacular. Heizer considers this briefly, then adds: "Maybe we should go look at Railroad Valley. It's one of the longest in the Great Basin. We can drive through the mountains, go up the valley to this one pass that I've never been through, then head back here. Lotta miles, though."

We pull out three or four maps, and though Beth and I aren't anxious to impose on his hospitality, we'd love to spend the day with Heizer just driving around. So, once again in the Dodge pickup, we take on a circumambulation around part of the valley before entering a canyon, passing along the way scattered traces of abandoned ranches. I can never look at fenced-in land, or for that matter any settlement in Nevada, without wondering where it is in its life cycle. Nevada has seen roughly five hundred towns come and go since the mid-1800s, a reflection of how human endeavor plays out against limited resources in the Great Basin. As we drive through the valley, we can see a deep set of scars on the lower flanks of a mountain, part of a mining scam from earlier in the decade. The con man who seeded the mine with gold and duped investors into buying shares was eventually caught and sent to jail, but no one has the time, money, or force of law to come in and repair the highly visible damage left behind on the treeless side of the mountain. The disturbance will remain visible for decades, an interesting and instructive contrast to *City*, which from an equal distance is all but invisible.

A few cattle are cooped up in a corral, awaiting the disposition of a cowboy who is nowhere near in sight. Once we reach the partial shade of the canyon there are a couple of cabins and even a mobile home scattered up the road, one a rustic getaway for an urbanite who has colonized the former remains of a ranch. This remains easier territory for the contemplation of nature than it is for the running of livestock, no matter the scientific advances in husbandry. Besides periodic droughts, the creep of halogeton, increasingly numerous coyotes, and the occasional marauding mountain lion, the sheep and cattle of the Great Basin face the vagaries of a volatile marketplace, whereas scenic contemplation is a limited commodity with a steadily rising commercial value. Both uses of the land have their environmental tradeoffs, however; the road building, plot grading, and visual pollution of vacation homes as troublesome as overgrazing.

Several miles up into the range, at something higher than sixty-five hundred feet in elevation, we take a right-hand fork in the road and make the climb over to another drainage. Heizer leans out of the cab, scanning the mostly piñon and juniper forest into which we've ascended. A few big Jeffrey pines stand here and there, second-growth timber recovering from the incursions of the nineteenth century. Once over the ridge separating the two canyons and headed down to a creek, Heizer starts pointing out stands of both dead and living mountain mahogany.

"Old 'hog," he says, pointing out the windshield. "That dead wood standing in there?—probably several hundred years old. We used to come up here every year, early in the fall, and haul out cords of that stuff for firewood, it burns so slow and hot. Too much trouble now, and we use coal." He stops the truck. "Maybe we should take just a little for a barbecue, though."

Beth and I pile out and pick our way over to a sizable snag, more of a large dead bush than a tree. Without much difficulty we dismantle the brittle remains, some of which is already down, and drag it over to the truck. All around us steep reddish brown cliffs step up to the ridges, volcanic ash flows solidified over time and pocketed with numerous caves and fissures. It's a mountain scene found the length of the Great Basin, from its southern extremities in the Mojave to where it closes off in southern Oregon, the tectonic stresses that produced the alternating basin and ranges accompanied by volcanic activity throughout the millennia.

Back in the truck we continue down to the creek, marked by a line of dense foliage, then bear uphill, continuing our climb through the mountains. The going is steep and the diesel engine labors steadily in low gear, but the road is a good one, originally the stagecoach route that passed through Tonopah on its way to San Francisco from Denver. Now it is frequented by campers, hunters, corporate mining engineers on the prowl, and people harvesting piñon nuts in the fall. Heizer peers at intervals into the tops of the piñon pines, pointing out the proliferation of small green cones sitting heavily on the branches. "Going to be a good year," he judges. "Not the best one I've ever seen, but a really good one." Toward the very top the grade gets progressively rougher, and we shake our heads over what it must have been like to get a team of horses up here, much less a stage and passengers. Presumably, they got out and walked.

We pause at the top, and Heizer backs us into a single campsite where we'll have lunch on a bed of soft pine needles in the shade. The map shows our elevation to be more than seven thousand feet. The floor of the desert, just visible between bends in the canyon walls, lies at least twenty-five hundred feet lower.

"This is the epicenter of the Great Basin," Heizer declares. "At least, according to the geology books I have." I knew that the central upwelling of crust underlying the formation of the Great Basin was located in this part of the region, but I hadn't ever expected to be sitting on a pivot point of the void with its master artist eating peanut butter and jelly, and at first I'm doubtful of what seems too easy a literary coincidence. Then I remember that the Heizer family has been intimate with the geology of the West since the late 1800s. One of his grandfathers was chief geologist of the State of California, and the other a renowned mining engineer and general manager of Nevada Massachusetts, an English-owned gold mining company that was based in Reno. In fact, given his family's history in the state, Michael considers it a fluke that he was born across the border in California. In compensation, it seems to me, he takes pride in his knowledge of geology in the Great Basin, maintaining a library of earth science books to back him up.

Heizer, having finished his sandwich, leans back and rests his forearm over his eyes, not so much asleep as simply checked out for a few minutes. It's obvious he's enjoying himself, but is easily tired by the driving, and I'll offer to spell him a little later. Beth turns over a small piece of white chert she's found nearby, chipped from a point by a native sometime in the last ten thousand years. I stand, brush off, and head up a faint wagon trail following the ridgeline. Within less than a minute there is no evidence that anyone else is around, and I've stepped into a wilderness. The trail subsides into stony ground, and I step left, away from any trace of passage. It's easy to see why prospectors complain that they can no longer explore in the area because of the rampant growth of the underbrush. When the tall timber was cut out of here in the 1800s, the denser piñon-juniper forest with its brushy understory began to take over. Under protection by the Bureau of Land Management it firmly established its hold, and now, once off the old track, the brush is thick, dry, prickly. The atmosphere is still with not even a birdsong or a contrail disturbing it.

Looking through the gap below, I can peer down to the far playa, an empty white page from up here. Although I don't know what we'll find down in Railroad Valley, I do know that what looks like an empty space awaiting the inscription of our passage is far from devoid of presence, human and otherwise. As throughout most of the Great Basin, life and history are present in the valley, but simply in a way much less visible than what we are accustomed to, allowing us to mentally eliminate it, to frame it outside the picture we want and need to see. The historical changes in the valley, the ones we have been able to keep track of and measure ourselves against, have occurred only in the last 170 years, a rapidity typical of the American West. Although somewhat arbitrary as demographic milestones, the frontier had no more been opened officially in 1862 with passage of the Homestead Act, than Frederick Jackson Turner declared it closed in 1893, a theoretical change in status that nevertheless generated instant nostalgia throughout the society. The result is that we tend to consider the West as a mythical territory: in our imagination, cowboys and cavalry continue to cohabit the desert with cocaine smugglers and aircraft on maneuvers.

Our national character was forged, in no small part, by the notion of exploration and settlement, by the story we told ourselves about the conquering of an empty frontier, about the pushing forward, mile by mile, of civilization. The desert was the trial we endured before reaching the promise of California and the West Coast, a characterization that not only has some truth to it, but also has been reinforced through the stories we tell ourselves and the lack of perceptual evidence to contradict them.

The desert, and our various inabilities to perceive it, allow us to imagine that such empty places really existed and that the story was true—and often to erase the occupation by Native Americans. I gaze out across the desert and know I can imagine myself as Jedediah Smith, the first Euroamerican to cross the Great Basin and to see, in 1827, the playa below. I can construct a story about his self-reliance and the nobility of his quest for the Rio Buenaventura, presumably a dangerous exploration undertaken on behalf of civilization, and then imagine myself in his place. Or, I can call up Frémont, the next white explorer to venture through, twenty-seven years later in 1854 on his fifth great journey around the West, as he crossed through the pass where Mary cut down the juniper tree. I have no direct memory, obviously, of these men, only of their published reports and maps and the numerous books and movies made about them. They have been mythologized by our culture as part of the national story, which I've been ingesting since I was a kid in grade school.

The Great Basin is a harsh environment that has been trying to the survival skills of everyone who has lived in it, whether the Indians, the explorers, or the miners or ranchers—men and women often genuine and even courageous exemplars of self-reliance—but Railroad Valley is not an impossible place. Some authorities go so far, in fact, as to describe it as one of the wetter valleys in the Basin. Although the temperatures can range from 30 below zero in the winter to 115 degrees or so in the summer, and the total precipitation in some years can be limited to only four inches on the playa, the Grant and Quinn Canyon Ranges to the east of the valley receive as much as thirty-five inches annually, enough to fill two perennial streams and perhaps as many as ten intermittent ones, all flowing out of the canyons such as the one we're about to descend. Several springs in the valley even hold endemic, if threatened, species of fish. Botanists have counted at least 250 different kinds of flowering plants in the valley, and although that's far lower than the 970 plants cataloged in that archetypal basement of the Great Basin to the south, Death Valley, it's still a healthy and diverse biotic community, though not exactly an easy place to make a living.

According to current estimates, several waves of nontechnological peoples inhabited central Nevada for at least 11,500 years prior to Euroamerican settlement. They hunted giant ground sloths and mammoths ten millennia ago, made tools out of wood, bone, antler, and stone, and by a thousand years ago were either trading for or producing their own pottery. Railroad Valley was used as a seasonal hunting ground, and may even have been inhabited at times when the climate was favorable. When Frémont went through the valley in the 1850s, however, he was advised by the Mormons in Utah to avoid traversing this part of the Basin for lack of water; and it is true that he didn't see another person for the three hundred miles between western Utah and the Sierra Nevada. But by 1866 silver had been discovered at the southwestern corner of the valley and the town of Reveille was built. The valley has been mined throughout the last 125 years for everything from silver and gold to salt and oil, and some of the land claimed that decade has since been occupied continuously by ranchers, prospectors, cattle rustlers, schoolteachers, attorneys, and miners.

On the other hand, the valley is 120 miles long, and the mountains on either side range from 7,000 to more than 11,500 feet in elevation. There are now only two communities in the valley, the Duckwater Indian Reservation, which was established in the 1940s and holds about 185 persons, and the town of Currant, population officially around thirty. Apart from a few assorted ranchers, the surrounding thirteen hundred or so square miles is mostly uninhabited. The nearest towns are Ely, fifty miles northeast, and Tonopah, roughly ninety miles to the southwest. In terms of historic time, the most lively days of the valley were in the late 1800s, when the mines were going full bore and portable sawmills were set up in the nearby mountains. Apart from a small oil boom in the 1950s, and the subsequent twenty or so field hands maintaining the pumps, the population has mostly been in decline ever since.

Although the desert is not a blank slate, it's empty enough in comparison to what we are used to that we're prone to transform it in our imaginations into a literal void that happily receives our mythic inventions, which range from the Virginian and the Lone Ranger to the space operas that have evolved from those stories, such as *Star Wars.* Not only does the dissonance we experience in looking at the desert prevent us from examining it too closely, we're actually anxious to edit out awareness of its history and biotic community. We want, apparently even need, to see it as that void that helps define us as a people. The more crowded the planet becomes, the more contested the supposed nobility of our history, the more we need the void as a physical purity to reassure us that all is not lost. So desperate are we to maintain a connection to the myth of frontier, that uncorrupted state of mind where we still have a chance to heroically reestablish ourselves in a garden without sin, that we bring "the final frontier, space," into the Great Basin, declaring that the aliens are here.

BACK AT THE LUNCH SITE, Beth and Mike are much as I left them a few minutes ago. Heizer gets up in slow stages as Beth and I reload the coolers into the bed of the pickup. The road down from the summit is even steeper than our approach up from the east, and we ease out in low gear. We quickly leave behind the cool, open vantage of the heights for the brush-choked canyon, the high walls of which to the south I think are rhyolite, but lower down and to the north are limestone pocketed with caves. On the outside passenger side of the cab, I hang over the edge of the road and count large tree stumps left over from the last century, as well as the occasional cache of rusting tin cans. Beth manages the complicated array of maps, pads, the altimeter, pens, and a bag of hard candies for sucking on in the heat. Heizer is driving one-handed down what is, at times, more of a dirt embankment than a road, telling stories about driving up this pass in winter, though why anyone would attempt it in several feet of snow in anything less than a Humvee is a mystery to me.

In early afternoon we reach Railroad Valley, and Heizer points out the Bordoli Ranch. Almost entirely hidden by lush cottonwoods, the ranch was originally called Italian Springs, but was bought in 1897 by Martino and Santina Bordoli. Their family owned the ranch until 1958, just one year after seven-year-old Martin Bordoli, grandson of the original owners, died of leukemia. The Bordolis had been featured in *Life* magazine as early as June 1957 in an article that questioned the safety of nearby aboveground nuclear explosions. Brokenhearted and angry over the loss of their son, whom they considered a casualty of fallout from the Test Site less than thirty-five miles away, Martin's parents sold the place and moved. The ranch has once again achieved notoriety as the more recent site of the infamous Casey cattle-rustling operation, which John McPhee wrote about in the *New Yorker* in 1993. But for me, though rustling is as integral a part of the livestock scene in Nevada as a rodeo, the ranch is more important as a touchstone in the history of how we mistreat the Big Empty of the West.

Again, like outer space, a frontier into which we assume we can simply shoot off nuclear waste if we need to, the Great Basin is an earthbound analog; it is a terrestrial space in which we presumed to blow up and distribute the most toxic substances on the planet because we thought it was so large the stuff couldn't turn around and bite back. We were wrong—there are now more than fourteen hundred toxic areas that need cleaning up on the Test Site, some of which are leaking radiation into the groundwater that may slowly move south toward Las Vegas—but we continue to consider the desert a safe place to dump nuclear and other hazardous wastes.

It's bad enough that hundreds of square miles of the Basin have been made uninhabitable for the ten-thousand-year half-life of the plutonium we've scattered about within the boundaries of the Test Site, but we also spread airborne radiation from atmospheric tests clear across the country, apparently raising the incidence of thyroid and other cancers in the Midwest for the remainder of the century. What Railroad Valley experienced from the testing was even more severe, and so willfully bizarre it reads now almost more like science fiction than fact.

The Atomic Energy Commission had been looking for an excuse to move its bomb tests from the remote Pacific atolls to a less expensive land base for some time, but not until America entered the Korean War was public perception judged favorable enough to do so. Paranoia plus public relations overruled common sense. In December 1950 the Air Force approved use of the Las Vegas Bombing and Gunnery Range for the tests;

President Truman signed off on the deal a few weeks later, and in late January the first atomic device was detonated on the floor of the Nevada desert. Following this fast track to apocalypse, perhaps more than two hundred aboveground tests were conducted until July 1962.

The Nevada Test Site, just sixty-five miles northwest of Las Vegas, was chosen over alternative possibilities in New Mexico, Utah, and northern Nevada not because it was the most remote, but because the prevailing winds blew straight into the void of the Great Basin. The officials acknowledged that the area was inhabited, but at a level less than anywhere else in the country over the longest distance, thus allowing maximum dispersal of radiation with minimum exposure to major civilian populations. It was a risk equation that's been used ever since.

The winds in southern Nevada prevail from west and southwest to east and northeast—right up the Reveille, Railroad, and Sand Spring Valleys. The ranchers in those valleys would get their children up at four in the morning to view the tests clearly visible in the predawn light, even though some of them were conducted 125 miles away, clear across the Test Site near its far western edge. Dust from the subsequent mushroom clouds sometimes coated everything in the valleys, blocking out the sun and sending chickens into their henhouses to roost. By one account, prospectors walking through Reveille Valley after the tests got such high readings on their Geiger counters that they thought they had discovered a fortune in uranium deposits. It was just fallout on the sagebrush.

Cattle and ranch hands developed radiation burns on their exposed skin from the fallout; dogs and sheep went blind and, along with the locals, lost their hair. In 1979 a Nevada newspaper estimated that somewhere between sixteen and twenty thousand people living within three hundred miles of the Test Site were directly exposed to fallout from eighty-four aboveground tests, and Martha Bordoli stated that at least fifteen of the seventy-five or so people who lived in Railroad Valley during that period had already died from or were suffering from cancer. Despite the eventual establishment of an extensive network of air sampling stations throughout the region, such as the one in Heizer's yard; despite the development of cancer by even some of the officials since monitoring the activity; and, despite the twenty-five to fifty thousand dollars in stipends paid to compensate more than a thousand victims of the fallout and their heirs, people still argue about whether or not fallout from the tests really harmed anyone.

Driving by the Bordoli place sobers my otherwise jubilant mood. The dozens of radiation monitors scattered throughout this part of the state aren't a joke, any more than are the bombers and fighters that target farming structures in the valleys for war games. The military is a constant, usually low-level presence in the background here, and I wonder about the exposure that has been spread pervasively across much of the state. The radiation levels that are up in the groundwater on the Test Site, for example, show contamination spreading much more quickly and widely than previously thought. Radioactive waste has been stored there for decades, and there are no ironclad assurances—even after fifteen years of studies and tests costing more than $3 billion—that when Yucca Mountain opens up as a high-level repository for nuclear waste there won't be an increase in unexpected releases of radiation into the environment. It is a dangerous combination, our cognitive difficulties in assessing the true nature of the desert compounding the lies we tell ourselves in minimizing the dangers of nuclear waste. The fallacy of the risk equation will become all too apparent once a major population is affected, such as that of Las Vegas.

About the time I finish scribbling a few notes to remind myself to look up some of the facts and figures about atomic testing in the '50s, my pad and pen meeting only on every other bounce of the truck over the washboard we're experiencing, Heizer points out the playa that shimmers in the heat before us. Behind us, south, the valley just rolls off the horizon. Ahead and to the north, past the blank white sheet of the playa, the land rises toward the boundary of the Duckwater Indian Reservation. Ten miles west a cluster of volcanic hills marks the official rim of the valley; thirty miles beyond that the summits of the Hot Creek Range rise a mile above the valley floor, defining the visual basin. It's this combination of the two, the unbounded north and south with the distant but defined escarpments to the west and east, that makes the space so large in human terms. Long enough that we cannot see its ends, yet just narrow enough that we can intuitively triangulate our position and understand the reach of the valley floor, we are greatly humbled. Whereas in most parts of the world you're lucky to see a few hundred square miles from the vantage point of the heights, here we are near the bottom of the valley—yet can see more than a thousand square miles, a contrast closely related to the one evoked by *City* with its bounded space underneath the boundless sky.

As always, when defining our relation to landscape spatially, the temporal side of the equation has to be taken into account, and here, too, the naked structure of the land puts us "in our place." Geology is evident everywhere there is a contour line. Once your eyes are used to the overall great flatness, slight horizontal disruptions reassert themselves around the rim of the valley as gravel bars defining ancient shorelines. You can trace the prehistoric beaches from which native peoples fished ten thousand years ago. Looking up at the surrounding ranges, hundreds of millions of years of strata are displayed. Deeply preconditioned by landscape photography of the West, which since the mid-1800s has sought to portray it as a region of monumental geological antiquity, our individual and racial life spans are thrown into sharp contrast here with the land itself. Where the geological clock is disguised in other regions by forest or ocean, field or ice, here it surrounds us, forming the very walls of our vision.

It's all lunar and lunatic as we roll north, paralleling one of those desiccated gravel shorelines that belonged to the thirty-by-fifteen-mile pluvial lake that once covered this end of the valley, one of a pair of local Pleistocene bodies that slowly dried up over thousands of years, leaving behind only the salty, dry lake bed. What looks from a distance to be a structure hundreds of feet tall out in the middle of the valley turns out ten minutes later to be a lone cottonwood sucking up some underground water, its size magnified by our need for vertical relief. The playa starts just past the tree and rolls on like an advertisement for the moon. Despite the rattling of the pickup bed, the steady deep chugging of the diesel, and a wind leak that has erupted somewhere in the frame of my window, the impression outside is one of stillness. Then Heizer sees something off to the left and brakes. He waits for the dust to catch up and blow past us before putting the truck in reverse for thirty yards.

"Something worth looking at here." Like most people who live in the desert, from sheepherders to sculptors, Heizer is always curious about abandoned structures and the narratives they hint at in a landscape that otherwise offers little physical evidence of such. He turns off the engine—and the air-conditioning—opens the door, and steps stiffly out. I do the same, my legs creaky from bracing against the floorboards. Beth follows. Gasps. Almost gets back in the truck. It's hot with that kind of dry convection that makes contacts stick irretrievably to your eyeballs within seconds. Heizer sends me out through the sagebrush to a low structure built into the side of a wash that's about two feet deep. Beth walks with me for a minute, then drops back to the shade of the pickup. Heizer and I are used to this, more a mental game than a physical one, simply knowing in advance how the heat feels. Although Beth can move with composure in summertime Washington, D.C., through humidity so high it equals the temperatures, a climate in which I become supremely dysfunctional, she's not ready for the arid triple digits of the playa border.

I stop at a tiny cellar built into an embankment. Constructed out of what might be cottonwood logs, a roof still partially covering the interior, it's an ideal home for black widow spiders and deer mice infected with hantavirus. There is no water here now, but looking back into the Grant Range with its line of nine-hundred-foot-high limestone cliffs atop Troy Peak, then tracing the nearest canyons downward, it's easy to guess that this old springhouse was situated on one of the intermittent streams and possibly dates back as far as the 1860s. I see a couple of old tin cans and a rusted stovepipe flange; otherwise, the place is as picked clean and bleached out by heat as a cow bone. Taking a full 360-degree inspection of the surroundings, the isolation of living here more than a century ago is almost unimaginable. Although there were hundreds more people subsisting in the valley then than now, there were almost no roads nearby to speak of, save those to the mines. Food was worth more per pound than the ore. Desperate, I think to myself. Desperate.

Back in the truck with the air-conditioning going full blast we keep on our northerly heading toward the only current extractive labor of note in the valley, the oil fields. Nevada, unlike other western states such as California and Wyoming, isn't usually thought of in terms of oil wells, but ever since Clarence King in the 1870s identified oil-bearing shales in the northern part of the state, companies have been exploring on and off for the stuff, and even drilling some sporadic wells. In the early 1950s, though, Shell Oil got serious in Railroad Valley and in early 1954 brought in the state's first regularly producing well. By September of that year more than four thousand leases for the area had been awarded, and though most them were worthless, a few proved spectacular. The Grant Canyon Well #3, for instance, was at that time the most productive onshore well in the lower forty-eight states, bringing up thirty-eight hundred barrels a day. In 1995 total production from the several fields in Railroad Valley was approaching 38 million barrels, making it obvious why the National Park Service gave up considering the valley and its surrounding mountains as a potential site for a Great Basin National Park, choosing instead the Wheeler Peak–Lehman Caves area far to the northeast.

As we approach the fields, a dozen or so pumps lazily nodding their heads in the heat, our dirt road splits. Its original path, which continues straight north into the town of Currant, is overgrown with shadscale and sagebrush. The bend to the left, which enters the oil field, is identified as the Railroad Valley Road, and looks well traveled. It's not the way we'd planned on taking, a western diversion halfway across the valley, but we're leery of taking on what looks like an abandoned track. Heizer pauses, squints, and turns left.

The pumps stand out in the middle of the desert without any surrounding fences, and there's no evidence of anyone in attendance. It's rare in our society to come across undefended industrial structures, and tempting to drive over to one just to touch it, but we have a long way yet to go, this being more of a driving than a walking tour. Passing the few pipelines and what seems like a remarkable lack of clutter for an active oil field, I think about the difficulties of finding and transporting oil here.

Nevada is located in a great overthrust belt of older strata overlying younger ones, a zone stretching south out of Canada clear to Mexico, and the same formation responsible for trapping the oil found in Wyoming. That part is easy: overthrust equals oil. What isn't so easy is that the strata here have been folded so many times over that the bulk of the hydrocarbons may have evaporated millions of years ago. Overthrust notwithstanding, the tectonic deformations of Nevada geology and consequential difficulties in resource exploration here are daunting.

First there's the transportation issue, starting with getting the stuff out of the ground. The drills have to penetrate thousands of feet of gravel and fine sediments, which leads to erosion in and fouling of the drill holes. Then there's the fact that much of the product here isn't free-flowing, being too low-grade and almost as thick as tar; it has to be heated with steam before it can be pumped out. The pipelines we're passing don't go any farther than nearby collection stations where the stuff is pumped into trucks. Until a refinery was constructed at the Tonopah airport only a few years ago, the crude was driven to refineries as far away as Grand Junction in Colorado and Bakersfield in California. Overall, it seems to me to be about as economically improbable to pump oil here as to raise sheep, but people manage both, at least for short periods of time.

The road west from the field is much broader and freshly graded, obviously for exactly those tanker trucks, which in earlier days used to overturn frequently, thus providing regular employment for those locals willing to clean up the resulting mess. Now midafternoon, it is with something akin to amazement that we come across the first pavement we've seen all day, U.S. Highway 6. Running from Bishop in Owens Valley to the west, through Tonopah and east to Ely, where it ends, it's one of only three roads to traverse the central Great Basin in Nevada. Ahead of us are the relatively low and dry peaks of the Pancake Range; south and left is the playa, its nearby edge a wildlife-management area for migrating birds.

Heizer doesn't so much stop as simply change mental gears as he turns to the right, back north toward where the valley rises gradually but inexorably to the horizon. The truck cab is suddenly dozens of decibels quieter. The first cars in Nye County came through in 1903, but prior to the 1920s almost no one in Railroad Valley had ever laid a hand on even motorized farming equipment, much less a car. Oddly enough, though, the Great Race of 1908 from New York to Paris actually passed through the valley, the American team bogging down in alkali and quicksand halfway across. The route was briefly considered for the first transcontinental highway, but lost out to what is now U.S. Highway 50, which has been labeled the "Loneliest Road in America." If U.S. 6 had been the route, it would have been lonelier. Much lonelier. There are fewer than half the number of towns surviving on this route than on its counterpart to the north.

Taking the highway for only about twenty miles and as many minutes, the relative peace gives me a chance to reflect on what remains the most valuable resource yet extracted from underneath the valley: water. The northernmost subdivision of Las Vegas is, as the crow flies, 160 miles south and across the Test Site. In 1989 the city applied for 246,500 acres of groundwater rights from as far away as 300 miles north (a much longer reach than even the legendary 175–mile-long water grab into the Owens Valley made by Los Angeles in the 1930s). The fossil water that's been accumulating under Railroad Valley since the last ice age is, for all practical human purposes, a nonrecharging resource. It's under siege from Las Vegas, which already overdraws its allotment of Colorado River water—and with a population due to double sometime in the next decade.

If Las Vegas builds up a dependence on this northern aquifer, which will dry up just as surely as its midwestern counterpart, the Ogallala, there will be an urban collapse of stunning magnitude. Even if Las Vegas were to trim its extravagant habits of using roughly twice as much water per capita than Tucson, and even if it were to switch from watering its lawns and golf courses with potable to gray water (uses that currently consume 60 percent of city water), there is a definite growth limit the city will reach soon based on available, renewable water supplies. In light of the prodigious two-acres-an-hour development rate in Las Vegas that the real estate people maintain, it seems the message is not getting through.

None of this even begins to address what would, of course, happen to the streams and springs in the valleys of central-eastern Nevada, and the precariously balanced ecosystem they support, all of which would simply dry up and blow away, just as they have in the lower Owens Valley. An increasingly common alliance of ranchers and environmentalists have filed some preemptive strikes in the legal battles, but it is a near certainty that Las Vegas will continue to seek the water. The struggle can only intensify over the years, and it's hard to see how virtually a handful of locals could forestall forever the thirsty millions down south.

This is another one of the primary by-products of our failure to perceive the desert on its own terms, instead of through the lens of our expectations. We think a large, empty space equates to an opportunity for urban growth, the extreme outcome of which is the fantasy we call the Las Vegas Strip. But, given that deserts worldwide now support around a sixth of the planet's population, a percentage that in the next century could rise, astonishingly, to as much as 50 percent, this outlandish example of such a catastrophic water withdrawal based on population pressures may prove to be just a sign of things to come. It remains amazing to me that John Wesley Powell, the great explorer of the Grand Canyon and one of our country's most important public scientists, basically warned Congress as long ago as 1877 in his *Report on the Lands of the Arid Regions* against the transfer of water from one watershed to another, or from one hydrological basin to another. He knew that the intermountain West was mostly a desert with insufficient water to support more than a relative handful of communities; preventing water transfers would have been a logical governing factor on growth. Las Vegas, sitting just within the borders of the Colorado River drainage system, would have had to live within a much smaller hydrological sphere if Powell's philosophy had prevailed, and would certainly have not been able to contemplate taking water out of the most severely circumscribed hydrological region in the country, the Great Basin.

My speculations about water, arising whenever driving around the arid West, are cut short by our arrival in Currant. Since the 1870s, Currant has sat at the crossroad of east-west and north-south routes through the valley, which explains why it had one of the first two and only gas pumps within easy driving distance. The road from the northwest comes through the Duckwater Reservation, and the road northeast goes to Ely; a network of dirt roads veers in from the remaining quarters, and we'll take one of them to continue our tour. There are no signs of life this afternoon, but it's rumored that the Freemen have moved down from Montana and are now squatting in the few scattered buildings and trailers that make up the dusty town. If so, they're probably isolated enough in a county with so few law enforcement resources that they might actually be left alone for a while.

After consulting a couple of maps to make sure we're taking the right dirt road, we leave the pavement behind for the remainder of the day and head back up into the mountains on one of the few roads in the entire region that Heizer hasn't driven. He's looking forward to it, tired but curious, leaning back against the seat and scanning the scenery.

This leg, the shortest of the four, appears to be in direct contrast to the rest of our journey. We're neither in high mountains nor on the exposed valley floor, but driving up and down through low hills. We pass an astonishing layer of red volcanic tuff under the predominate limestone of the high peaks; nearby there's reputedly a rock shelter where more than a hundred mysterious red tally marks were painted on the rocks by prehistoric peoples. Then, snaking through a narrow, dry creek bottom, we pass one of the three vehicles we've seen all day, occupied by a group of college students from California studying the bizarre geology.

The hillsides around us are studded with three-foot-tall white PVC—polyvinyl chloride—pipes, the ubiquitous claim markers of international mining companies that stick up out of the ground as if ventilating the earth. Heizer stops the truck while I get out to examine one, but the claim information suspended on a wire inside the plastic tube is unreadable. Nevada, though it may not be populated very densely, has been prospected down to the square inch, about 250 geologists deployed around the state at any given time looking for mineral deposits suitable for mining.

Where gold was present but too dispersed to be economically feasible for mining in the last century, heap leaching can now be profitably employed. Instead of following rich veins of ore, huge earthmovers simply tear down entire mountains containing low-grade deposits, piling the dirt into heaps over which a weak cyanide mixture is sprayed. As the chemical percolates down through the piles, it picks up the microscopic gold for recovery in the precipitation ponds waiting below. It's an efficient process that has made Nevada one of the largest gold-producing regions in the history of the world, though it has killed a lot of birds using the Great Basin flyway from Canada to Mexico, which mistook the poisonous ponds for fresh water. Most of the cyanide pools are now covered by netting, and environmental concern has shifted to the deleterious effects on groundwater, as yet not fully known.

Another worry is how all of this widespread teardown is making Nevada look. It's not so much that the majority of residents are worried about scenic values in a place they jokingly refer to as having been forgotten by its creator—most of them have never seen one of the mines up close and in person. But Nevada mining is subject to federal and state environmental laws, and the mining companies are required to post bonds to ensure that they return their properties to a state suitable for grazing, wildlife, or other recreational and industrial uses. The Anaconda Minerals Company even commissioned Heizer in 1980 to do a makeover of its huge site in Tonopah, and he prepared drawings for what would have been a truly massive effort. *Geometric Land Sculpture,* a project that would have required the moving of 100 million tons of mine tailings over twenty years, was eventually canceled, much to his relief. He did go on to make *Effigy Tumuli,* a sculpture comprised of five huge totemic mounds on a 130-acre mesa overlooking the Illinois River, a former mining site, but he insists that his work only coincidentally has anything to do with reclamation. Heizer does care about the responsible use of land and the status of its health, but he is constantly aggravated by the confusion caused by people identifying his sculpture with land issues, as if his work were somehow mere landscape decoration. The mined-out places are, however, logical building sites for him, opportunities to move dirt around into sculptures where the land has already been disturbed, and where someone will pay for the machinery and labor. "Material is place, place is material." In a way, his sculptures are a continuation of the extractive efforts, this time mining the excess materials for meaning instead of minerals.

Just before we come out of the hills, emptying out into the remote arm of yet another valley, the tidy structures and corral of an old ranch come up on our right. None of us knows anything about it, only that it's noted on the map and almost too pretty to be true. Nestled in a green spot below the hills with an open view to the north, it looks like a slightly tattered Pony Express Station from a movie. Such postmodern confusions proliferate all over the West, where our nostalgia-fed appetite for dime-store novels and more than seven thousand movies about the region have not only given us a set of romantic images, but also made us suspicious and even cynical about our preconceptions. Thus, I can't tell what I'm looking at, so closely does it match my expectations for how a nineteenth-century station should appear. Is it an abandoned ranch or mail station? A historical artifact, an old movie set, or the hobby of someone from Las Vegas who is re-creating one of the above? We drive by, speculating for story, but unable to answer the question until we can look it up.

Soon we're out on the slightly downsloping flats and looking for the right choice out of the many dirt roads converging on us. Pausing at each intersection and consulting three different maps, we finally choose one track that just looks more traveled than the alternatives. I'm scanning the book of Nevada maps in my lap, a collection I know to be only minimally reliable in some areas. The Bureau of Land Management has more than ten thousand miles of roads on property it maintains, and keeping all of them straight on maps takes much more care and money than most commercial mapmakers can expend. "Mike, why are there so many roads through here? There are at least three parallel ones shown running down just this side of the valley."

"Because every ranch needed its own road to get in and out. Some of these roads are over a hundred years old. This one, I think, is an old sheep track that they still use for driving flocks down to a watering tank."

We ride mostly in silence for twenty minutes or so, tired and cramped from sitting in the truck for so long, but also in admiration of the colors that are starting to come out now that the sun is getting a little lower in the sky. The water tank comes into view right on schedule, and we make a jog to pick up a high bench road. Late in the afternoon we reenter Heizer's valley, passing a power line that is the only point of entry here for the transmission grid that covers most of America. Electricity and phone lines weren't brought into Railroad Valley until the 1970s, and not out here until about a decade ago. Heizer is still independent of both and plans to remain that way.

It's 6:25 P.M. when we pull into Heizer's yard. We've been gone almost six and a half hours and driven more than 150 miles, averaging about twenty-five miles an hour for the day, hardly the seventy-five or so most drivers maintain when crossing the Great Basin. I have less than one full page of notes, testament to both how unpredictable the road surfaces were as well as how visually fastened to the landscape I've been all day.

As Beth and I unpack the truck and wash up for dinner, I frame a conundrum: squaring the void. That is, we've circumnavigated about two hundred square miles by tracing a rough rectangle on some of the emptiest land in the country. Likewise, we have accumulated a series of observations and facts about both the space and time of our passage, a geometrical literary figure that proceeded from the here-and-now, through the far geological past and multiple horizons of human occupation in the area as we toured Railroad Valley, and then returned to the present while discussing the recent advent of a nearby power line. We've followed a literal map in order to form a cognitive one, which is built of experience and memory. I could now sit down and trace both our route and its environs on a piece of paper, accurately enough that someone else could use it to repeat the drive, and I can also tell a story about what we saw.

Yet, it's an empty feeling, as if we've driven around something and not into it. Just as the ancient mathematical quest to square the circle is doomed to failure, I have only traced a contour line in my mind, the outline of a thought. The perimeter and enclosed surface area of a circle are measured by the infinitely indeterminable number of pi, whereas the same dimensions for a square are completely and cleanly finite. You can't derive through geometry a square exactly equal in area or circumference to a circle, only imagine the possibility in your mind. I can't begin to inhabit the territory we circumscribed until I re-create it in the indefinite territory of my imagination through the act of writing it, relying upon memory and constructing a narrative.

The Chinese word for landscape is comprised of two elements, *shan* for mountains and *shui* for water. The ritual for the propitious placement of buildings and gardens is *feng shui,* wind and water. Nowhere are these principles more evident than in the desert, a space in which these contradictory and complementary elements play out their relationships in full view of the observer. Surmounting the cognitive difficulties is the challenge.

In order to distinguish, for instance, the spatial and temporal scale of the changes wrought upon mountains of the Great Basin by the erosion of wind and water, you have to be able to gauge how large the mountains, the gullies, and the crenelated ridges really are. To do so means you have to climb them and establish, for yourself and through direct contact, how long it takes to trace their features, and thus what size they are in proportion to your body. Every other knowledge of the terrain, hence of the landscape and possible relations to it, is theoretical. To experience the desert through such methods is an unlikely prospect for most people.

What I am beginning to sense is that the closest we can come to understanding the land without actually walking and climbing it is, oddly enough, not through the science of measurement, through cartography, but through art, whether it is classical Chinese landscape painting or the immense sculptures of Michael Heizer. But though the former uses clouds, atmospheric fading, and progressively overlaid outlines of topology to evoke a psychological distance parallel to that actually in the mountains, thus bringing forth the awe-full nature of large and empty space, the latter establishes the bedrock geometry underlying cognition. Landscape art can only represent the void and architecture only simulate it. Heizer's sculpture allows us to understand why we react the way we do precisely because it is not about landscape, but our actual perceptual and cognitive processes. It articulates the void and allows us to enter it.

For now, though, it's time to wash up for the dinner that will soon be on the table, maybe a barbecue cooked over some of the mahogany we've unloaded from the truck. A stroll afterward under the stars would be nice. The night sky here, in what is some of the clearest atmosphere on the continent, is so prolific with stars that, even without a moon, it's bright enough to walk in the desert. It vaults above you in three dimensions instead of the usual two, an illusion so deep it's dizzying, and you have to concentrate to keep your balance when tilting back your head to look. Then it will be time to go to bed and to sleep, that vast interior place where rectangles and other shapes will float and lock together in dreams, forming an imaginary landscape in which it might be possible to actually square a circle.

THREE

&

On the last morning of our visit, I walk out to *City* once more just before dawn, this time without the accompaniment of the coyotes. Heizer has suggested that, instead of viewing the sunrise from atop one of the berms, I catch it from below, perhaps from down in the pit as it rises behind *Complex One,* the vantage point of a photograph once taken of the sculpture. I'm a little later this morning than the last time, so the lines of *City* are more defined as I approach. Maybe it's an aftereffect of the ride through Railroad Valley, or simply the fact that it is still not light and that I am thus walking through not only the void of the Great Basin, but also another void known to all of us, the night. Whatever the cause, I realize one of the reasons that anything constructed in the desert tends to have such visual and metaphorical importance for us: the desert has no middle ground. It lacks the natural features or built structures that allow us to focus on that part of the landscape where normally our vision, hence our imagination, spends most of its time. It's another example of our dissonance with the Great Basin.

As a species, we have evolved a way to split visual information into two streams, one feeding data into a shape analyzer that helps us decide what something is, the other one into triangulating where it is located. The dates for when our cognition, upright posture, toolmaking, and rock art all evolved are matters for supposition, the only clear pattern being that those horizons in our development are constantly being pushed further back in time the more we learn. But all of them apparently developed when we were living on the edge of and on the African savanna, a rolling plain covered with tall grasses and featuring clumps of trees and water holes. The primary shape analyzers and distance-measuring devices of our brain evolved to engender our success in the forests and on the mixed terrain of the African plains. When we step into the desert, we are genetically ill-equipped to instinctively perceive it correctly. We have to think about it.

Our eyes traverse the land in a complicated series of staccato movements, "saccades," that constantly sweep the field of vision, organizing contours between light and dark, selecting shapes and details. The binocular parallelism of our vision and elevated stance enable us to measure our distance from what, it turns out, is a very limited menu of basic shapes. Out of perhaps as few as twenty-four basic geometric shapes our brain organizes the entire world, a place in which gravity has preordained there will be right angles. Thus begins the process that immediately converts land into landscape, and then translates landscape into a mental map.

All creatures react to their environment by using various senses to recognize boundaries and thus define the spaces around them, part of their essential survival repertoire. Although single-cell organisms might define their space through temperature or pressure, and choose their paths accordingly, humans engage space primarily through vision. We might stand on the side of a road in the country, for instance, and visually establish a horizon line around us by a set of far mountains seen in front and a low hill behind. Our feet would rest on a level surface with a ditch to the left and a white line to the right, boundaries marking, respectively, the edge of the road and the beginning of dirt, and the realm of traffic where it's not safe for us to enter without first checking carefully with both eyes and ears for cars ahead and behind. Perhaps a quarter of a mile away sits a barn with its yard enclosed by a fence. We would recognize private property, as well as the enclosure of animals, and know to exercise caution and courtesy when approaching. Although we couldn't see the back of the structure, a windbreak on the other side might indicate a house, and already we would be deep into constructing a cognitive map of the territory, automatically marking and projecting out danger zones, available resources, and probable lines of travel.

All of this data first would be assembled by the two or three eye movements made per second back and forth across our field of sight, then reassembled into a survival-ranked hierarchy based on our experiences and social conventions. Our vision is a matter of physics, genetics, and social constructs, hardly a simple mix, and the desert screws it all up.

The floor of the valley here doesn't offer up much in the middle range of our perception. There is the foreground—the sand underfoot and our shoes—then either bare earth or millions of apparently identical desert plants that fade quickly into an undifferentiated ground of muted color. That's all, until our vision hits the far background, the horizon. There are seldom structures, no constructed boundaries, hence no middle ground upon which the eye can settle even momentarily in order to establish a left and a right, a front and a back separate from our own body. We have nothing to which we can easily relate.

History is space and space is history, it is said, and events not only occur in space, but actually construct it, at least as far as our memories are concerned. History "takes place." The emptier the space, the less history we perceive. Without evidence of events, save those of geological occurrences mostly eons ago, we are also temporally unanchored. We're hungry for artifacts, for ruins.

Anytime we see a vertical disruption of the desert floor we have at least a spatial reference for the middle ground, hence our position in space, and usually time, as well. If it's a tree, we're able to relate our body to its height, distance, and life span. If it's a structure, we're doing roughly the same thing, adding onto the process an estimate of historical scale derived from our guesses at when was it built, by whom, and for what purpose. Without all of that we're drifting about, thrust back into a sphere of spatial perception about on par with a baby, who is concerned with and can concentrate on only the territory either within physical reach or at the natural limit of vision, whether that's a bedroom wall or a horizon. We can orient ourselves to basic directions and that's about all, too meager a body of information to buttress our sense of self against the universe for long. This is another reason science fiction plays so well when Hollywood sets it in the desert. Not only are we conditioned to see it there by almost a century of convention—the Mojave arm of the Great Basin being the nearest and most open space available to Los Angeles, hence the cheapest setting for alien fantasies—but there are few other visual referents to get in the way of the action, to intrude everyday scale and normality into the deliberate disorientation of the audience that makes them more susceptible to accepting the suspension of logic.

City is a structure built in the middle ground of a desert valley, and as such there is no competition for our attention. Like the poet Wallace Stevens's proverbial "Jar in Tennessee," it orders all around it—or, rather, enables us to do so, though as a work of art it holds a few caveats for us. Viewing *City* is not as simple as looking at telephone poles or a barn on a farm. If, for example, you don't know the size of the sculpture, it can be very confusing: the valley looks much smaller than it really is; your walking time up to the leading edge of the site seems to take forever. And if you are not aware it's an artwork, you might at first glance mistake it for a munitions storage site or the traces of an ancient civilization, another set of cognitive twists that are quite forgivable. *City* doesn't look like what we expect of art; it's too big and geometrical, too unexpectedly both a part of and apart from the land in which it sits.

I make it to the bottom of the pit just as the sun is coming up through that low pass to the east, a stream of light aimed at the opening between the first and second complexes. *City* is not in any sense a megalithic calendar, but capturing the sunrise from a specific point establishes a simple field of geometry in which the sun penetrates and links the background mountains, the midground of the sculpture, and the foreground of my own vision. It's a unifying moment that establishes the principles of visual space and the passage of time, the latter as both the daily rising of the sun and its seasonal alignment. Light fills the pit and pushes away the darkness, replaying the displacement of mass when the pit and complexes were created.

THE SUN NOW illuminating the valley, I walk back to the top of *Complex Two* in order to compute another mental triangulation, and I set my hiking compass on the concrete to take a bearing. I have been bothered, in rereading an earlier description of *City* by another author, at the assertion that the sculpture is aligned along a precise east-west axis, which somehow doesn't jibe with my own internal compass. I remember Heizer saying, during my first visit here in the fall of 1989, that he simply studied the site for months and then eyeballed the orientation so the piece would pick up as much sunlight as possible throughout the year. Sure enough, the compass shows that *City* is rotated about fifteen degrees off magnetic north, closer to how a greenhouse would be situated at this latitude in order to pick up maximum solar energy than to the cosmological ideal of an urban grid.

This reminds me that the United States Geological Survey (USGS) 7.5-minute quadrangle for this property shows another skew in the surroundings. The map, which covers more than twenty-eight hundred square miles, shows almost entirely white space with predictably sparse contour lines, a pattern interrupted only by the rocky heights of a small mountain range through which, to conflate the map with the territory, the sun has been steadily rising. Small patches of pale green indicate growth exceeding the height of the sagebrush, probably juniper.

Like all the sixty-thousand-plus topographical maps published by the USGS, the great grid of the modern world is traced out across the valley in fine black lines, demarcating the hours and minutes of latitude and longitude. Settlers in the region staked their property lines in the 1860s based on compass readings for magnetic north, a widely used system based on common sense, but one that was overruled in 1873 when the government redrew all the maps based on orientation to true north. You can still find fences in Nevada with posts stepped along the original lines, and as I spread the map out in alignment with my compass, I see that Heizer's roads, surveyed by him to trace a square around his property, are likewise a-kilter to the grid on the map, and set to magnetic north.

More than a mile above me in elevation, the handsome face of a tall peak in the region is standing in the morning sun. Less a sharply defined summit than the high point of a ridge that crests for eight miles on or above the ten-thousand-foot contour line, it reputedly hosts a fine stand of huge bristlecone pine, members of a species that in some cases grow up to almost five thousand years old, among the very oldest living individual beings on the planet. First reported by John Muir in October 1878, it is a sight both Heizer and I would like to see, though neither of us is likely to get around to it.

Muir was one of the guides for a massive surveying effort carried out by the U.S. Coast and Geodetic Survey. Their objective was to survey a twenty-five-hundred-mile arc along the thirty-ninth parallel of latitude in the United States as part of the Transcontinental Triangulation Series, the lofty mission of which was to measure the size and shape of the earth, a project not completed until 1895. This peak was one of the substations used to establish the triangles, which could run up to a hundred miles on a side, and an elaborate trail was built up it so that the ten thousand pounds of gear required to establish a signaling station could be placed on top (including the thirty-inch-long glass barometers used to measure elevation). Utilizing mirrors mounted in iron frames to reflect sunlight from summit to summit through a complicated and precise system of theodolites, the heliotropers bounced light across a hundred miles off nothing more than a three-inch piece of silvered glass twice a day, from sunrise until eight in the morning and again from four-thirty in the afternoon until sunset.

Nowadays it's done with lasers monitored by digital computers and with sophisticated satellite-borne radar systems, but triangulation remains the basis for the mathematics of surveying, whether for maps or for laying out *City*. Refined for use in the modern world during the seventeenth century in France, and quickly exported across the Channel to England, the subsequent rectangular grid soon began to propagate around the world. By 1777, the surveyor who had become the first president of the United States, George Washington, appointed one of his mapping colleagues to the army, beginning a long tradition continued by Thomas Jefferson when he created the U.S. Army Corps of Topographical Engineers, as well as the Coast and Geodetic Survey. It was to the former of these institutions that a young and ambitious army officer, John Charles Frémont, found himself attached in the 1830s.

After making his first tentative forays west tracing the upper Mississippi and Missouri Rivers under the tutelage of Joseph Nicollet, an old-school immigrant French scientist, Lieutenant Frémont was ready in 1842 to lead his first expedition. He was charged with mapping a route through the Rockies suitable for use by settlers, and hired a moody but very capable German cartographer, Charles Preuss. On the way to his jumping-off point into the wilderness, he also engaged the services of a scout who would become one of his most devoted partners, Kit Carson. Not much mapmaking seems to have occurred on the journey, and Frémont even managed to lose most of his scientific collections in a river-running episode. Instead, Frémont went mountain climbing, dragging his party up what he mistakenly declared to be the highest mountain in the Rockies. Although the expedition may not have been of primary historical significance, it established two important facts. One, Frémont was willing to diverge from his orders for the sake of exploring unmapped territory. Two, he was inclined to gain the advantage of height in order to survey his surroundings, not always the case with his more traditional and sedentary colleagues.

In 1843, by then a seasoned explorer, Frémont set out to lead what would become one of the most significant geographical explorations in the history of the country. He would convince Charles Preuss to rejoin him, and together they would make the first accurate survey of a trail penetrating the deep West, marking their progress by shooting star positions each night. Breaking camp in late May of that year from the site that would later become Kansas City, and once more in the hands of Kit Carson, they made their way to the Oregon Trail, the intended subject of their mapmaking. But first, Frémont felt compelled to make a supposedly unauthorized excursion south, probing toward where he thought the legendary Buenaventura River might be. In August his party camped along the shores of the Great Salt Lake; Frémont declared it to be a body of water residing within a huge interior basin and with no outlet to the sea, the first time such a judgment had been made by a scientifically trained surveyor. His journals reveal that he was exhilarated by the experience of circumnavigating part of the shoreline, as well as by taking a boat out to an island in the lake—and by not being swallowed in the process by the mythical whirlpool that some of his men thought existed in the eerily buoyant waters, perhaps connecting the lake to the Pacific Ocean through some fantastic subterranean tunnel. (If the Buenaventura couldn't be found on the surface, the popular imagination of the time allowed for it to flow underground.) Disappointed at not finding a trace of the river that would lead from the Rockies to the Pacific, he nonetheless wrote approvingly in his journal of standing high above the Great Salt Lake in the presence of abundant water flowing out of the Wasatch Mountains. His description of the potential lushness of the surrounding countryside, possibly rewritten by his wife, Jessie, in more imagistic terms than the original, was one that would help convince the Mormons to settle there four years later.

During the remaining months of that autumn Frémont's party traveled back north and then west in order to rejoin the Oregon Trail and terminate their explorations at Fort Vancouver, an outpost located on the Columbia River just opposite the present-day site of Portland, Oregon. When Frémont's report and Preuss's maps of their journey were published in 1845, their thorough and accurate documentation of the Oregon Trail greatly increased the westward flow of the pioneers and earned Frémont the status of a hero in Washington, D.C. What's often overlooked, though, is what he did on that trip once he had fulfilled his official obligation. Dragging the ever reluctant Preuss with him—who, apparently having had enough of both Frémont and the West, would rather have returned east the direct way—the intrepid leader politely ignored his orders once again. Or, perhaps he was just implementing what many have speculated may have been his secret and unwritten military mission, which was to furtively extend strategic knowledge of the interior in preparation for driving off the English and Spanish from the West Coast. In any case, and with the assistance of Kit Carson, Frémont took a party southward through central Oregon and toward its boundary with Nevada, fortunate in the long run that the stubborn topographer insisted on taking exacting measurements each day.

On December 16 of that year Frémont stood at the edge of an escarpment more than a thousand feet above the valley below, gazed east, and realized that he was on the opposite edge of the same "Great Interior Basin" that he had defined when standing on the bluffs above the Great Salt Lake. It was a fantastic moment in American self-discovery, an intuitive triangulation wherein Frémont realized that the Wasatch on the east, southern Oregon to his north, and the Sierra on the west enclosed a single geographical unit of immense size that was a self-contained void. It remained for him only to complete his circumnavigation of the Basin the next spring, after recuperating at Sutter's Fort from a near-disastrous midwinter trek across the Sierra into California, to determine once and for all that no Buenaventura existed.

When the boundary of the Great Basin had been roughly traced, however, the vast majority of its interior was still just blank paper; even if Frémont had laid to rest the myth of the Rio Buenaventura, the allure of the mysterious region was still growing in the American imagination. Frémont and Preuss, in bringing topographical techniques to the interior, started one of the great cartographic rushes of the nineteenth century, part of a larger intellectual movement that could trace its roots back to the Greeks and Pythagoras. Naming the world "the cosmos," a word that literally means "order," the Greek mathematicians took it for granted that the universe was a measurable entity. They observed the path and periodicity of the sun from different locations, and thus established the equator of the planet. That allowed them to mark off latitudes, and every western cartographic grid since has flowed from that baseline circumference of the earth.

It was the second-century Alexandrian geographer Ptolemy who noted that cartography wasn't just a set of equations describing relationships in space, but a pictorial representation as well. And pictures of land, whether a painting, a photograph, or a map, are notoriously biased in favor of the maker's preconceptions. Each of them picks a point of view by virtue of assuming one vantage point from among many others, and then excluding the majority of our visual perception of the surroundings with the inevitable frame—a frame that can be the camera lens, a gilded piece of wood, or just a museum wall. Even those supposedly supreme examples of the objective grid, the USGS maps, contain unnamed ironies and anomalies so manifold they could, in all statistical likelihood, never be definitively listed. For one thing, there never exists a completely accurate set of maps covering the country at any one time. The processes of geology may be slow compared to human life spans, but they're fast enough to change the course of a river in a season, to erode a mountainside into a new configuration within the long seconds of an avalanche, or to swallow up whole towns in pyroclastic flows. There are USGS maps of the Great Basin that show lakes where none any longer sit, and that represent fences that are now underwater in reservoirs. Not to mention the fact that there's no way government mapmakers can keep pace with the road building, housing developments, and overall revisionist terra-forming of American capitalism, despite our faith in their use of our tax dollars to do so.

The other minor problem with maps is that they actually do attempt to square the circle, to overlay a sphere with a rectilinear grid. This is an honorable and useful effort that nonetheless results in numerous accommodations on maps and globes, such as the sizable and often-noted exaggeration of Greenland relative to the rest of the world. In Great Basin maps this leads to small disparities in the grid that cause surveyors to adjust property lines, and for the national grid of square-mile sections to jump abruptly on some sheets in order to account for the curvature of the earth.

Maps lead us to believe that we understand where we are, and though they help us toward some consciousness of actual space, they can create a series of assumptions that can prove ultimately fatal in the desert. Knowing that we can grid off its space on paper, for example, leads to the belief that we can grid it off with asphalt. After all, it's ground that's been measured, hence we think we know the dimensions necessary for extending our habitation. However, the map says nothing about the flow of water or time, nothing about how the grid of streets will interact with alluvial drainages, and groundwater with radiation. Our cartographic imperative is a direct corollary to the doctrine of Manifest Destiny, which in the last century held that the land was ours for the taking, that America's higher purpose was to use the land so we could infinitely people it. The map grid that Frémont brought to the Great Basin is an ancestor of our overextended irrigation canals, which crisscross the desert on a pattern aligned with the maps, and of the metastasizing urban supergrids of cities such as Las Vegas.

Sitting atop *City* this morning, the sunlight well down the mountains now and filling the valley below with warmth and the rising scent of sagebrush, I take as always solace in a belief that art is a counterweight to such presumptions. You can't look at any work of art located within the context of the land—whether it is a picture representing it, or, in this case, a sculpture residing on it—without being made aware of its frame. The art places you, as a viewer, standing in front of it (or on top of it!). You establish a vantage point, one mostly directed by the artist, but also one you construct by choosing where you stand and for how long, for the experience is as much a function of time as of spatial placement. You see what has been included in the art, and wonder about what has been left out, a cognitive exercise intimately related to the business of visually identifying boundaries, whether geopolitical ones or simply that white strip next to you on the road.

In the realm of *City,* I am led to speculate on the sacred geometry of the Mesoamericans and the Egyptians, as well as the more secular outcome of mathematics in maps from ancient Greece. I trace trapezoids from the sculptures to the nearby mountains, and thus physically and mentally identify myself with the environment, a reflection measuring my state of mind much as the heliographers measured distance across the mountains. And, above all, I am led to consider the twin issues of size and scale—of how large our efforts are in moving cubic acres of dirt, of how small our effect, of how large the valley. This spatial realization is accompanied by its temporal counterpart, the scale of an hour spent with *City* contrasted with historical time and the processes of geology apparent in the hills all around me.

Although *City* is a work of material art wherein Heizer reinvents the formal language of sculpture, it also happens to be situated in the middle of a Great Basin valley. It can't help but strike a balance in our vision with the lack of visual cues in the desert. As such, it reclaims our perception, places itself between the viewer in the foreground and the nonself of the horizon, and in so doing reconstitutes our cognitive processes.

I remind myself, standing slowly, still stiff from the drive yesterday, that *City* isn't set on a place, but is a place; it is a set of complex and inspirational geometries emergent from, yet independent of, the land. It is simply what the artist, what Heizer, wants to see realized before him. Because he has constructed his vision so powerfully, even though he has not yet completed the work, we see it, too. Heizer has made the void visible by the only means we know, surrounding it by perceptible form and making geometry and nature coextensive. He has turned void-the-noun into void-the-verb.

If the void remains resistant to my efforts to capture it, accepting definition indirectly and only through my describing what I find scattered around its perimeter, *City* is the first exhibit in my contention that the void is an imaginative construct necessary for us to place ourselves in the world. We need a perceptual frontier over which we can peer in order to imagine that there is still an unoccupied space to go into, at least in our imaginations if not in reality. We need a space where the grid fails to cocoon us in an outered version of our bodies, fails to carve it up into the commodity of suburban lots. We need a space where our customary perceptual protocols fail, and we find ourselves in the presence of some other, some nonhuman sensibility. The Great Basin is one of the few such spaces we have, a fact that only increases the resonance we experience around *City*.

This morning Beth and I will drive out the long dirt road to pick up a two-lane highway, then later in Utah join the traffic on one of the interstates as we drive to a rendezvous with her daughter. From there we'll traverse into Colorado and the next day transfer to a four-wheel-drive vehicle to climb onto the Cimmaron Ridge, spending a few days with friends in a cabin above ten thousand feet and without any telephones. Nowhere on that long trip, however, will we be outside of, away from, or off the national grid charted by Frémont and his successors. Not until I'm back in the Basin later this fall will I have another chance to examine how the void manifests itself, not by escaping the grid, but by examining in person how its lines came to be drawn. Setting out by Jeep and on foot, I mean to go to what is roughly the opposite corner of the desert and to retrace some of Frémont's path and the history of cartography. This time, instead of standing on an artwork that successfully coexists with/in the void, I want to walk the visible outline of a science that, although it, too, uses geometry as its basis, has failed to come to grips with that emptiness we find so desirable, yet so elusive, that we have turned it into myth.

THE GRID

Indeed, the making of such a map is an interesting process. It must be exact. First, the foundations must be laid in observations made in the field; then the reduction of these observations to latitude and longitude; afterward the projections of the map, and the laying down upon it of positions fixed by the observations; then the tracing from the sketch-books of the lines of the rivers, the forms of the lakes, the contours of the hills. Specially is it interesting to those who have laid in the field these various foundations to see them all brought into final shape—fixing on a small sheet the results of laborious travel over waste regions, and giving to them an enduring place on the world's surface.
— John Charles Frémont

The long chain of simple and easy reasoning by which geometers are accustomed to reach the conclusions of their most difficult demonstrations, led me to imagine that all things, to the knowledge of which man is competent, are mutually connected in some way, and there is nothing so far removed from us or beyond our reach or so hidden that we cannot discover it, provided only we abstain from accepting the false for the true, and always preserve in our thoughts the order necessary for the deduction of one truth from another.
— René Descartes

Make straight in the desert a highway for our God. (Isa. 40:3)

℞

FOUR

⚘

TRYING TO KEEP UP with Alvin McLane is a bad idea unless you're a competition-ranked cross-country runner. I'm paying dearly this morning of October first for all my sins, not least among them my original laziness when faced with laps around the track in grade school. McLane is an avid hiker, climber, caver, and skier who has lived most of his life out-doors since growing up in the "hollers" of West Virginia. He's also the person who probably has walked over more of Nevada than anyone else in history, and although this morning I can't decide whether it's a blessing or a curse, I've had the unique experience of climbing and hiking with him for more than twenty-five years.

About five-foot-eleven with receding black hair, a stocky build, and a nimble gait that has more in common with a mountain goat than a human, McLane at sixty-three has the distinction of being an accepted authority on a number of things Nevadan, from its mountain ranges and caves to the routes of the early explorers, John Charles Frémont included. Through all his wanderings during recent years he's kept a scrupulous record of the rock art he has seen, both the pictographs painted on and the petroglyphs pecked into rock surfaces. At nine-thirty this morning, the sun still over the Nightingale Mountains to the east, we're threading our way through a maze of tufa on one of the ancient multiple shorelines above Winnemucca Dry Lake, once part of the ancient Lake Lahontan. The ten- and fifteen-foot-high boulders look like giant brain coral, but are in reality precipitates of calcium carbonate that settled out of the waters in the giant Pleistocene lake. And almost every surface is covered with incised petroglyphs.

Scientists still don't have a reliable dating technique for rock art, though the rate of repatination—how fast the desert varnish re-covers pecked or scratched surfaces—shows promise. Instead, they rely on the indirect context of materials found nearby, but this much is known: The shoreline we're exploring was one of many created by the Pleistocene lakes, which were at their highest fifty thousand years ago. At the retreat of the last ice age, around fifteen thousand years before present, the climate began to warm, and the waters receded even farther through the end of the Pleistocene, around ten thousand years ago. Sometime between fifty thousand and ten thousand years ago humans migrated out of Siberia and across the land bridge of the Bering Strait, probably in more than one wave, and made their way down into what would someday be the western United States.

Paleo-Indian presence in the region has been documented starting approximately at eleven thousand five hundred years before present; the cuplike depressions and caves in the tufa were used as shelter in sites such as this throughout Nevada starting as early as nine thousand years ago. Direct evidence of habitation around Lake Winnemucca dates back sixty-seven hundred years. Some of the rock art is deeply cut into the rock here, but the lines are dulled by centuries of weathering. Many of the petroglyphs are worn down almost to nothing, visible only in the acutely angled light this morning that picks up the faintest contours and shadows. Even where the rock has disintegrated into huge chunks on the ground, petroglyphs lie face down in the soil. This is an old site.

I carefully run my right hand for balance along the rocks, a pad and pen in my left, as we pick our way through the tufa, pausing only to note where we should return for a photograph. I place my hands gently because, though the tufa faces have weathered, every broken edge of the crystalline formation is razor sharp. Tufa has been known to slice standard eleven-millimeter climbing ropes into threads thin enough to use as sutures. I wouldn't be using my hands at all if Alvin wasn't in such a hurry, intent on getting us over to the dark west side of the formation. The viewing conditions would be better in the afternoon, but he's excited about showing me the first grid of the trip.

Alvin's dog, a gray and wiry six-year-old mixed breed named, appropriately enough, "Petroglyph," or "Petro" for short, runs ahead and disappears behind a low gap in the rocks. Alvin swings left and I to the right, searching for a specific glyph called "the sun and the net" by archeologists. When we find it, that's indeed exactly what it appears to be: a round body covered with a gridiron. To its immediate right is a field of interwoven diamond shapes running horizontally across the rock. A metaphorical interpretation might be that the artist, by holding tight the image of the sun, ensures its return tomorrow on the other side of the rock. The net is a classic prehistoric grid, proposed by some to be a predecessor of rock calendars that first counted off and then, eventually, came to predict the arrival and departure of the seasons. Others have interpreted the grid to represent the Milky Way and its alignment with the rising and setting of the sun. It's part of the metagrid we have constructed for our entire perceived universe, a perfectly logical and metaphorical place for us to begin this trip into one of the most barren and remote corners of the Great Basin.

Back on the front side of the rocks we prowl among the numerous examples of rock art. Alvin, who's been coming here since the 1960s, still discovers new petroglyphs every time he visits, and today is no exception. I find nested arcs, radiating lines, and multiple grids that could represent anything from celestial observations to migraine hangovers. The latter is not as far-fetched as it sounds, some rock art specialists speculating that the gridiron, lattice, and hexagonal patterns derive directly from the structure of our optic nervous system. The patterns could have been carved after experiencing the hallucinations known as "entoptic phenomena," which are seen during altered states of consciousness, a not uncommon state of mind in the desert to begin with, and one traditionally enhanced by Indians through the ingestion of various mushrooms and fermented plants.

The more traditional interpretation of the grid symbols, however, was made by Michael Heizer's father, whose 1962 book written with Martin A. Baumhoff, *Prehistoric Rock Art of Eastern California and Nevada,* offered the first categorization and classification of the symbols based on scientific method. Heizer and Baumhoff separated examples into Great Basin Representational and Abstract, the latter containing geometrical figures that they further subdivided into Curvilinear and Rectilinear. The first category of abstracts includes circles and meanders, forms that occur throughout western North America. The second category, however, which is comprised of gridirons, cross-hatching, and forms that are called rakes, one of which appears directly above "the sun and the net," is found only in the Great Basin.

It was Dr. Heizer's contention that the primary fact of existence for Paleo-Indians in the harsh aridity of the Great Basin must have been the securing of food. Little time and energy was left over for, among other things, the labor-intensive activity of pecking and scratching images into rocks, which meant its most likely subject would have been obtaining food. Because he found Great Basin rock art occurring most frequently near hunting and fishing sites, and often featuring imagery specific to game, he postulated that the grids and rakes represented the nets and fences used to divert and capture animals and fish.

It's a typical Robert F. Heizer analysis, built upon a meticulous accumulation of circumstantial facts: the number of undigested bones found in prehistoric coprolites, the layering of dust and silt in caves during the dry periods, and the mapping of rock art sites within their geographical contexts. The interpretation seems borne out by examples here, at what must have been a fishing camp, with the skeletons of fish carved near the grids, although it's not necessarily inconsistent with my metaphor for symbolically catching the sun. It's also an analysis subject to much discussion as the years go by, people offering alternative theories from the entoptic hallucinations to metaphors for rainmaking to extraterrestrial communication as the source and/or meaning of the images—the latter an example of precisely why, in his monograph discussing rock art to the southeast in Lincoln County, Heizer noted with dismay our apparent need for a world of the imagined to coexist with reality.

As we wander through the tufa, I bear in mind that my interpretation is very much the product of personal speculations on how we use the grid to understand and relate to the void of the desert. My notion could bear at best only a literary relationship to the literal one of the artists. In fact, even calling the carver of a petroglyph an "artist" is to superimpose an unlikely historical role upon a prehistoric individual, who for all we know may have been a hunter, a weaver, a shaman, an accountant, or a grocer for the tribe.

By now Alvin has taken as many photographs as he needs to, and we walk back to his 1995 electric-blue Jeep Cherokee parked nearby. It's the least-fancy four-wheel vehicle owned by anyone I know, and totally in keeping with his modest lifestyle. His only enhancement has been an upgrade to truck tires in order to discourage punctures. Many of its fifty-three thousand miles acquired over the last two years have been on roads like the ones we'll be driving later on this trip, all dirt and sharp rocks. He's yet to lose a tire.

As we drive back down to the highway, pausing briefly at a series of rectangular stone breastworks erected by emigrant Chinese fishermen in the late 1800s, I am as content as I can imagine. Across the road is dry hardpan, a lake bed that no longer has any source of water from outside the valley, holding only briefly the runoff from surrounding mountains and rain falling directly in the basin. Winnemucca Lake at its highest modern level—when it wasn't part of the greater Lake Lahontan—covered about ninety square miles and was eighty feet deep, receiving its water most years as overflow from Pyramid Lake, a body of water located behind us to the west and on the other side of the mountains.

Pyramid was the deepest point of Lake Lahontan and is now its largest remaining remnant. Its exact size and depth depend upon the annual volume of its source, the Truckee River that flows north out of Lake Tahoe for more than a hundred miles, but the lake is roughly thirty miles long and ranges from four to eleven miles wide. Its deep-blue appearance is a total shock in the arid surroundings, and it once substituted for the Sea of Galilee in the 1960s Hollywood biblical epic *The Greatest Story Ever Told*. It was named in January 1844 by Frémont, the first white man to see it; he compared its enormous, almost 350-foot-high triangular tufa formation on its eastern shore to the Pyramid of Cheops. The geology of the West invariably evoked comparisons to the monumental architecture of antiquity in the minds of the nineteenth-century explorers, which helps account for some of the contemporary confusion between landscape and art that viewers experience when encountering the large geometries of Mike Heizer's *City*. The sculpture, which deliberately brings forward ancient building forms, in turn reminds viewers of those gothically eroded shapes in the desert West that we continue to describe as "ruined castles."

The Truckee, which Frémont stumbled across five days after sighting the lake, is the most litigated river in America. By the end of 1844 it was the route favored by emigrants on their way to California, who followed it into the lush meadows that would later become the Reno-Sparks area. It now serves as the only major source of water for the cities' quarter-million residents. Since 1905, when the U.S. Bureau of Reclamation built its first dam in the country to divert some of the Truckee into the desert communities of Fernley and Fallon for farming, the river has been unable to supply enough water to cause Pyramid to overflow. By 1939 Winnemucca had become the playa it is today, a dry lake that is wet only intermittently. Pyramid itself dropped a hundred feet in depth within eighty-five years, and was threatened with extinction by increasing upstream withdrawals to meet the demands of urban growth. The Paiutes living on the Pyramid Lake Indian Reservation sued for water sufficient to sustain their tradition-al food source, the huge cutthroat trout and unique prehistoric cui-ui fish, and negotiated a settlement in 1990 protecting them.

The settlement temporarily halted decades of litigation over water rights, but left out the desert farmers, who became even more upset when a federal ruling sent all overflow water in the system directly to Pyramid Lake, thus bypassing their irrigation ditches. Currently, the farmers are suing the developers in Reno, simply avoiding the Indian issue and attack-ing the users most likely to appropriate what little water they still receive.

Despite the poor odds facing the rural residents down south against the Las Vegas water grab, they probably have a better chance to protect their water than do the farmers relying on the Truckee. The growth of the urban grid has been overcoming the agricultural one throughout this century, the most vulnerable farmers being those dependent upon irrigation to support what is essentially an indefensible idea, the raising of water-thirsty crops such as alfalfa in the middle of the desert. The growth of Reno generates greater economic benefits for a larger number of people than does farming in the desert, which requires federal subsidies—and political power will fol-low the money. None of this affects Winnemucca Lake, however, for which it is decades too late.

All this history comforts me this morning as we drive through the des-iccated basin, not because I'm happy about the conflict, but because I understand it, having lived in Reno from 1959 through 1993. Across the playa from us is a deeply crenelated peak that I climbed in the spring of 1976. Mount Limbo isn't especially tall, and a group of us tackled the four-thousand-foot scramble only because Alvin had suggested it. With only touches of third- and fourth-class climbing at the top, it was not exactly a technical challenge, but it was the first time I'd climbed a peak out in the middle of the desert, and it was exhilarating. I could see west to the Sierra ridges holding in Lake Tahoe above Reno. Standing before me were the mountains around both Pyramid and Winnemucca Lakes, then northward the chain of playas stretching out into the Black Rock and Smoke Creek Deserts. I could, in short, see a large chunk of the 8,665 square miles once covered by Lake Lahontan. The prehistoric bones of the region were laid bare by the view, and I suddenly understood the intertwined histories of Great Basin hydrology and habitation.

As we drive this morning along the old shorelines, the wave-cut terraces stacked up for five hundred feet around the valley like concentric bathtub rings, Alvin relates a story for almost every peak, rock, and granite face within view. Anything that's sufficiently vertical has his interest, and he's either climbed it or plans to go check it out. This, too, is part of my history and why I'm making this trip with Alvin. It's not just that he's led trips into the Black Rock for numerous other writers and scientists, but that he locates his place in time and space through many of the same stories as I do. We've read the same exploration journals from the nineteenth century, climbed together some of the peaks Frémont walked past or stood upon, and have talked for years all around the void and the grids we impose on it. Alvin knows exactly what I'm after and where to find it.

Nevada Highway 447 stretches out in front of us, a ruler-straight road that will take us to the edge of the Black Rock Desert that I had first glimpsed from the summit of Mount Limbo. More than a million square acres in extent, it has been called the only "absolute" desert in America, a sterile flatland where, apart from its transitional margins, nothing grows. Ever. The silts washed down from the surrounding mountains and filling up the basin for tens of millions of years are more than nine thousand feet deep and far too alkaline and salty to support anything green. Among the earth's estimated fifty thousand arid basins with interior drainage that we define as playas, the Black Rock Desert is second in overall size only to the Great Salt Lake Desert in Utah and to the playa of Lake Eyre in Australia. Besides being one of the three largest playas in the world, the Black Rock is the largest dry lake bed in America and the flattest land in North America. The efforts to set land-speed records shifted there from Utah's Bonneville Salt Flats in 1983 because, although it's smaller, it's even drier, and topo maps for the Black Rock show zero contour lines for a significant portion of its sixty-five-mile length. The interlocking squares of the national grid, the one-mile-square sections that cover more than 70 percent of America, are shown on the Black Rock maps with dotted lines, which indicate that no exact measurements have ever been surveyed on its ground. For me, the playa that John Hart in his *Hiking the Great Basin* calls the "barren among the barren, wastes among wastes" is the metaphorical heart of the void.

WE PULL INTO GERLACH, a town embraced on three sides by alkali flats with a population between 350 and 700, depending on which guidebook or sign you believe. No one disputes that it has five bars, however, most of which seem to be open this morning. We're 107 miles out from our starting point in Reno, and Alvin decides to top off the tank, this being the only gas station we'll see for two days—the only one, in fact, within the empty ten thousand square miles of far northwestern Nevada. I go around back to find the bathroom. While sitting on the toilet I find a large black widow watching me from her perch beside the door hinge three feet in front of my knees.

I go hot and cold about black widows, knowing that they're a useful pest-control element in the environment, but never happy to see one within close range. When I'm done I leave this one alone. She's not on my territory, and desert rules apply in Gerlach, where, as the sign boasts, "the pavement ends and the West begins."

Back in the Jeep Petro is sitting next to a rear side window in a small space hollowed out of our gear. As we pull out of the gas station he calmly watches what is, for Gerlach, a rush hour. Normally in the first week of October the only people we'd see would be a handful of tourists passing through and the regulars, a smattering of local ranchers and employees from the Sheetrock plant down the road. Hunting season won't start until the end of the week, but there is already a proliferation of recreational vehicles in town, spectators here to witness the Americans and the British duel over the sound barrier on the Black Rock, as good a reason as any for the town to be jumping. We're hoping that we'll be allowed across the playa this morning, that they're not running the cars and haven't, as a safety precaution, closed it off.

The road splits just north of town, NV 447 going north by northwest up to Oregon, and a smaller road, NV 34, that we take northeast alongside the edge of the valley. Our entrance to the playa ramps down 3.3 miles past the turnoff, this morning guarded by a cheerful young Brit with a walkie-talkie. He tells us that they haven't decided if they'll try a run today or not, depending on the wind. They'll give it until noon, but if the wind gets above fifteen miles per hour they have to pack it in for the day. He waves us through, and we coast down onto the flat.

Driving on the Black Rock is unlike moving in a car anywhere else I've been, and I always look forward to it with both anticipation and nervousness. It's either the safest place in the world you can drive, or the most dangerous. Thousands of trips are made across it each year—but people also die out here on a regular basis. It's safe because there's nothing to hit and you can't get lost in the middle, the tops of the surrounding peaks visible at all times. Unless, of course, you leave your car, in which case the vehicle can become almost mystically invisible, lost to your vision in a flatland without any middle-ground reference points whatsoever. It's also hazardous because it's an immense area where it can get very, very hot; should your car break down, there are no emergency services or water even remotely within walking distance.

When it gets wet, it's even more dangerous. After the standing water disappears the ground looks dry, but underneath the surface it's an endlessly deep goo that, should you try to drive on it before it's had a chance to thoroughly dry out, which people do every year, your vehicle will simply sink until its oil pan is resting on the ground. There it will stay until the playa consolidates and a team can come extract the remains. Those are the practicalities that have killed people in the past. Then there are the perceptual problems, much the same as seen in Railroad Valley, but magnified.

Alvin has chosen, more or less at random, one of the half-dozen tracks leading toward the middle of the playa. There aren't any roads out here, just shallow ruts that develop during the summer, then are erased every winter by the brief but sometimes violent rains and the runoff from the mountains. Within twenty minutes water can stand on the playa in a single sixty-by-twenty-mile sheet, a thick liquid of suspended silts that is only a few inches deep. As the playa dries out, desiccation fissures will form, ranging in width from a few millimeters to several feet across, and fracturing the hardpan into irregular geometric figures, a complicated polygonal pattern that scientists have yet to understand. The desiccation polygons of the

Great Basin, formed by the relentless hot/cold–dry/wet cycles, can measure anywhere from a few inches to six hundred feet across, the larger patterns not noticed until the advent of aerial photography.

At this time of year, however, before the first of the storms, the surface is unbroken and the tracks are still firm, proliferating in several angles out from the entry ramp. Our destination is the Black Rock itself, a four-hundred-foot-high point of vertically tilted sediments that stands at the far end of the playa, and one of the few distinctive landmarks offered the eye in any direction. It served as a marker for Frémont as he came south from Oregon and out of the High Rock Canyon, became the significant signpost for emigrants using the Applegate Trail, and is our guide this morning. In between is the void with all its cognitive dissonance.

If becoming fatally mired is a recurring danger on the Black Rock, other more subtle hazards for the mind exist. In Heizer's valley it is possible to at least partially overcome the initial dislocation of distance and scale. The sagebrush slowly asserts itself as a visual element, and your eyes organize the valley around the trees on his property and the residing geometries of *City*. In Railroad Valley the horizontal playa is balanced by nearby mountains and the presence of the oil wells at its northern end. In both places you can find optical anchors, as minimal as they are, and the driving is relatively slow. On the Black Rock there are no such anchors. It's said that you can see the curvature of the earth here, the supposedly dead, flat alkali curving out from underneath you on both sides, as if you were standing on top of an almost imperceptible swell. The fact that the bases of the peaks are hidden from view when you are in the middle of the playa supports the visibility of the curvature. Your eye just slides around the immense basin with nothing to stop it. A tin can three hundred yards away is mistaken for a car miles off, the emptiness overwhelming any previous experience with size and scale. Radical misjudgments are the rule.

Alvin calmly eases the Jeep up to sixty miles per hour. Then sixty-five, seventy, faster than we were driving on the highway. Watching the playa over the hood induces a faint motion sickness, the smooth off-white surface rolling up to meet us as if it were a sheet of paper in a typewriter. The disjunction between perceiving the ground to move but the far-off horizon to remain fixed produces a feeling akin to seasickness, which is triggered by the same kind of failure we experience on board a ship as we try to reconcile what we see, the fixed walls of a cabin, with what we don't, the rolling motion produced by the waves outside.

Behind us floats the inevitable plume of dust that anything moving out here lifts off the playa; behind that, a faint haziness rises from the ground, evidence of the wind picking up. Out in front of us are two unexpected vertical masts, and we strain to distinguish what they are. To the right a Stars and Stripes is flying, which marks the camp for the Spirit of America, a forty-four-foot-long, four-and-a-half-ton jet-powered car in which sixty-year-old Roger Breedlove had hoped to be the first person to break seven hundred miles per hour on the ground. Breedlove is basically a California hot-rod enthusiast who hobbled together massively powerful but relatively low-tech cars to set the four-hundred-mph land-speed record in 1963, the five-hundred-mph record in 1964, and then the six-hundred-mph one in 1965. He made his consecutive string of records on that other great playa of the Great Basin, the Bonneville Salt Flats, and he's come out of retirement in order to face the challenge offered by the British. He's having mechanical and financial troubles out here, though, having blown compressors and fuel pumps, experiencing aerodynamic instability, and clocking an official speed so far of only 391 mph last Sunday. Now, three days later, he's anxiously awaiting the next move by the Brits.

Richard Noble is the man who brought twentieth-century land-speed racing to the Black Rock in 1983, breaking Breedlove's record at just over 633 miles per hour. Last Thursday his thirty-five-year-old driver, an Oxford graduate and Royal Air Force fighter pilot named Andy Green, flew through the record in Noble's car at 728 mph, shattering Breedlove's initial goal. Now both teams are shooting for the sound barrier, which, at this altitude and depending on the temperature, hovers somewhere around 750 mph.

I use the verb "flew" to describe Andy Green's accomplishment because that's what he's doing, piloting a decidedly high-tech, fifty-four-foot-long, twelve-foot-wide, ten-point-two-ton monster, its body slung between a stubby pair of 110,000-horsepower Rolls-Royce jet engines—essentially the same as those used in the Navy's F-4 Phantom jet fighters that chase bombers around the Nevada desert. Noble's car has an estimated top speed of 850 compared to the 230 mph your average Indy car turns around the track. Such speeds on the desert have more to do with the hand-eye reflexes of a fighter pilot than those of an automobile driver. It's also a plus having someone pilot the Thrust SSC who is accustomed to regularly breaking the sound barrier. No one knows what will happen if Green or Breedlove manages to drive through the barrier at ground level, and some automotive writers have speculated that the shock wave could lift the car off the ground and into a short flight that could have only one extremely unfavorable outcome for the driver.

While I'm relaying this stack of statistics from a newspaper article to Alvin, he chooses to veer slightly left toward the British camp, which is substantially larger than the American one and has more activity. A small inflatable hangar is surrounded by orange pylons, more of which block off the beginning of the fifteen-mile racetrack. About sixty vehicles, mostly RVs and four-wheel drives, are sitting in the roped-off area where we park. Walking over to the hangar, I check out the western horizon, which is now obscured by a thickening dust cloud as the breeze continues to build. I don't think they'll be running today, although the crew is swarming over and under the car; in fact, I don't think we'll be staying here for long at all if the long white cloud over my shoulder grows much larger.

The car is, well, larger than its numbers. Painted black and so low to the ground that I have to get on my knees to see the wheels, the two engines are as tall as the crew members. The fat nacelles dominate the car's sleek body, which terminates at its far end in a tail with stabilizers, looking like it also was borrowed from a jet. The Thrust SSC sits under the inflated yellow shell, its black stiletto nose and dual intakes a threatening profile that reminds me of the black widow at the gas station. I sidle into a group of journalists, a guy in blue overalls patiently explaining the differences to them between the power train of a conventional car and that of a jet engine.

Alvin, in the meantime, is talking with a couple of Bureau of Land Management (BLM) employees he knows who just happen to be out here on their day off, checking out the action. Like many people who work in the desert, they'd rather spend their free time here than in town, being as they are addicted to the void and all its anomalies. Alvin is discussing the sites we'll be visiting over the next two days, a controversial "elephant" petroglyph and an earth figure, or geoglyph. Behind him the dust cloud has turned outright ominous, blocking out the entire southwestern end of the

playa. I break away from the lecture on the arcane mysteries of jet propul-
sion, hoping to convince Alvin we should leave.

Just as we pull out of the lot a few minutes later, and back onto one of the
tracks headed toward the Black Rock promontory arising at the playa's far
end, the first tentacles of what is now a full-blown dust storm sneak into the
encampment, the Union Jack snapping, the other spectators also heading
back to their cars. On the fringe of the outpost we pass three small airplanes
and a microlite used to check out the course. I hope they're lashed down.

BACK TO SEVENTY miles an hour, Alvin steers with small movements that
arc us gently away from the racecourse that is marked out with long lines
of lime as if it were an athletic track. The white lines for the British and
black ones for the Americans are uninterrupted by a single contour line on
the map or on the ground. The Jeep floats over the eerie alkali bed, and I
keep my eyes fixed on the Black Rock Range ahead of us, its dark prow
marking where we'll hit the Applegate Trail. Alvin continues to reel off
names of peaks and geographical features, pointing out a band of white
cliffs named Frémont's Castle, high on a distant mountain range. I wonder
if Andy Green has any time or inclination to learn names embedded in the
surrounding terrain. Certainly not while he's driving, his speed guaranteed
to obliterate any narrative except its own.

As we approach the Black Rock Range with its dark forepeak, the desert
splits around it, continuing on both sides for miles, and the ground is broken up by phreatophyte mounds, small bushy hummocks collecting sand
at the edges of the playa. The salt-tolerant bushes stabilize small dunes
blown here by windstorms like the one we've temporarily outrun, though
the mounds are a phenomenon that has been in decline throughout the
West for the last hundred years. As the mounds rise higher the roots of the
plants have to grow deeper in order to reach water; when the mounds get
too high, the bushes die and the remains are eventually blown back down
into the playa. Botanists speculate that widespread groundwater pumping
in the West has lowered the water tables just enough that the plants can't
reach water once on a mound. The decline of groundwater levels may also
account for why playas are growing throughout the region and desiccation
polygons becoming more frequent.

In any case, science aside, this is the only green we've seen since venturing out onto the playa. Dodging through the mounds we skirt the Black Rock Spring on our left, a bitter water hole surrounded by orange-brown tule reeds. This was the spring sought by emigrants who chose to cut off north from the California Trail, taking the Applegate variation leading to Oregon and northern California. The Black Rock Spring is only the first and southernmost of a series of hot springs arising along a fault line that we'll trace to the north up the left-hand arm of the desert, backtracking the path of Frémont's exploration that opened the trail.

A historical marker sits where the original wagon ruts are still visible, and the wooden ruin of an old sheepherder's rig lists to one side nearby. We stop for a look around. Dragonflies hover over the dangerously hot water, and Petro whines, unable to go for a dip. The sign has been peppered by a shotgun blast, which sets the normally equanimous Alvin into a fit of exasperation. "I just don't know how people can do that," he sputters. "What were they thinking?"

I've never heard Alvin swear, and don't now, but know well the tone he gets when people exercise gratuitous violence. He's a man who has survived calmly in the outdoors and in hazardous conditions throughout his life, and he has no time for people demonstrating how invincible they think their firearms make them. Underfoot are numerous rimfire .38-caliber shells from someone target practicing with a handgun. The brass casings rest amidst what is defined as a heavy lithic scatter: hundreds of chert and obsidian flakes on the ground, evidence of Indians camping here and making tools over a long period of time. It's a conjunction that is an instant cliché, it's so loaded with obvious ironies.

Now eleven-thirty, the dust storm is fast approaching, and it's time to find a sheltered spot for lunch. We head for the next set of springs and then the remains of Harlin City, far enough to the north in the western arm of the Black Rock that we might be out of range of the silts sucked up off the playa by the wind.

Our route follows, more or less, the old wagon route up the slowly rising elevation of the valley, leaving the alkali dust for loose alluvial gravels. Forced to cut across the banks of numerous small watercourses, we find it tortuous going but never steep enough to demand four-wheel drive, yet forcing Alvin to shift constantly from first to second gear as we rock stiffly from side to side over the uneven ground. Once again, as with Beth and Heizer in the mountains above Railroad Valley, I marvel at the stamina of people traveling in the nineteenth-century West, the contrast between their slow passage and the nearly supersonic ground flight of Andy Green another ready-made irony.

Served poorly by faulty maps and imperfect guidebooks, arrogant wagon masters and slowly weakening animals, the emigrants rode and marched across this rough, empty terrain for mile after mile each day, from spring to spring, hoping that the water would be drinkable. Over the intervening years their trails have been picked clean by souvenir hunters, but they used to be littered with the bones of expired livestock, iron hardware that had rattled itself to pieces, and every imaginable household item abandoned in an effort to lighten the loads. The racing crews, by contrast, commute to Gerlach's motels on motorcycles and in air-conditioned RVs.

A few minutes past noon we're at the historical marker for Harlin City, another target well used by the sharpshooting joyriders. Alvin positions the Jeep hood-first to the wind, which we've failed to outrun, and opens up the back; we huddle on folding chairs in what protection there is. Cheese, chips, salsa, soda, the essential high-sodium food groups of the desert traveler. Beats taking salt tablets, I think to myself. We have gingersnaps for dessert, clean up, then go looking for the remains of the town. Harlin City wasn't much, more a proto-town built on a wish and a prayer for what turned out to be a false assay for silver in the hillsides above. All that's left are adobes melting in the occasional storm, and some foundation walls built of handsome red blocks quarried from the cliffs to the east. By now the air is silting up, the dust storm a large one that's covered the entire playa and is blowing clear over the peaks around us, a good four thousand feet higher. We can't see across the seven or eight miles to the other side of the desert valley, so decide just to keep heading north.

The road curves east and climbs farther on the alluvials, a little smoother now that we're up off the valley floor, but I'm still brushing off alkali from my writing tablet every time I make a note until we're almost at the turnoff for Soldier Meadows. It's two-thirty, and we're fifty-five miles from the playa, finally out from underneath the airborne alkali. Behind us the solid wall of windblown dust obscures the view south. To the northeast the first ranch we've seen since Gerlach is nestled in the trees by Soldier Creek. Incorporating the outbuildings of a nineteenth-century army fort, the ranch is now a bed-and-breakfast, and according to Alvin a pretty exclusive one at that. That might help account for the sudden improvements in the road, including major grading to improve the drainage from numerous nearby springs. This is as far north as we'll go for the day, and the first order of business is to find a campsite before taking on any further explorations.

Prowling around in the nearby hills identified on the map as the Black Buttes, we settle for a site next to the warm creek below the mouth of Chukar Gulch, a place Alvin remembers from earlier trips. More than twenty hot springs are identified in this one drainage, the water flowing down to join Soldier Creek and then on to Mud Meadows Reservoir, an unremarkable pond used by the cattle grazing the open range. Left to its own, all the water here would simply drain into the arm of the Black Rock that we've been following, eventually sinking into the soil.

Much to Petro's dismay we leave the campsite before he can go swimming, and go back down the valley a short way before turning west on a dirt road toward the high volcanic plateau. Cutting down from the higher ground is a series of spectacular defiles, one of which, High Rock Canyon, is near legendary. First used by Frémont as his path down into the Black Rock, by the following year it had already become that part of the Applegate Trail used by the emigrants to climb out of the desert. We'll drive its notoriously rough road tomorrow morning. For our pleasure this afternoon Alvin has planned an excursion into the lower reaches of Fly Canyon, a smaller gorge that Frémont would have found impassable, a route barred by a series of perfectly round potholes that water drilled into the bedrock during the last several eons. High Rock Canyon is, in fact, the only canyon descending to the desert that is navigable by wheeled vehicles.

The entrance to Fly Canyon is hidden from the road, and when driving you have to approach it over a lateral ridge running parallel to the streambed. Cresting the rise, the road then drops precipitously down into the meadows below the canyon. Alvin takes it in first gear, the Jeep tilted so sharply over on its side at one point that it feels like we're going to roll over and down the side of the hill rather than drive down the road. At the bottom it's all sage and blooming rabbitbrush that, as the land rises and becomes damper, are replaced by willow, wild roses, and thick wild rye so tall that it's over the top of the Jeep. It feels as if we're in Africa, an impression only enhanced by the tawny form of a large coyote bounding up what looks like an impossibly steep slope between the volcanic cliffs now rising up on our right. The road ends where the cliffs from the left join in, pinching down so tightly that the canyon sides almost touch. Petro considers it only fair that we have to walk, since he had to leave the campsite so soon, and he bounds out in search of water. Alvin rolls his eyes, prepared for what's coming.

Just at the mouth of the canyon there's a shallow cave with carbon stains on the ceiling, lithic scatter on the floor, a pack rat midden in one corner, and wire twisted around a large stone, what's left of an anchor to a coyote trap. It's a compact and dense record of usage, evidence of how difficult an environment the Great Basin has been for its inhabitants. Favorable habitats tend to be few and used over and over again throughout time by all manner of living creatures.

Ahead of us the dark-gray and brown walls are stratified and folded intricately upward, overhanging and labyrinthine, in places only an arm's width apart. Alvin and I relish the chance to put our hands on the rock, test a few holds, and to imagine climbing routes up the nearly two-hundred-foot-high walls. Following Petro along the dry watercourse, we're immediately confronted by a steep water-polished staircase up which we scramble. Walking around a bend is to lose the rest of the world; except for a winding ribbon of blue above our heads we might as well be underground. The first pothole we come across is dry, a round sandy depression, but the second is several yards across and filled to the brim with a thick layer of floating scum through which Petro is joyfully plowing laps. This, I realize, was what Alvin had anticipated.

We look for a way around the water and on the right-hand side find a narrow ledge that ends right at the water level, but is continued by a board hidden in the brushy willows that bridges the gap to its next segment. At the far end of the pothole we climb up the rocks to the next terrace, Petro following only at the last moment, shaking politely out of range, then zooming past us. Not only is this a dog who loves to get wet, he insists on being first up the trail.

Alvin leads our way up through the gorge, carved thousands of years ago when a lake in the plateau country high above us had its natural outflow dammed by a landslide. The water backed up and overflowed into this canyon, augering out the potholes every place there was a ledge to flow over, or a bend in the walls to set up an eddy. On its way to Lake Lahontan, the water plummeted down hundreds of feet within less than a mile, one of the steepest watercourses I've ever seen. Clambering up a narrow watercourse in the Swiss Alps years ago, where the frigid runoff from the melting snout of a glacier was drilling similar holes, I can testify that the noise in Fly Canyon must have been bone numbing.

We circumvent the next large pothole by climbing up to a sloping ledge above the water, traversing carefully over to a rickety wooden ladder that leads back down to the next sandy level of the streambed, then descending. The ladder itself is an antique too weatherworn to stand on, but it provides an extra set of handholds while backing down the rock. Up one more dry but slick staircase and we find the largest pothole yet, maybe a dozen yards across, the foreboding surface of the dark water broken only by the water bugs skating on it. The walls are sheer, and getting around the pool would require backtracking to a break in the cliffs and a fifth-class ascent with a rope. Both of us had thought about bringing our gear, but independently had decided that climbing would have been a distraction. Still, as we turn around and head back down the canyon, we can't help but pick out a couple of likely spots where we could have started the climb.

DRIVING BACK OUT of the broad meadow at the canyon mouth and topping the ridge, we're very close to where Frémont came down from High Rock Canyon. This is essentially the view he saw on New Year's Eve of 1843 as he and his men rode down into the desert, just a few days prior to encountering Pyramid Lake and the Truckee River. It was a disheartening moment for the explorer, who had hoped to find a lake but instead found a basin so desolate that it actually frightened him to enter it.

Frémont's 1843–1844 expedition is the central historical pivot around which our understanding of the Great Basin revolves, his discovery resolving one of the last great mysteries of the continental interior. The maps that Preuss drew from the trip not only increased greatly the utility and safety of the Oregon Trail to the north of us, but also made feasible the Applegate cutoff into southern Oregon. Along with the California Trail, which followed the meager Humboldt River through central Nevada, the three routes carried by far the majority of the early pioneers to the West Coast.

A few years later, after the Civil War so dispersed the officers of the Army Corps of Topographical Engineers that it was disbanded, what was mostly left to accomplish was survey work. Hauling the necessary instruments over rough terrain required the deployment of numerous specialists with large support teams, as was the case with the heliotropers on the peaks above Railroad Valley. Frémont, though, was of that earlier generation of prewar explorers, reconnaissance specialists who followed in the footsteps of the legendary scout Jedediah Smith, and were sometimes led by others, such as Jim Bridger and Kit Carson.

In May 1804 under the sponsorship of President Thomas Jefferson, Lewis and Clark had been sent west to explore a possible route from the Mississippi River to the Pacific Ocean, continuing the tradition of government expeditions that were expected to live off the land. Although they had to rely upon a Native American guide, by the time Frémont came along there were mountain men with sufficient experience from working for the fur companies to act as scouts for the government explorers as they traversed and then mapped the West. Prior to Frémont, the usefulness of maps in the Great Basin was limited, to put it mildly. In the 1833 map by the Parisian cartographer Brué, for example, the Great Basin was crossed by nothing save the lines of latitude and longitude. In 1840 even David Burr, geographer to the United States House of Representatives, could identify what would someday be Nevada and western Utah only as a "Great Sandy Plain" on his official map. This was, admittedly, an improvement over maps from the early 1700s, which showed the region as "The Sea of the West," a gulf extending inland to the Rockies—and far better than the almost 250 separate maps of North America drawn from 1622 up to the early 1800s that still represented California as an island.

The first Euroamerican to enter the Great Basin was the Franciscan father Francisco Garcés, who came into the picture approximately 450 miles to the south. Garcés, among the most intrepid of all the early explorers in the Southwest, opened a trail from Arizona to California in 1771, thus helping to connect the Spanish outposts in New Mexico with those on the West Coast. It was in March 1776, while attempting to find a more northerly and well-watered route, that he left the drainage of the Colorado Basin just west of the present-day town of Needles and entered the Great Basin. After traversing the Mojave Desert and the dry white bed of Soda Lake, he found the modest stream that passes for the Mojave River and followed it upstream through the future sites of Barstow and Victorville. He left the Basin by descending Cajon Pass into the San Bernardino Valley, only to reenter it in May via Tehachapi Pass to the north on his return journey. Six months later the Fathers Dominguez and Escalante left Santa Fe and made a six-month-long traverse of the Colorado Plateau to the west, crossing the Colorado River and also entering the Great Basin, this time just south of the Great Salt Lake.

The achievements of all three explorers were remarkable, and although contact between the Spanish in New Mexico and the Utes living in the Great Basin was maintained more or less continuously afterward, theirs were the last official Spanish explorations into the region. The geographical knowledge they brought back was of value, but continued to misconstrue the region. Although they knew there was no inland gulf and that California was connected to the mainland, the fact that the Great Salt Lake was rumored to be a body of salt water only fueled their certainty that it was somehow connected to the Pacific Ocean.

The maps that Lewis and Clark drew for Jefferson, using knowledge gained on their two-year transcontinental journey to more accurately portray the lands north of the Great Basin, still used Spanish suppositions for the southern regions. As a result, their work showed the Mojave River emptying into San Francisco Bay, yet one more variation on the mythical Rio San Buenaventura. They had failed to locate a Northwest Passage, but clung to what seemed a reasonable hypothesis: some great river must, if not connect the Great Plains to the Pacific, at least flow west from the Rockies to the coast.

The first deep incursions into the heart of the interior basin were made because a fur-trapping party was attacked in Idaho during 1823 by members of the Blackfoot tribe, forcing the Rocky Mountain Fur Company to send Jedediah Smith southward the following year in search of safer territory. In the spring of 1824 he entered the Great Basin from the northeast and out of the Wind River region of Wyoming. At the same time the Hudson's Bay Company, attempting to improve the financial performance of its far western Columbia Department, sent Peter Skene Ogden down along the Snake River drainage and into the Basin looking for new beaver streams. Ogden made four extensive trips through the region from 1824 through 1830.

Although the Great Salt Lake had been discovered a few months earlier by either Jim Bridger or another fur trapper, Etienne Provost, Ogden stumbled across it in 1825, but couldn't identify it. In March 1826 General Ashley of the Rocky Mountain Fur Company left St. Louis for a six-month trip to the Great Salt Lake, and that spring Jedediah Smith led a canoe party for him around the lake, which took them twenty-four days to circumnavigate. The main purpose of the foray was to locate the lake's outlet to the sea, presumably the Buenaventura. Although the men found no outflowing river, they assumed that they had simply missed it.

The next year Smith recrossed the Great Basin via the Mojave, passing close by the Santa Fe Trail pioneered by Garcés, and wandered up the Central Valley of California, seeking the Buenaventura without success. His return journey across the Basin in 1827 was the first trek completely across central Nevada made by a Euroamerican, and the route he followed went by the south end of Walker Lake and then ran roughly along what is now Highway 6 in Railroad Valley. Despite Smith's far-ranging and fruitless exploration of the territory where the Buenaventura was supposed to flow, and his subsequent statements that no such river could exist, belief in it by others persisted.

It's easier to understand how this could have happened when one remembers that the Great Basin is so large that the explorers couldn't wrap their imaginations around it. It didn't help that the pattern of watersheds dividing the Great Basin from the Snake and Green River drainages, which flow into the Columbia and Colorado Rivers, respectively, is sometimes marked by no more than gentle swells in the land. Peter Ogden, on his fourth and last series of ventures across the Great Basin in the winter of 1829–1830, wandered from one watershed to the next. He discovered what Frémont would later name the Humboldt River, which flows down from the Ruby Mountains in northeastern Nevada and runs west before trickling out into the marshes and salt flats of the Humboldt Sink—but mistakenly thought it somehow connected to the Great Salt Lake—this from the man who, by that time, had spent more time exploring the region than any other!

The country was a recursive labyrinth; it all looked alike, even to experienced travelers. Although the decade of the 1820s had seen virtually every major stream, valley, and mountain range in the region identified, it was relatively too meager of water to sustain much of a beaver population, and it was soon trapped out. The fur trappers either redirected their efforts back northward, or retired east to their homes, despairing of anyone ever finding the Buenaventura. But they had penetrated America's harshest desert and found the most direct route to California, which was becoming a desirable destination in and of itself.

In 1832, less than two years after Ogden had abandoned the field, Joseph Walker and the Frenchman Benjamin Bonneville teamed up for what would become a three-year expedition and one of the most important trail-making trips through the region. Proceeding west from the Great Salt Lake and following the Humboldt River, Walker took between thirty-six and forty men across the Great Basin and over the Sierra to the very rim of Yosemite Valley; on the return trip he took an even larger party across. Bonneville's maps of the Walker route established the Humboldt River as the most accessible path across the desert. Magazine articles about the Bonneville-Walker exploits by the famous writer Washington Irving led directly to a young teacher, John Bidwell, putting together the first wagon train to California in 1841. Out of five hundred people who signed up to make the trip, the thirty-five people who completed it, including the first two white women, Mrs. Benjamin Kelsey and her daughter, were the leading edge of overland emigration to California.

In 1845 250 people in five separate parties crossed the Great Basin, part of the slowly rising tide of population pressure from eastern America that would necessitate better maps not only for the journey itself, but also for an enhanced strategic understanding of the territory. The United States was engaged in increasing competition with other countries, most notably the Spanish, for a west coast that would complete its reach across the continent. In 1848, of course, all hell broke loose with the gold rush to the western slope of the Sierra. It has been estimated that some twenty-five thousand people were strung out along trails across the Great Basin during 1849, most of them following the Walker route, or a close variation, along the Humboldt River.

When Bidwell and his partner, Bartleson, led their party to California, the map they used showed the Great Salt Lake being drained by two rivers, both supposedly larger than the Mississippi. Lewis and Clark had explored to the north, and Lt. Zebulon Pike to the south in "New Spain" (later renamed New Mexico), their trips in reality military reconnaissances only disguised as explorations, but the Great Basin remained more the province of cartographic imagination than of survey mathematics. Every major commercial map published of the region in the first half of the nineteenth century, starting with English cartographer Aaron Arrowsmith in 1810 through the 1840s map by David Burr, shows a Buenaventura River draining the desert. It was as if national pride could simply not allow a void to swallow progress on its way to the Pacific. If a grid of latitude and longitude could be projected over the entire West, as already appeared on the 1834 Brué map, then surely geography must follow in a like and orderly manner. The land would, "by God," be divided and conquered via a divine waterway of good fortune, just as the Tigris and the Euphrates flowed out of the desert highlands of Turkey through the Edenic river valleys of Mesopotamia and on to the Persian Gulf.

Arrowsmith in 1834, in fact, had based his very popular map upon Ogden's expedition of 1828–1829. He fancifully connected with a dotted line the Humboldt River in the center of Nevada to the Sacramento River in the Great Valley of California, calling the whole hypothetical system the Buenaventura. Arrowsmith's map, in turn, was reproduced almost unchanged in 1838 by the Army Corps of Topographical Engineers, a service newly formed as part of a bill authorizing the president of the United States to occupy the Oregon Territory.

Jed Smith had deduced several critical features of the Great Basin, but left behind only the most circumstantial evidence to guess at what he surmised. Although he shared his notes and maps with other explorers of the era, he died before they could be published, and they later disappeared. Albert Gallatin published a map in 1836 that includes accurate representations of such features as the Mojave River, as well as names used only by Smith for various other rivers and lakes, suggesting that he must have had access to the scout's documents. In his article regarding the region, which his map served to illustrate, Gallatin observed that the Great Salt Lake had no outlet. Although Gallatin persisted in showing the Basin being drained to the north by the Humboldt, which he proposed connected to the Owyhee and, thence, the Snake, he had begun the process of breaking down the myth that connected the Great Salt Lake to the Pacific Ocean. David Burr apparently also had before him a map by Smith when preparing a chart showing the route of Ogden's 1826 foray. Gloria Cline, in her thorough account, *Exploring the Great Basin,* even holds that a Smith map informed the 1845 Frémont-Preuss map of the region. Along with other scholars, she suggests that Smith, had he not perished during his trip along the Santa Fe Trail in 1831, would have made the mapmaking history that was to become, instead, part of Frémont's career.

When Frémont set out on his second expedition in 1843, he started by following what was becoming the well-known trail to the Great Salt Lake via the Wind River Mountains. He was familiar with at least the Gallatin map, as well as with two charts made by U.S. Navy commander Wilkes, who had been sent out to survey the West Coast in hopes of finding a navigable river draining into it from the interior. Wilkes could find no such thing south of the Columbia, and his maps show that he, too, was deeply skeptical of a river flowing out of the Great Salt Lake. Nonetheless, Frémont carried with him a fervent desire to discover the fabled river, a belief he shared with his father-in-law and patron, the powerful senator from Missouri, Thomas Hart Benton.

Frémont's charge from Benton was to connect the Wind River territory he had surveyed previously in 1842—when he climbed what he thought was the highest peak in the Rockies—with the work of Wilkes, accurately mapping the Oregon Trail along the way. By setting Frémont on such a course, Benton was repeating the strategy employed by President Jefferson with the Lewis and Clark expedition, using exploration as both cover and tool in the diplomatic extension of empire. Jefferson, who himself had been a surveyor and was the son of a surveyor, knew the power of the cartographic grid, and had once actually given Senator Benton one of his maps. Benton learned the lesson well, knowing that if Frémont and his cartographer, Preuss, could return with an accurate road map to the West, emigration would be encouraged and enabled, thus unifying the central West into a territory secure against the British and the Spanish. It had long been an accepted truism that the only way to know a territory was to bring back a map so that others could reach it. To map the land was, thus, in no small measure to claim it.

What distinguishes Frémont's efforts are the aforementioned taste for climbing up on high vantage points as well as his refusing to let fiction stand in the way of facts, an attitude enforced by his meticulous cartographer, Preuss. Prior to commanding his own expeditions, the young lieutenant had already established himself as a valuable member of the Topographical Engineers in the War Department through his work on a reconnaissance of Cherokee country in the south. In 1838 the Topographical Bureau was over-hauled to form the U.S. Army Corps of Topographical Engineers, an expansion fueled by the increasingly broad western military frontier, as well as the Seminole War in Florida. Warfare, as always, depended upon reliable maps. Frémont found himself under the supervision of a remarkable immigrant scientist, the Frenchman Joseph Nicollet, who, had he lived long enough, would have been perhaps the greatest cartographer of trans-Mississippi America. Even so, he commanded the first expedition of the new corps, and was the only civilian to lead an army survey until the 1870s.

When the Frenchman Nicollet trained Frémont in the methodology of scientific exploration along the upper reaches of the Mississippi, he not only inculcated in his young assistant enough discipline and patience to take accurate astronomical observations, but also introduced him to a practice new to the interior of the continent: using a barometer to measure elevations. This was critical. Using what was, in more modern terms, an altimeter to take consistent measurements of elevations above sea level enabled Frémont to do more than simply trace a path across the grid, but to develop contours of the land itself, an organic reality often in direct contrast to the rigid grid. Where a map with no elevations can be read as simply a flat plain to be traversed with minimum effort, the addition of elevations showed why a river flowed the way it did, as it dropped from the high peaks and followed downsloping valleys. It made the land three-dimensional, a strategic and tactical advantage discovered by Napoléon, the first modern military commander in the West to have access to topographical maps, a fact of which leaders in Washington were aware.

When Frémont and Preuss climbed up on the gravel benches above the Great Salt Lake in August 1843 to take barometric readings high on the eastern edge of the Great Basin, they could compare the height of its rim with the valley floors. In December of that same year, this time on a ridge in the far northwestern corner of the Basin and just days before entering High Rock Canyon, they would take another set of readings, compare them with the previously recorded elevations, and realize they were once again on the rim of the same interior province.

Still, even after unifying the region in his mind, Frémont wasn't completely convinced that the Buenaventura did not exist. First, he had to descend into and cross the Black Rock Desert and make his way over to the eastern slope of the Sierra just south of Lake Tahoe, forcing his way across the mountains in February snows. After recuperating, he and his men continued down the remainder of the Sierra on its western side clear to the Old Spanish Trail, thus tracing the entire one-thousand-mile mountain barrier separating the Great Basin from the Pacific watershed. Frémont was, finally, forced to concede that no river ran from the Rockies through the desert and into the ocean.

After proceeding east in April 1844 to the springs at Las Vegas, a traditional resting spot on the trail to Santa Fe, Frémont's party made their way into southwestern Utah, and then on to Utah Lake just south of the Great Salt Lake. Frémont had, by the end of August, circumnavigated the entire Great Basin and with Preuss recorded elevations the whole way, fully recognizing for the first time the extent of what was the totally enclosed province. In so doing, he definitively laid to rest one of the most persistent legends of the continent.

Frémont was an explorer in an age of faith that later would crash in the second decade of the twentieth century, belief in neither God nor Darwin being sufficient to prevent the slaughter of the First World War. Although the focus of worship was shifting in the mid-1800s from religion to science, as scientists such as Sir Charles Lyell, the preeminent English geologist of the time, pushed back the age of the earth, and Darwin the age of the human race, the culture of Frémont's time still believed unhesitatingly in certain representations of the world as being definitive—maps and art among them. Tens of thousands of emigrants were prepared to accept at face value the fifty thousand copies of Preuss's Oregon Trail map that the government printed, and many of them followed the map west. Immensely popular paintings a little later in the century, huge panoramas by artists such as Albert Bierstadt and Thomas Moran, were reproduced as lithographs in magazines that were read by millions, the operatic landscapes inspiring still more people to undertake the overland journey. Whereas now we might tend to view the Frémont-Preuss maps and nineteenth-century landscape paintings as metaphors for the unknown and our culture's relentless drive to dislocate itself, at the time they were taken solely as literal guides to reality. They were superseded as representations of the West only by photographs, yet another evolution in the technology of representation. The images taken by survey photographers such as W. H. Jackson and Timothy O'Sullivan were so steady and resolute in their gaze that by the end of the century they had replaced paintings and lithographs to become the accepted standard for the truth of the West.

MY OUT-LOUD MULLING over pathfinding and mapmaking in the Great Basin ends as Alvin stops the Jeep down on the flats below our campsite. He's spotted a pipe jutting up out of the sagebrush and wants me to see a physical manifestation of the grid that Frémont helped pull over the Great Basin. He also wants to check out the chain link fence surrounding a rectangular portion of the desert through which the stream from our campsite spring flows. The water here is warm, maybe three feet wide and at most eighteen inches deep, banked on both sides in lush grass, sagebrush growing incongruously next to it. "I think it's desert dace," he says. "They're a species of fish endemic to Soldier Meadows, only an inch or two long, and this is probably an exclosure keeping out the cattle."

Sure enough, there's a 1997 Department of the Interior marker on the fence. A few hundred yards upstream we can see more chain link protecting another stretch of the riparian habitat. Like the spring fish found in Railroad Valley and the cui-ui sucker fish in Pyramid Lake, the dace is a species isolated in its environment by the drying up of the Pleistocene lakes. Just as the mammals and insects of the mountain ranges have evolved away from each other on their biogeographical islands, so have the fish in the Great Basin's valleys.

A few yards past the exclosure is a vertical pipe set in a cairn of stones, a support for the brass section corner cap with 1946 stamped on it. It's a General Land Office marker with a cross of cardinal lines inscribed on it along with a warning that removal will cost the offender a $250 penalty. The one-mile-square sections laid out across that 70 percent of America not in the original colonies, which had been surveyed by the earlier and highly irregular systems of metes and bounds, was the result of Jefferson—ever the surveyor—instituting the United States Public Land Survey in 1785. The nationwide effort to divide all public land into equal portions fell out of his overarching notion that democracy was based on the ideal of the citizen-farmer. Every free citizen was to have equal access to equal lands, an idea hopelessly impractical even east of the isohyetal line, which marks roughly where more than twenty inches of rain begins to fall a year and irrigation is usually unnecessary. In the West, where it may take hundreds of miles to collect enough water to maintain even a small herd of cattle, and where the geographical distribution of rain is highly irregular and determined by the placement of mountain ranges, the idea was magnificently absurd.

The portion of the survey conducted by the General Land Office that covers Nevada started from the West Coast—rebounding, if you will, back across the continent from the closure of the frontier—and plotted every square mile it could in the Great Basin, starting first with the valleys and working its way up the hillsides, but never really conquering the unnerving and obviously untillable playas such as the Black Rock. This particular section corner has its cardinals extended by pieces of white plastic held down by rocks, remnants of a large white cross marking the spot for the USGS aerial photographs used in the compilation and ongoing correction of its topo maps.

"What you have to do, when putting in one of these newer markers, is to destroy the original one by scattering the stones," Alvin comments, turning over a large one as he speaks. "Yow," he exclaims, quickly lowering the rock again to cover the black widow on its underside.

"Must be all the moisture this year," I observe. "More plants, more insects, more spiders."

"Maybe." Alvin is noncommittal. "Anyway, what I was looking for was the original stone with the cardinal directions marked on it by grooves cut in the rocks. Sometimes when there weren't rocks around, they'd even use a wooden post, and you can still find them."

Jefferson's national survey pattern, spreading outward from an east-west line surveyed where Pennsylvania, Ohio, and West Virginia met, was designed to make possible the infinite replication of settlement, a repetitive set of nesting squares that was derived from thirty-six-mile-square townships, every other township subdivided into thirty-six one-mile-square sections of 640 square acres each. Later, these were further divided into quarter sections of 160 acres, which became the standard size for a family farm (and a size against which that intrepid explorer of the Grand Canyon, John Wesley Powell, argued fiercely, knowing full well that in the arid and semi-arid West such a small parcel of land would almost never be sufficient to support even a single grazing cow).

There are quarter-section markers out here, too, and it is remarkable that Jefferson's agrarian idealism, barely practical for the eighteenth-century Midwest, would be so consistently present in the contemporary West. Looking at an 1897 map I have at home of Nevada and Utah, it's simply astonishing to see the national grid propagating across the terrain regardless of topology, tribal reservations, or the patterns of traditional landownership (yet, leaving blank the deserts of both the Great Salt Lake and Black Rock). It's worth remembering that Jefferson, an enlightened gentleman scientist familiar with the geopolitical advances being made in France, also proposed a national system of roads in 1806, though Congress didn't get around to passing the Federal Highway Act until 1916, supposedly in an effort to improve postal delivery.

The rectilinear Jeffersonian grid manifested by our sectional survey, the most extensive regular division of land in the world, allowed the peaceful plotting of 5 million farms during the nineteenth century. It made possible the transfer of land in relatively straight corridors to the railroads, and eventually the establishment of the interstate freeways. It guided the paths of transcontinental telegraph lines, which, like the railroads, first linked up in the Great Basin—and then the routes of power lines, telephone wires, and fiber-optic cables. Placing my hand on top of a General Land Office marker is like plugging into the far end of the national nervous system. It gives me shivers.

It's almost five-thirty when we get back to our campsite spring, set up the tent, and unstuff our sleeping bags. I bring out the chairs while Alvin prepares our dinner: a can of soup, cheese, chips, salsa, soda. Gingersnaps for dessert. The repetitive simplicity is nothing if not economical. I top it off with an antihistamine to combat the effects of the blooming rabbit-brush. Afterward we drop our clothes on a piece of plywood resting on the edge of the spring before lowering ourselves into the clear and slightly steaming pool. At our backs there's a board to rest our heads on, the small retaining wall of rocks piled up to form the pool only a couple of feet beyond our toes. The dust storm thirty miles to the south is still visible, still blowing over the peaks, but up here the wind has dropped to a light breeze, and an overcast is moving in from the west over northern California. We don't talk much, and it's almost dark when we get out. It's early, not yet eight-thirty, but too much trouble to build a fire, so we just go to bed, leaving the flaps and bug screen tied back, the tent open to the fresh air.

FIVE

෫

THE INSIDE OF my left bicep is burning when I wake up, and for a moment I don't move, thinking that I have just been sleeping on it at an odd angle. I've had my arm outside my bag, being plenty warm in the lofty down, but as the burning gets worse by the second, I decide I'd better investigate. I bring it up to my face and gingerly palpitate the flesh with my other hand: slightly puffy and hot to the touch. I put my arm back down and quickly run through the possibilities. We're too far north for fire ants, so it's a scorpion sting or a black widow bite. Dumb of us to leave open the bug netting in such a wet place, I think. Alvin is lightly snoring, and I tilt my head to look outside.

I freeze. Under the shoulder seam of my T-shirt something is moving. I don't think, just grab and squish. Whatever it is stops moving, but the fabric is soaked in that one spot, and I can't sit up fast enough to pull off the shirt. Alvin keeps snoring. In the beam of my flashlight I can pick out the distinctively jointed legs of a black widow and some body pieces. Training the light on my arm, there's nothing to see except the slightest reddening over an area the size of my palm. No hole, no popping veins, no venom oozing anywhere. I shove the shirt into a corner, check around for other multilegged life-forms and, finding none, lie back down.

Single black widow bites are very seldom fatal to an adult, but multiple bites can be problematic; the only question is whether or not she got me more than once on the bicep. I have no way of telling, it's a half-day's drive to get to a hospital, and I'm full of antihistamine, which might help. I decide against waking Alvin and go back to looking outside.

The overcast is broken, and Orion, my favorite constellation since my father showed it to me as a child, is rising to the east. I'm in the middle of where I want to be—the desert and working on this book—so I zip up the bug net, then lie back and try to enjoy the compound void of night in the Great Basin. My arm now feels as if it's been stung by the largest bee in the world, and the elbow aches slightly. Other than occasionally flexing my fingers to see how my reflexes are doing, I just lie still. Attempting to think of a simple distraction, I decide to review what I'm doing out here in the void, the first topic I can bring to mind.

Nevada and western Utah, the majority of the Great Basin province, are among the emptiest places in the country, but they're coming under increasing population pressure. Having served for centuries as terra incognita, resisting exploration and understanding, and literally standing outside of our cognition, the desert here still baffles us even as we bisect it with interstates and surround it with instant suburbs. I think it's a beneficial bafflement and one we want to keep; I believe that we desire and actually need physical voids on the surface of the planet, big empty spaces into which we can travel in order to see ourselves.

The primary way we handle the void—how we physically and imaginatively manipulate it so we can travel safely through it to the other side—is to impose the most basic of all rectilinear geometries upon it, from petroglyphs to maps to highway signs. I've organized this trip with Alvin around finding different traces of the grid, a narrative armature around which I can wind my investigation of the relationships between the void and the grid. Tracking down petroglyphs and section corners is to find parts of the grid that Frémont and others have brought into the void.

The evolution of maps is inextricably bound up with that of ourselves and with the development of both spoken and written languages, all based on an intimate relationship with land that becomes very tortuous when we abstract ourselves from where we live. Perhaps the origin of maps lies clear back with animals complex enough to remember a sequence of places through which they had traveled, a route from one place to another. Certainly, evolution seems to favor creatures who retain such an ability, whether it's through the migration of birds guided by the memorization of constellation patterns rotating around the Pole Star, or the dances of bees as they communicate to each other how to locate a food source. Different senses are employed by different species to compare surroundings with remembered routes and territories, from the sonar of undersea mammals to the olfactory clues used by four-legged predators. As humans, we locate ourselves through stereoscopic vision, and, when standing upright and elevated off the ground, cannot but help triangulating ourselves from here to there, inevitably heightening our egocentricism along the way.

Whenever it was that modern Homo sapiens sapiens evolved, usually estimated to be sometime after two hundred thousand years ago, our race apparently came equipped with very much the brain we have now. We already had both the well-developed vocal tracts and prefrontal cortex needed for speech, but also a cortex with more than half of its mass devoted to a system of visual perception organized around the ability to distinguish borders and outlines. It seems a logical speculation, and one made increasingly by cognitive scientists, that mapping and language were concurrent abilities already in place. Our neural system had by then evolved enough not only to take in vast amounts of visual information—100 million bits per second transferring from the eye to the occipital lobe—but then also to filter out most of it, a much more sophisticated task allowing us to organize through contrast and boundary recognition those handfuls of shapes we understood as the immediate environment—shapes that were, by virtue of their reduction in our minds and their small number, more easily remembered.

We see—that is, build in our minds a representation of the world—by creating hierarchies of shapes based on boundaries that occur when two or more areas of differing visual intensity abut one another, an activity some scientists interpret to mean that we actually organize our spatial memory as maps, and even that the brain itself is arranged topographically. This is a theory that dovetails neatly with what we understand must have been the increasingly intense level of competition for food and safe shelter as the human population doubled and redoubled, making imperative the hunt for new resources in unfamiliar territory. Our brains had to acquire the ability to memorize and recall particular spaces so we could first return home, then get back to the new source of food. And, thus, we turned land into landscape, space into place. Once one place was linked to another in sequence, then remembered as a progression, a mental map was formed. A survival skill.

Much of what we have recorded of speech by members of preliterate cultures seems rooted to landscape: stories about moving over it through danger in order to reach food and shelter, to family and tribal histories, all of it tied mnemonically in a mutually reinforcing pair of skills to specific places. Even at the end of the twentieth century it remains true that people from cultures with strong oral traditions, once they are separated from their homelands, whether Eskimos in the eastern Arctic or Apaches in Arizona, lose touch with their native languages and the specific knowledge of the land embedded in it. Speech and the very specific placement of the senses, hence "sense of place," are continually discovered to be more important to each other than we think.

Mental maps, those highly personalized charts we carry in our individual minds that enable us to function from day to day, now include the routes we use in walking to school and driving to work, the trails remembered by hikers and hunters from year to year, and even the labyrinthian paths through cyberspace, many of which are now digitally configured as analogs to physical spaces—sites as places we can remember how to reach. Our minds hold certain features in the landscape as larger or smaller, closer or farther away, according to our familiarity with them and the importance we accord them, variations that occur in the mental maps of an Eskimo, a child in Chicago, an adult in London. When people are asked to put their mental maps to paper, they often bear only a vague spatial relationship to reality (or to a printed map), but they are organized so well that, not only do we remember them, but we can also communicate them verbally to someone else when asked for directions.

In Mesopotamia around 8000 B.C. precursors to the world's first-known writing were put into use. Small handheld neolithic clay counters impressed with strokes, they were used to keep track of the modest agricultural trading that started to occur once basic communal living made it possible to establish settlements, which in turn led to an availability of surplus food. By the fourth millennium B.C. the numerous settlements of the Near East had elaborate trade networks; the consequent need for full-blown written record keeping had been systemized into cuneiform writing. At the same time, maps showing the squared-off division of property lines came into use. Personal property, landownership, and the abstraction of value for trade had all become common, making necessary an agreed-upon system of record keeping. Writing and maps were the key ingredients of such a system. By 2500 B.C. the society of Babylon was so complex that public financing was required to maintain it, and maps were being used as the basis for taxation.

Both maps and writing continued to develop from tools that merely described what was known to exist into much more powerful instruments able to predict what might exist, part of our human exploration both intellectual and geographical. The invention of mathematics for tallying crops and predicting the periodicity of celestial events had a direct bearing on the story, as well as having cognitive roots in common with language and mapping. Although there is evidence for many human migrations from one part of the globe to another, one reason western expansion figures so heavily in the myths and history of our culture is that the very origins of that progression are embedded in our Arabic numerals, our Roman alphabet, and our European cartographic conventions. Even at the level of individual languages, our Euroamerican culture's specific knowledge of the world was once tied to physical realities and specific locales as intimately as is the nature of snow in the tribal dialect of an Eskimo. The phrase "once in a blue moon," for instance, was commonly understood to refer to those years when a full moon appeared twice in a month. Now it's an anachronism drifting slowly out of usage as we have more and more night sky blotted out by city lights.

But, though Eskimos still rely on their language to preserve knowledge critical to survival in the Arctic environment, even as they chase prey with snowmobiles, our various forms of written communication have drifted still further and further away from the environments in which they developed. In mapmaking, that pictorial branch of communication whereby we share the shape of the land, the history of that abstraction is readily available to anyone with access to a historical atlas. And, though the purely personal mental maps of someone living in Los Angeles may differ only in the details from those of his or her tribal ancestors, the evolution of formal cartography demonstrates clearly how we have increasingly overlaid land with the grids of power, political as well as technological, in order to continue to transform land-based resources into wealth, and to transfer that value from one place to another.

It's three A.M. by the faintly glowing hands on my watch, and although my arm is as sore as when I woke up, it doesn't seem any worse. I'm sleepy enough to ignore both it and the thoughts about maps and grids, about art and land. I unzip the bug net for a look outside: Orion has disappeared behind a fast-moving bank of clouds. As I snuggle back into my bag the first drops from a squall line fall on the taut nylon of the tent, and I fall asleep to the reassuring and regular patter of the rain.

By SEVEN O'CLOCK, and although Alvin is still asleep, I'm ready to get going, surprised that my lack of sleep last night isn't keeping me in bed any longer. Then I add up the hours between when we went to bed, the spider bite, falling back asleep, and now—and realize I've still managed about eight hours of sleep. I pull on my shorts and unzip the bug net, careful to thoroughly empty out my shoes before putting them on—please, no more spiders!—then exit the tent. Petro, who leaves the tent with me, runs off through the sagebrush. Alvin rolls over, not awake but getting there. Outside, the ground is completely dry, no trace of the rain remaining, evidence of how pervasive the aridity is here. As I rummage through the Jeep for a clean T-shirt, I notice that the coordination in my left hand seems a bit slow, and that my arm is still sore and hot to the touch. Although it's not as painful as last night, I also dig up an Advil and down another antihistamine for good measure.

I get the stove going to heat up water for coffee, enjoying the view of clouds resting on all the surrounding peaks. A slight breeze wafting steam off the creek is all that's left of yesterday's wind, and it looks like the clouds will burn off the mountaintops by midmorning. Alvin joins me, stretches, and together over coffee we look at the maps to confirm our route for the day. Passing by the road we took yesterday to Fly Canyon, we'll stay on the main track that leads into High Rock Canyon, a gorge I've read about and had described to me by fellow Great Basin aficionados, but never visited. It will be a slow drive, the road listed as the roughest in the state by some guidebooks, so we don't dawdle over our cereal. This time Petro has no reluctance in leaving the campsite, apparently as eager to be on the road as we are.

Our route first takes us across the valley and up onto a ridge above Fly Canyon. In the early-morning desert calm a brace of chukar, Hungarian partridges imported to this country in the 1930s, bursts out of the sagebrush and into noisy flight. As we climb up the ridge several more of the sturdy, well-camouflaged birds break out ahead of us. We're following the emigrant route, the old wagon ruts first on one side of us and then the other. At the top there's a notch in the road where the emigrants lowered their wagons by ropes, the slope ahead far too steep for oxen to manage, though the Jeep does fine in first gear and a bit of heavy braking. Alvin has something special to show me before we go any farther, and we pull off for a short hike down into the upper reaches of Fly Canyon.

First we tromp off to the left and onto flat basalt, the bedrock underneath the rhyolite cliffs that the river cut down to. Basalt is pretty hard rock, but the water drilled potholes large and small into it all along its path, and we once again find ourselves climbing through and around several before ending up at a wall-to-wall pool just above the one that blocked our passage yesterday afternoon. It's a nice piece of geographical symmetry that I appreciate, but it's not all that Alvin has to show me. We turn around and scramble back up to the rim of the canyon, at this point only fifty feet above us, the gap in the cliffs we ascend a hostile barricade of thorns, sharp rocks, and loose dirt. At the top several twelve-gauge Winchester shotgun shells are scattered amongst chert, obsidian, and even rhyolite flakes. There's no telling how much time separates the two groups of artifacts. "Could be two hundred years, could be five thousand," replies Alvin to my question. "The flakes don't weather very fast."

Now we head upstream, Petro ranging ahead and out of sight, and within a couple of minutes we're at the world's largest pothole. From the top of its upper lip it's an eighty-foot drop to the dry sandy bottom; from where we're standing, at the outflow on the lower rim, it's around nine or ten feet down. Petro has taken the plunge, this time into sand instead of water, and looks up at us, expecting us to follow him. Alvin and I look back at Petro and then at each other. The pothole is 150 feet wide, severely undercut by several feet completely around the rim. We could jump down into the sandy pit, but without a fixed rope there's no guarantee we could climb out of what would be an awkward overhang. Alvin pushes back the cap on his head, and I sit on a nearby rock.

Alvin first surveyed the pothole for the National Park Service in late 1968, when he held the contract to catalog and submit locations in the Great Basin for possible designation as nationally registered natural landmarks. He nominated the pothole, which he determined to be the world's largest, but it didn't make the final Park Service list. He was able to lower himself down into the pothole then to measure it, but it looks to him like the pit is deeper now.

"Petro, come on, let's go," Alvin calls and walks back from the lip, hoping the wiry dog can find a way out. No such luck. Petro races around inside the pothole looking for ledges, but we're standing on the only possibility, which is far too high for him to jump up to.

The only thing we can think of is to hike back to the Jeep and see what we can tie together. I'll help lower Alvin, he'll lift Petro as high as he can for me to grab him, and then we'll worry about getting Alvin out. As we leave, Petro sets up a worried barking, obviously concerned that we're abandoning him. In the rear of the Jeep we find a couple of leashes that might do the trick—but by the time we're only halfway back to the pothole, Petro is trotting up the hillside. We look at Petro, he looks at us, we all look at each other.

"How did you do that?" Alvin asks the dog, who wags his tail happily. Alvin and I are completely mystified how a dog could jump nine-plus feet straight up in the air, catch a ledge with his paws, and then haul himself out. Once more back at the Jeep, Alvin gives Petro a drink of water, but before we drive off and into the mouth of High Rock Canyon about three miles up the road, wonders out loud if we should toss the dog back into the pothole just to see how he got out. I'm relieved to see that he's only half serious.

Leaving behind Fly Canyon, the road actually climbs up along the streambed until it is directly above the break in the cliffs through which the water flowed. We can peer into the start of the canyon to where the water was forced through a sharp S-curve, which presumably set up the eddy that eventually augered out the giant pothole just below it. The road continues to rise up to High Rock Lake, which this morning has standing water in it and is packed with waterfowl on their way south. Alvin is amazed to find water here this late in the year, a testament that the summer in northwestern Nevada was just as wet as at Heizer's place several hundred miles south. We take a quick detour so Alvin can photograph the birds, and he points out to me the massive landslide at the south end of the lake that forced the water to back up and then overflow into Fly Canyon.

We're in rolling hills as we resume driving north, still following Frémont's route, and the hills begin to close in only gradually. The sandy track is well graded now, but when Alvin first came through here in the late 1950s, shortly after moving to Reno, it had only the two original ruts. The sagebrush hasn't changed much, though, from Frémont's description, and is almost as tall as the Jeep. At the actual entrance to the canyon and with no evidence of any gorge yet in sight, a large BLM sign proclaims: "Area of Critical Environmental Concern—prehistoric, historic, scenic, and wildlife values." At least this announcement hasn't been shot full of holes.

Once past the sign, the road immediately gets more serious, tunneling through sagebrush that cuts off all views but those of the dark-brown volcanic rimrock beginning to build up around us. White patches atop the buttresses show where numerous raptors have roosted, preying on the plentiful wildlife that inhabits the canyon. We burrow up out of the sagebrush, and the country gradually widens again into a grassy valley. As we come around a bend at the far end, however, a phalanx of imposing rock suddenly towers three hundred feet above the the the "high rock" section of the old trail. I take a picture of the cliffs and can't help falling into that nineteenth-century habit, comparing them out loud to ancient Egyptian temples. Alvin agrees and drives slowly forward, not because the road is rough, but to savor my reaction.

Pulling up next to the towers, we pause frequently, craning our necks to follow old lines Alvin either attempted to climb thirty-five years earlier, or thought about trying. The rock is intricately shattered almost everywhere. "Pretty loose stuff. I'm not sure I'd want to try a route here."

"Well," Alvin replies, pointing to a crack system on the face of a tower, "it did get pretty scary up there. I left a piton and just rappelled off." Alvin seldom retreats from a vertical challenge, but he's survived four decades of climbing and caving precisely because he does know when to back off. His admission confirms my opinion of the unstable faces and gullies around us. "I'd hate to be here during an earthquake," I mutter under my breath.

We park at the bottom of the second pillar and go looking for a "sign" in the void, which is to say, language in the landscape. Pecked into the rhyolite is:

George N. Jaquith,
July THE 16th, 1852
from WIS.

It's a good example of how American pioneers in previous centuries picked a prominent vertical in the landscape and wrote evidence on it of their passage. It also reminds me that people have been leaving their names on the Egyptian pyramids for four thousand years. I hope that the inscriptions there, though, haven't been peppered with a shotgun blast, as these have. Alvin has that look on his face again, and I, too, find this late-twentieth-century mark of cultural illiteracy very sad.

On nearby faces we find the weathered remains of other names painted in 1852 with soot and axle grease. Below us is a simple breastwork, a chest-high wall of rocks that offered the emigrants both shelter from the winds and some measure of security against the possibility of Indian raids. Parallel to the rocks, it squares up my perception of the landscape, attracting and containing my sight, and I'm compelled to clamber down and step inside. Just regular and straight enough to almost imply the word *architecture,* the primitive shelter is a reminder of the many ways in which we use geometry to fortify ourselves against the void, to combat the cognitive dissonance, to ward off the fear.

Farther up the canyon Alvin stops again, this time leading me under the base of another pillar and into a cave. It, too, was used by the emigrants for shelter. On a slab that they tilted up in the middle of the small chamber as a kind of mock-stela are more names, as well as what are supposedly the Masonic insignia of a square and a compass. Even as I'm again thinking about earthquakes and how much I hate caves, I'm admiring evidence of the grid even here. Alvin, after taking a photograph, asks me if I want to climb out through a crevice in the back, and I decline, adding fear of black widows on top of my earthquake paranoia.

As we progress slowly up the canyon, still following the wagon ruts as they pass up a hill, then through a series of acute bends and a narrow gap that Alvin calls "The Notch," the country once again widens out, this time into a high valley with numerous subsidiary gorges and defiles. I can't call the vegetation lush, but the sagebrush are enormous and the grass plentiful. The lack of water and forage during the crossing of the Black Rock killed innumerable oxen, one wagon-train leader writing that, upon his arrival at Black Rock Spring in 1849, access to the water was blocked by the carcasses of 150 oxen and several mules and horses. High Rock Canyon, with its flowing water most of the year and plentiful grass, was welcome notice that from here on the path north into Oregon would be easier.

Before tackling the final portion of the canyon and climbing up onto the volcanic plateau, we break off into one of the side canyons. The road ends in a thick tangle of willows. Time to pull out the folding chairs and tuck into our favorite lunch: chips, cheese, salsa, soda. You'd think I'd be getting tired of this stuff, but in fact it tastes better and better.

Somewhere above us in the canyon is the peculiar "elephant" petroglyph that Alvin wants to examine, and after a hike and some mental triangulation off nearby land features, we find the right boulder. Roughly five-by-six feet, the flat rock reclines eastward on the hillside. Five petroglyphs are pecked into its surface, four abstract elements and the "elephant." It's definitely a pachyderm, but what kind is hard to say. The eleven-foot-tall mammoths that lived in the Great Basin, remains of which have been found in the Black Rock, disappeared from here between twelve and ten thousand years ago during the last two millennia of the Pleistocene, part of a widespread extinction of mammals that included mastodons, the Shasta ground sloth, prehistoric camels and horses (the latter not returning to the North American continent until reintroduced by the Spanish), and carnivores such as dire wolves, the huge short-faced bear, and sabertooth cats.

Various theories have been put forth to explain the extinction, including climate changes at the end of the glacial age and the advent of mankind upon the scene, or, more probably, a combination of both. If the climate change to the current aridity was alone responsible for the extinctions, it's hard to understand why, for instance, there are now approximately thirty-two thousand wild horses roaming the Great Basin, a growing population the government has trouble controlling. The timing of the disappearance with the migration of people across the Bering Strait from Siberia, a movement also climate related, is too close to be easily dismissed, making many people very curious about this particular piece of rock art.

Alvin spends ten minutes or so looking at the separate glyphs from different angles, pondering the geology of the rock, and the sharpness of crystals and growth of lichen in the pecked areas. Each of the petroglyphs appears to be equally aged, which is to say, not very weathered, and the abstract figures look as if they're within traditional imagery. He peers at the down-curving tusks and upraised trunk of the hand-sized pachyderm, the lance in its side, and the exact placement of its feet. Based on all this, his reaction is to consider the figure one made by a historical Indian instead of an aboriginal one, or maybe someone running cattle up here during the last century. He doesn't think it likely that an emigrant took the time to peck it out, the site being way too far off the trail. Perhaps, whoever the artist was, he once saw an elephant in one of the numerous circuses touring the West during the last century and a half.

Taking out his camera and tripod, pads, pencils, compass, and measuring tape, Alvin settles in to more thoroughly examine and then document the piece, a process that will take an hour or so. I begin to wander out from the site in ever widening circles, noticing what up here is a thin lithic scatter, but one that grows very dense lower down by the streambed. The hillside we're on forms a point between two small watercourses, which, Alvin has pointed out to me, makes it a good camping ground—and from his personal experience, the most favorable conjunction in which to find worked stone. I think about Robert F. Heizer's theory regarding petroglyphs being found near hunting sites, and how the watercourses here must still channel down deer from higher up.

My circling brings me up to a section-corner marker, this one dated 1919, and I'm taken aback first by how early the date is, and then by its very presence. The emigrants might not have bothered to come up here, but the General Land Office was scrupulous, not missing any spot it considered arable as it went about dividing up the terrain, as if the grid could conquer the desert and turn it into Jefferson's "garden of the West."

Picking up a piece of worked obsidian, probably a skinning tool, I notice almost absentmindedly how well it fits my right hand but not at all my left. Next to me is a large green rock set into the hillside, serpentine I think, its top squared off as if it had been milled, and I wonder if it's an artifactual surface that was used for working stone, or just a geofact, a product of nature. Probably the latter, but it reminds me of the breastworks down the canyon, and that makes me consider how the rectilinear grid manifests itself not only in maps, but also in gardens, art, and architecture. I sit on the square stone, not the most comfortable perch, but good enough while Alvin surveys the petroglyphs below me, afternoon sun glinting off his compass.

THE RECTILINEAR OR right-angled grid is one of the most persistent and intractable memes of the human mind, not only because it is an idea that seems to leap from mind to mind, but perhaps also because it is based in the evolution of our cognitive abilities. A meme, which was named by the evolutionary biologist Richard Dawkins, is defined as an idea that survives, as if it were an independent organism, by replicating itself in different forms from mind to mind, and is subject to natural selection. The grid has proved itself to be a superior meme by its tenacity across both time and cultures, one reason being that it is based on the square, a shape that human beings recognize more quickly than any other because of its lack of ambiguity. It has sharply defined edges and corners and carries the most basic of attributes it is possible to find in a shape, an inside versus an outside. The square is a bedrock form in the neurological lexicon of our boundary recognition and contrast, and is essential to how we perceive shapes; the grid is robustly anchored, therefore, in the hardwiring of our cognitive abilities.

The square is also symmetrical of aspect in all directions, having an equal top and bottom, a left and right, a front and back. Translated into three dimensions, a cube is the space we most easily envision. We see the shape even where it doesn't exist, squaring up angles that are approximate and evening out the sides of anything that comes close to the shape. The gestalt of the square, its complete form that we intuit instantly, is a compelling one. Looking at the front of a square or a cube, we can't help but simultaneously envision the rear, which is invisible to us. Only the circle comes close to being so universally recognized and, though more ambiguous to our hierarchical system of vision, is the second most perceived shape around us.

The square, however, has the advantage of being easily stackable—it adds to itself and multiplies more easily in the mind and on paper than a circle, a triangle, or any other shape you can think of. We call it a "gnomon," a parallelogram the corner of which, when it is removed, retains the parent shape. Which is presumably one reason that, despite the fact that the rivers and valleys and hills of Mesopotamia weren't straightedged, property was nonetheless divided into squares and rectangles: it could grow or diminish in a form that was legally, as well as perceptually, unambiguous. Applying a related principle to map grids, we call them "graticules," a lattice that can be proportionately enlarged or shrunken, increasing or decreasing the scale.

The architecture of Mesopotamia likewise evolved into a very specific design that paralleled that of the fields and, therefore, that of the maps. Although pretechnological people have left behind much evidence of round structures, at some point when communal living reaches a certain critical mass, as do the buildings, the technology goes square, whether in the adobe of Mesopotamia or that of southwestern America. The gnomonic principle was applied first to structures, rooms added to rooms, and then to urban design, houses added to houses. By the time Titris Hoyuk was built along the Euphrates, a city of ten thousand people circa 2500 B.C., streets first were being planned and then built to establish the basic grid of the town, a pattern that was subsequently filled in with uniform rectilinear housing built around communal courtyards.

The walled courtyards grew to include a fountain in the middle, an analog of and homage to the fertility of the fields and streams nearby that made life possible in the arid lands of the Near East. The house thus became both closed and open, an enclosure that provided shade throughout the day. It was a functional yet highly symbolic interior environment that acknowledged the surrounding heat and aridity, as well as the ever present and marauding nomads. It was also a garden that paid homage to Eden with water flowing from a central and protected source that was channeled out through four rivulets oriented to the cardinal points. This divided the square courtyard into subsidiary quadrants, a design calculated to observe ritual appreciation for the water. It was an enclosed Edenic grid, and Persian rugs recapitulate this divine geometry in endless gardens underfoot. The very word *paradise* derives from old Persian for enclosure, and in Greek and Latin takes on the meaning of garden or an enclosed park.

The extension of this domestic geometry outward to urban spaces eventually spread throughout the world, regularizing what had been haphazard and narrow tracks into street grids. As Yi-Fu Tuan put it in what is arguably the seminal book on the subject, *Space and Place: The Perspective of Experience:* "Human beings not only discern geometric patterns in nature and create abstract spaces in the mind, they also try to embody their feelings, images, and thoughts in tangible material. The result is sculptural and architectural space, and on a large scale, the planned city."

The Persian paradise garden is the visual principle underlying the floor plan of Western civilization, and its spread can be traced to monuments as far apart in time and space as the Sumerian Ziggurat of Ur (2250 B.C.), the Persepolis of Persia (circa 540 B.C.), the Taj Mahal (A.D. 1632–1654) in Agra, the Mosque at Cordova, Spain (A.D. 785–987), and the street grid of Los Angeles. The original Spanish colonial grid laid out in L.A. in 1781, for example, was directly derived from instructions given in a book at the Archive of the Indies in Seville, according to D. J. Waldie in his memoir of the Lakewood subdivision that is titled, appropriately enough, *The Holy Land.* The Seville collection of royal ordinances was based on a book written by the Roman architect Vitruvius around the time of Christ—the grid of classical Rome itself influenced by the Near East, which had become part of its empire. It was, as Waldie observes, a "grid that came from God," the product of a desert monotheism. When Brigham Young followed Frémont's description to the shores of the Great Salt Lake, which the explorer had called "bucolic," and moved the City of Zion to Utah, he reconstructed a numbered street grid laid out by the prophet Joseph Smith in 1833, which prescribed a city one mile square that was meant to replicate into the infinity of sainthood.

The Greeks attributed the origin of geometry to the Egyptians who, they claimed, had devised it in order to annually reestablish agricultural property lines erased by the regular flooding of the Nile. It's difficult to assert that geometry arose as a consequence of desert economics, but perhaps not such a stretch to see how the influence of mathematics could have spread so readily on a land as blank as a sheet of paper. Likewise, it's more than mere coincidence that the pyramidal geometry of Egypt resides on open desert, as does the geometry of Michael Heizer (and, of course, one of the largest standing pyramids on the planet, the Luxor Hotel-Casino in Las Vegas).

It's an old habit, geometry in the desert, whether it shows up in Navajo rugs and Hopi sand paintings, or Australian petroglyphs and Persian rugs. When the landscape is so bare before us that we cannot ignore the fact that most of the universe around us is empty, we invent systems in order to hold it in our minds so we don't, either literally or psychologically, lose ourselves in the void. The Persian rug is part of what has grown into a magnificent Islamic tradition utilizing sophisticated and recursive geometries in the decorative and fine arts. Its patterns of architectural detailing executed in tiles are like the maps of heaven, and have as much to say about the psychological realities of the desert as do USGS quadrangles about the physical ones. The power of Islamic prayer is reinforced through kneeling upon a rug, thus placing oneself in the garden, a richly imagined courtyard providing refuge from the existential silence of the desert. As has often been said, it's no wonder the world's great monotheisms arose in the desert: one creator with a vast and impartial design favoring those who find and utilize water.

The oldest known artwork discovered to date is a huge series of thousands of circles pecked out on a sandstone monolith in northwestern Australia. If the estimated age of the carvings is correct, at seventy-five thousand years old and twice the age of the Ice Age animal drawings in France's Chauvet Cave, they even may be the work of pre–Homo sapiens hominids. The bark paintings of Australia's Aborigines are, among other things, complex representations of territory and songlines, the maps of myths ritually memorized in songs and then sung while one walks, both re-creating the land in front of oneself and acting as a guide to religious sites and water. It's hard not to speculate on the relationship between the two kinds of artwork; whether or not there is any direct lineage is not so much the question here as is what might be the cognitive affinity to impose precise geometries on natural features, especially in the arid regions of the world.

I pause for a moment from my writing to check on Alvin. He has his measuring tape stretched across the petroglyphs, his compass screwed onto the tripod, and is busy sketching the petroglyphs to scale in his notebook of graph paper. He is, in essence, mapping art, obviously still absorbed, and I return to my speculations.

Archeologists of the mid-twentieth century, puzzling over Anasazi petroglyphs that are more than a thousand years old, were baffled when trying to interpret abstract squiggles pecked in the desert varnish atop a mesa in the Southwest. Not until one member of their party noticed that the lines matched the contours of the very mesa upon which they were standing were they able to decipher the drawing, a topographical map of the area. The problem of identification stemmed from a confusion between art and mapping, which is not only rooted as far back as the Near Eastern conflation of geometry with myth, and with garden with rug with prayer, but has precedents in more recent western practices.

Until the end of the nineteenth century, art was still a visible part of cartography, not totally subsumed by the rectilinear mathematics of the USGS maps we use today. Artists in that earlier century were very much key personnel in scientific expeditions and explorations; painters and photographers accompanied the surveyors to the tops of the highest mountains, down the deepest canyons, and across the apparently trackless deserts. Religion, art, and science were still, for the most part, reconciled into one system of belief that judged the universe to be the masterpiece of a supreme Artist, and it was only natural that artists should, along with preachers and geologists, interpret the handiwork. Even when Sir Charles Lyell, the great geologist of the age, pushed back the origin of the earth's features by millions of years, it was taken as scientific evidence of divine infinitude. Maps were the visual evidence of that mind-set, the increasingly accurate triangulation of landmasses still accompanied by fanciful scrollwork and bordered with illustrations of the latest and most fantastic geographical features of the region. Prior to that, European maps for centuries were more often than not executed as aggregated drawings of local topographies, miniaturized mountains shown to surround the tiny buildings in cities. During the Renaissance mapmakers were often artists, Albrecht Dürer and Hans Holbein being just two of the more famous examples.

The map and the grid have been formally associated for so long we forget that it is possible to have a map without a grid, reminded only when looking at maps drawn by preliterate people wherein features are traced by contour, instead of located within a coextensive system of lines where all the intersecting points are equal.

The oldest known map is, not surprisingly, from Mesopotamia around 2300 B.C.—around the time that urban spaces were being designed as grids—and shows rectangular settlements next to watercourses. A Babylonian map has been found that shows the world as a circle geometrically divided, and the cartographic grid shows up for the first time on Greek maps of the fourth century B.C. A Chinese map from the third century B.C. is reported to have been drawn on silk, and it's been thought that the weft and warp of the fabric may have been another origin of the map grid. A Greek geometer designed a globe representing the earth as a sphere in 355 B.C., and little more than a century later Eratosthenes deduced the circumference of the terrestrial globe to within two hundred miles of actuality and divided it with regularly spaced lines.

By 150 B.C. Hipparchus had drawn equally spaced rectilinear intersections on flat maps, suggesting that they be fixed on astronomical measurements, essentially the same system that Frémont and Preuss brought to the Great Basin. Ptolemy in the second century A.D. proposed a world map based on latitudes and the as-of-then unmeasurable longitudes. Two thousand years before the United States Public Land Survey was begun, the Romans mapped their empire with a rectilinear survey from North Africa to Great Britain.

The first maps to be printed were made in Italy in 1475, and were based on the Greek text of Ptolemy's *Geographia,* which had been smuggled out by refugees fleeing the Turkish expansion into Byzantium (Istanbul). Ptolemy's text, based in no small part on the work of Hipparchus, included suggestions for breaking down the world into sectional maps, and contained thousands of coordinates for locations based on approximate latitude and longitude. Within ten years copies of Ptolemaic world maps were becoming widespread throughout Europe, coinciding nicely with the refinement of mathematical perspective in drawing and painting. The circulation of identical copies of gridded maps, of graticules based on geometrical figures wrapped around the spherical globe, reinforced the idea that the map had conquered the world, and that all that was left was to fill in a few blanks.

Math and maps really came together seriously in France during the seventeenth and eighteenth centuries when triangulation was adopted as the basis for national surveying. By 1783 French cartographers were suggesting to their English counterparts that both countries use the same scale of triangulation. It was a conversation Jefferson could not have failed to notice, and the method was imported to America just in time for the exploration of the West.

This business of "getting some perspective" on the subject applies to both art and cartography at the most basic mathematical and philosophical levels. Perspective can be traced back to Paleolithic cave art, where the figures of some animals are superimposed over others, thus placing them in the foreground of the visual field. Superimposition and relative size—portraying objects more distant as being smaller than ones nearby—are the two simplest methods of perspective. Various other techniques of perspective were employed in ancient Greek and Roman art, but it wasn't until the fifteenth century that architecture and the figures therein could be represented in a fashion that was both geometrically correct and sensible to a viewer standing in front of a painting. Essentially, Renaissance perspective took a square and drew lines converging from it to a point on an assumed horizon, then divided the receding space with horizontal lines that grew closer and closer as they approached the horizon.

It was a sophisticated grid based on triangulation that allowed any object in the picture space to be placed accurately in relation to any other object in the same space. A viewer could now approach a painting and see a two-dimensional analog of three-dimensional space that looked real. A mathematical analysis of the painting could be used to measure how far apart the objects were in reality, just as could be done on a map, the cartographic grid serving a function similar to perspective. Both ways of representing the world visually, art and maps, were becoming systemized as they were based increasingly on more abstract mathematical methods. Both methods were also attempting to square the circle. The rectilinear grid of the map was wrapped around a spherical solid, while perspective reframed the circular perimeter of our vision into rectangular picture windows. Both abstracted us away from looking at land and into considering a landscape.

Untangling the grid from art and cartography can become an even more complicated task when we consider the history of pictorial representation. Who would deny the possibility that among the first visual marks made by man were lines drawn in the sand by one person showing another how to get to water, to food, to shelter? And at such a point in our cognitive development, who knows whether or not the map, the picture, was considered separate from the territory it represented. Michael and Susan Southworth, in their *Maps: A Visual Survey and Design Guide,* define maps as representative objects that can exist in two, three, or even four dimensions, portraying both space and time. They argue a map can be "verbal, numerical, graphic, photographic, sculptural, small- or large-scale, static or changing. It may represent things, places, people, ideas, qualities, or activities in space or in time. Anything that can be spatially or temporally conceived can be mapped." Using this definition, it is possible to categorize almost all visual art as maps of one kind or another, objects that chart emotional and intellectual landscapes as well as geophysical ones.

Such an enlarged categorization is not at all strange when examining, for instance, the behavior of the great nineteenth-century American landscape painter Frederic Church when he unveiled his encyclopedic natural-history painting of South America, *The Heart of the Andes*. Church framed the nearly fifty-five square feet of canvas with black drapes and potted specimens of the exotic plants depicted in the massive landscape, a painting that very nearly did exactly what the artist claimed it would: present to the viewer a natural-science catalog of the region. Visitors, who paid a quarter to visit (generating an astonishing three thousand dollars in one month for the artist), were handed opera glasses through which they were to examine the flora, fauna, and geology. This was no less a conflation of a picture with the place it represented than is an aboriginal painting that acts as a map.

With such precedents, is it any wonder that everyone loves a map? They remain for us the symbolic keys that both represent the mysterious and offer a way to unlock it. The categories become even more blurred if we take into account a view held by some art historians that abstract paintings by mid-twentieth-century American artists as diverse as Mark Rothko, Barnett Newman, and Jackson Pollock were figurative replications of the vast landscape sublime represented more literally by Church and Bierstadt and others of the previous century.

Accepting such visual representations for what they are—both painting and cartography being deeply framed strategies of a particular vantage point—is safer than taking maps too literally for what they pretend to be, an objective and disinterested analog of the world. As maps became more and more scientific in their methodology, refining their baselines and extensions into reliable guides to the position of things in the world relative to one another, we began to accord them more representation than they could bear. We thought that, for instance, once we surveyed all the rivers in the West, we could then engineer them as we pleased. But representing the current course of the Colorado on a piece of paper used to choose where to plant Hoover Dam is not all that's needed, not when the river is carrying so much silt that it could fill up Lake Mead and overtop the dam within a couple of centuries. Such misplaced trust founded on cartography not only generated the almost immediate need for another expensive dam upriver to delay the silt, but, when the Glen Canyon Dam submerged one of the most beautiful canyons in America, also started a lengthy reexamination in our society about the environmental costs.

The desert is valuable because, among other reasons, it is a naked landscape most unlike the majority of the lands we live in. Without trees and bushes in the way, and without the intervention of buildings, the corners of the national grid are visible, which leads us to consider the genelike meme upon which all our other grids are based and what effects they have on us. We can measure the desert mathematically. We can make maps of it and tirelessly revise them in order to plot out more accurately the heights of the ranges and the depths of the basins. But, in order to understand what it means to have one's ranch buried by the sands, or one's community become a ghost town, a map by itself won't do. The grid and all its engineered corollaries won't stop the sand from blowing or the water from being used up, and in fact may hasten those ends. The contrast between man-made control and natural chaos is manifest, the limitations of the grid all too evident.

In a sense, by virtue of its unadorned surface and the subsequent scope of our vision, the desert acts as an indicator region for the rest of the planet. Our perceptual assumptions about the world and the consequent changes we wreak upon it are often visible here before anywhere else. The cognitive dissonance we experience in the desert, as it upsets our everyday perceptions and habits of mind, can be an advantage if we allow it to lead us into reconsidering how we see the rest of the world, no matter where it is we live. We gain a new viewpoint, see where we live—and therefore ourselves—from a new angle. It's precisely the vision we need in order to calculate truly our effects on the planet before we spoil it to the point of our own extinction, if we haven't yet done so.

IT LOOKS LIKE Alvin is finishing his observations just as I do mine. As I walk down the hillside, I realize how enjoyably frustrating the subject of cartography has become for me. The proliferation of the cartographic grid has been going on for centuries, and is a topic occupying entire libraries. Still, I can't resist stopping and making one more note: look up the

Bedolina map from northern Italy, a town plan featuring multiplying squares that was carved into rock as early as 2000 B.C.

"Ready to go?" Alvin asks, though it's more of a call to get moving. Petro comes when called, and I'm faintly surprised he hasn't managed to find some water and get himself wet. The hike to the car goes quickly, and we're soon back on the emigrant trail. Crossing the valley and entering the canyon once more for its final narrows, we scare up a couple wild horses to our left. They're large, handsome animals, well fed this season, and they canter off ahead of us, sometimes using the road, sometimes going cross-country. They stay about a hundred yards away for a couple of miles, as if playing with the Jeep, and Petro whines softly in the back as he watches them. The horses finally disappear, suddenly and mysteriously, almost without our noticing so quickly is it done, so competent are they at surviving here. We continue on toward an intersection on the map, and Petro lies down for a nap.

When we turn on the road to the west that we think will take us back toward NV 34, Alvin expresses the hope that we've picked the right one and won't end up in a dead end. I have yet to get lost with Alvin leading, so don't worry about it, but simply enjoy the long climb onto the plateau. The road winds up into what is, strangely, an even more desolate vista than that offered by the Black Rock. Low, tawny hills roll away on all sides as if they had no end, and it's easy to believe that we can see straight into Oregon, only forty-two miles to the north. In front of us the low silhouette of the Hays Canyon Range marks the border with California. After wandering through the relatively tight enclosure of the High Rock gorge all day, traveling out in open country with hundreds of square miles visible in three states is exhilarating.

The sun is just low enough to glint off the glass broken alongside the road—but then I catch myself. Glass? Out here? Whatever is reflecting back at us is a consistent layer of material, and though it looks like the beer bottle shards found beside many Nevada highways, there aren't any bars or liquor stores within a half-day's drive.

"Alvin, what is that stuff?"

"Oh." He's not been paying any particular attention to the phenomenon. "That's obsidian. Those are chipped flakes. I've seen it where the lithic scatter goes for miles like this."

"So, stop the Jeep! I have to see this."

I open the door while we're still moving and hop out. Sure enough, the ground is paved with worked stone on both sides of the road extending back as far as I walk into the sagebrush.

"I can't believe this, there's so much of it." I keep bending down to pick up a piece, turn it over, put it back down, as if to reassure myself I'm not being fooled by some trick of geology.

"Notice how there are lots of cores here, the large pieces they used to flake off smaller pieces—but no finished tools worked on both sides, just leftover flakes?" Alvin directs my attention to fist-sized chunks of obsidian that have had flakes struck off on all sides. "This was an area where they did rough finishing to lighten what they had to carry. They took the flakes back with them to wherever they were camped, and finished them there."

"How many people did it take to do all this?"

"Well, there's two theories about sites like this. Either there were just a few people around for a long time, or a lot of people around for a short time." Alvin pauses. "But this much stuff in so many places? I think there were a lot of people around for a long time!" He laughs, knowing that it's a matter that may never be settled. I've heard it said that no more than five thousand Paleo-Indians could have been responsible for most of the evidence of prehistoric habitation left in the Great Basin. I've also read an estimate of as many as twenty thousand natives in the region in 1840. Neither figure is verifiable, nor are they necessarily related, but the latter one is a little easier to swallow as it is based upon eyewitness accounts, and it leads me (through the sort of amateur intuition that Dr. Heizer rightfully would have scoffed at) to believe Alvin might be correct. Walking back to the Jeep, I find a shotgun shell and a broken Budweiser bottle mixed in with the obsidian, evidence of the contemporary hunters.

Noticing numerous vehicle tracks flattening the brittle autumn grasses on either side of the road, we're at a loss to explain why they're here, much less why there are so many of them, until we starting counting the white PVC pipes planted by a mining company. Wherever there are siliceous volcanics, such as obsidian and chert, there's a possibility that microscopic gold will be found nearby in deposits sufficiently large enough to justify the enormous open pits and cyanide-leaching mounds used by the modern mining corporations. The Carlin trend, which runs like a crooked spine down fifty miles of Nevada, hosts a chain of open-face mines following the trail of gold dust, entire mountains reduced by the world's largest moving machines into a crude geometry of berms, as if in parody of *City*.

Whenever I see the white pipes I briefly consider pulling them out of the ground, as if such a simple sabotage could prevent even the possibility of earthmovers radically rearranging the scenery. One of the overarching purposes of the great mapping surveys run across the West after the Civil War, in the post-Frémont cartographic frenzy, was to trace geological features throughout the region in preparation for their exploitation, hence the name of the U.S. "Geological" Survey. Not much of the industrial attitude toward mining has changed in the last hundred-plus years, just the method of extraction and the filing of environmental-impact reports. It's hard enough to stop heap-leaching just outside Yellowstone and Glacier National Parks; this area wouldn't stand a chance, the synonymy of wilderness/wasteland in our cognitive vocabulary almost ensuring that we would allow the despoliation.

We've climbed from about thirty-eight hundred feet on the playa of the Black Rock to around forty-six hundred feet at our camp last night, and now top out around fifty-eight hundred. The extra two thousand feet puts us into a wetter zone where the Basques have been grazing sheep for more than a century, and Alvin says there are a series of "stone boys" up here, tall cairns built by the sheepherders. He's not sure of their purpose, but speculates that, because you can often see from one set to another, they could be directional guides through a terrain in which it otherwise would be difficult to orient yourself, given the lack of distinctive peaks.

Sure enough, we spot four of them atop the next ridge, and there's even a track off the road leading to them. Taller than we are and sometimes hosting capstones that are larger than the lower rocks and reminiscent of heads, the stone sentinels have obviously been rebuilt fairly recently, the color of the rocks on the bottom darker than those above. Three of them are lined up, pointing at some unknown location, and the fourth stands off to one side by itself. I note the presence of black widow webs in the rocks and shy away, my arm still sore.

I'm dressed in just a T-shirt and shorts, and definitely getting cold in the late-afternoon wind rising up the ridge, so we climb back in the Jeep and continue westward. On a straightaway below I spot a couple of pronghorns, the first time since visiting Heizer's last spring that I've seen one. Graceful quadrupeds that grow to only about three feet at the shoulder, they used to range over the entire midsection of the country. Delicate, trusting, curious, and apparently unwilling to cross railroad tracks, they easily fell prey to people shooting from the trains as well as hunters, on top of which their populations were ravaged by disease, overgrazing by livestock, and deliberate poisoning. The small herd up here was remote enough to escape widespread notice for decades, and in the 1920s and '30s a few conservationists convinced the government to help. The Sheldon National Wildlife Refuge was cobbled together just a few miles north of us out of public and private lands, the protection enabling the herd to grow to more than twenty-five hundred animals.

I see two more now, pacing us on the right at about twenty miles per hour, then four more, and twist around in my seat to make a count, suddenly picking out dozens of them. One group of seven or eight suddenly sprints ahead of us and bounds across the road. Another group does the same behind us, and we watch in astonishment as the entire herd springs over the road—none of them so much as touching the graded dirt—and then runs lightly down a small draw. Like the wild horses down below, the pronghorn seem to appear and disappear at will, more evidence of our inability to easily distinguish life in the desert.

Our road now begins to descend through a series of well-watered vales, sure signs of year-round ranching in the fences, water tanks, and small corrals glimpsed in the distance as we rejoin NV 34. The "High Rock Canyon" map sheet I'm using, one of the large hundred-thousand-scale USGS sheets that cover nearly seventeen hundred square miles, has almost no green on it. Although springs and creeks abound through here, there is no forest, just sere hills and canyons. NV 34 is a dirt highway wide enough to hold two large semis side by side and is clearly visible wherever it goes in the landscape. We turn left and start down what is the last segment of the crude parallelogram we're tracing.

It's not that we're bored, but our attention span is simply worn thin, and we're quiet as the Jeep heads south at a steady fifty mph, faster than we've driven since leaving the playa yesterday morning. The land slopes down, then gathers itself into the steep folds of Leadville Canyon, which after a few minutes empties out onto the Hualapai Flat, a valley that drains south through the low hills that divide it from the Black Rock Desert.

The upper two-thirds of the valley is pasturage for cattle ranches, and is ruled off by roads graded exactly on the section and quarter-section lines of the map, Jefferson's grid as prevalent here as in the fields of Iowa and Kansas. The first vehicles we've seen in almost two days pass us going the other way. All of them are four-wheel-drive utility vehicles or pickup trucks piled high on the inside with camping gear, or towing small trailers, the first wave of this year's fall hunters headed into the high country we've just left. Good timing, we think.

The lower third of the valley sinks into a small playa on the Fly Ranch, which gained some notoriety a month ago as the new home of Burning Man. Larry Harvey, a San Francisco artist who eleven years ago exorcised his disappointment in a love affair by torching a life-size wooden figure on the beach, was urged by friends to make it an annual ceremony. The next year they moved the location out onto the Black Rock, his friends invited a few of their friends, and by the time I got there in the fall of 1992 a thousand people were gathering on the playa to watch a forty-five-foot-tall skeletal colossus outlined in blue neon be consumed by a bonfire at midnight. Artists from all over the world came to build installations, beat drums, dance naked, and wear animal horns on their heads. It was riotous and neolithic, but although the energy of the crowd was unnervingly powerful, it was safe. Even the couple that year who landed their small airplane nose-first in the alkali walked away from the crash, were cheered, and then were handed glasses of wine.

Part of the attraction of Burning Man arose from the season. Coming at the end of the summer and the traditional beginning of the harvest, the rite had deep roots in European mythology, the Celts torching autumnal figures on cliffs above the sea each year before pushing them off the edge. The turning of the leaves and the lighting of the fire, the clearing of the fields and of the heart, the return from summer vacations to school—whatever your cycle, Burning Man seemed to have a metaphorical connection, and was quickly becoming irresistible to more and more people as they heard about it.

The other part of the attraction was the Black Rock itself, which was assuming ever more legendary proportions in the imagination of the arts community. People returned from Burning Man not so much with tales of midnight orgies around the dying embers, but with wide-eyed descriptions of the curvature of the earth and the sensation of being able to feel the planet revolve beneath their feet. They talked about walking out onto the playa, lying down on the ground, and thinking they were the last person alive on earth. And, of course, they lowered their voices and spoke gravely of the dangers—the heat, the blinding winds, what would happen if it rained while a thousand people were in the middle of the playa.

The year I went, Reno artist Jim McCormick had laid out nine hundred blocks on the ground to form a giant cross—or plus sign, depending on your vantage point. Each one-foot-square block was divided into one-inch squares in a perfect parody of the national grid. He lined up his X, his mark on the world, with true north, and with its eastern arm pointing straight at Burning Man. It was an intersection of art, map, and land that rose only an inch off the desert floor, was invisible from a few yards away, and reminded me of the intaglio figures traced out in the Mojave in California and on the arid Nazca Plain in Peru. Those giant drawings, which vary from animals to geometrical figures and mazes, were made by sweeping aside the dark stones, or desert pavement, to expose the light ground underneath. Although intaglios last for centuries, perhaps millennia if left undisturbed, and McCormick's work was only a three-day installation that reversed the figure-to-ground relationship of the prehistoric art—his work using dark lines laid out on the fine white dust—it had some of the same resonance.

Standing beside McCormick's schema, looking out past the upraised wooden giant and into the far reaches of the playa, was to be defenseless within the void, the presence of the art "articulating" and accentuating the emptiness. Around me stood hundreds of tents, a nomadic tribe of artists and onlookers gathered in the desert to invoke some serious partying, but also to ritualistically send up in smoke our pretense of ruling the void with rationality.

Driving by the much smaller, almost painfully constricted space of the Hualapai playa into which the event this year had been compelled to move by financial circumstances and insistent permitting agencies, I know the experience has been altered dramatically. No longer is the horizon of the festival an unbound theater of the dissonant, but a closed stage set. As the attendance has grown close to ten thousand people, the beleaguered organizers have been forced to set up a gate, charge admission, and turn over most of the proceeds to Washoe County in recompense for what have become essential emergency, medical, and law enforcement services.

I'm still complaining to Alvin about the shift in venue as we pass through the hills, our road running down to and then paralleling the Black Rock. I admit, though, that there's some virtue in containing the party to the smaller space behind us. Last year so many vehicles were on the Black Rock at the same time that people were running into and killing each other in car accidents, part of the reason the BLM and other government agencies wanted the event moved. Our cognitive inability to judge speed and distance in the void was an attractive feature of Burning Man, but it had proved once again a deadly one.

Ahead of us the great playa has gone a soft gray in twilight, the hills on its opposite shore glowing warmly in the last light of the day. It's an ancient sea of serenity, the only evidence of activity the faraway dust plume of a lone motorcyclist driving into Gerlach from the British racing camp. By the time we get to Gerlach it's dark and the town is hopping, but there's a table in the corner at Bruno's, and I order a plateful of their infamous ravioli. Sitting nearby with a blond companion, perhaps his wife, is Andy Green, the driver of the Thrust SSC. His lean face is so focused it's almost predatory in appearance, though he responds patiently to an older couple at the next table who pester him with questions. Dinner comes and I tuck into my pasta, Alvin setting aside the bones from his pork chops for Petro. In two days we've driven only 295 miles, more than half of them on dirt roads. My watchband is tight on my wrist, left arm slightly swollen from the spider bite. I'm tired and anxious to find a campsite.

Alvin, as usual, is relaxed about finding a place to pitch the tent. After dinner we poke around local dirt roads, making an inadvertent but thorough inspection of the Gerlach gravel pit before we find a superb spot on a creek with trees and running water. I didn't think it was possible to camp simultaneously within view of the Black Rock and earshot of running water, but here we are. By the time the tent is up Petro has taken a dip. It's nine o'clock and the only interruption all night is a coyote calling softly from the bank of the creek, trying to lure Petro away from camp. I look sleepily outside to make sure he's not tempted, and he lifts his chin only briefly to answer my gaze, as if to chide such a foolish thought.

Dooby Avenue West, otherwise known as Guru Road, parallels NV 34 just outside of Gerlach. At 8:45 this morning I'm hanging outside the Jeep window counting the hand-painted rocks bordering the dirt road, Alvin taking a tally of the stone boys, although these are only tall rock-pile imitations of the real thing up in the mountains. We're also keeping an eye on the playa. After breaking camp and on the way in to breakfast at Bruno's, we noticed that the entrance to the playa was closed, which means the Brits are running. The buzz in the cafe this morning had it that nine o'clock was the appointed hour.

Guru Road is an art project started well before Burning Man by a now-deceased local eccentric, DeWayne Williams. Laid out like a linear mock cemetery with small tombstones, it offers words of wisdom, messages to friends and loved ones, and political commentary. Folklorists call it a "visionary art environment." One rock installation is a series of concentric rings with a ground zero in the center, the rings representing blast waves moving over the landscape. Some of the messages are silly, some satirical, some just dates and names marking a marriage or a death. One statement encapsulates the assembled 675 stones: "Every Move You Make Makes a Mark," which is as true of the pioneers last century as Andy Green this morning.

We finish the count and pull back onto the highway, preparing to pass through Gerlach one more time as we drive around the southern end of the playa. In a few minutes we'll turn off on the Winnemucca Road along the southeastern rim of the flat, a route that will take us out to a newly discovered geoglyph site that a BLM archeologist has asked Alvin to investigate. At 8:50, just as we're passing the closed Gerlach Hot Springs, a long tube of dust suddenly blossoms out along the open playa to our left. No sound reaches us, nor can we see the Thrust SSC itself, which has taken five miles to get up to speed, passed through a carefully measured mile in less than five seconds, and then taken five miles to brake to a stop—the whole eleven-mile run lasting just over a minute.

We don't hear a sonic boom, so figure Green hasn't broken the barrier this morning, but it's enough for me just to see him pace off this particular mark. Besides, the rules say that, in order for a time and speed to qualify, you have to turn the car around and make another run in the opposite direction within an hour, the two speeds then averaged out for the record. It's possible we'll see him go again this morning.

Gerlach is almost empty as we pass through, everyone having gone out to watch the show, and at 8:58 we pull onto the Winnemucca Road. At first on a well-graded gravel surface while in Washoe County, within a mile we cross into cash-strapped Pershing County, and the road degrades into a rock-hard dirt washboard, far less pleasant driving than anything else we've encountered in the last two days. After almost an hour of eyeball-jarring rattles, and no sign that Green has been able to make a second run, we once again find ourselves triangulating off nearby features to locate what we think must be a rock art site. Two BLM people were supposed to meet us, but they must be running late, and Alvin thinks he can find the geoglyph based on their directions.

Up a slight rise and no more than a couple of hundred yards off the road we come upon the figure. Composed on the ground with rocks, around which the desert pavement has been scraped away in order to outline and highlight the assemblage, it's a bipedal creature surrounded by small boulders, some of which were obviously already in place, some of which have been added. Rocks darkened with desert varnish make up the limbs and head, and a light-gray slab of tufa represents the pelvis from which dangles either a penis or a baby. From each of the outstretched arms trail three downward pointing lines, and the head is pointy, almost beaked. Alvin doesn't give his immediate impression, but walks carefully around it several times first.

Breaking out his gear, he begins to survey the site, which measures out about twenty-three feet in length. Almost as if talking to himself, he comments: "I don't think this is all that old. The rocks just aren't buried enough in the dirt. And it's not out on the flats where you usually find intaglios—though that's not really what this is. There's nothing else around, either, no other petroglyphs or flakes. And it's not oriented to a cardinal direction, not even to King Lear Peak there to the northeast, though it's close."

He continues to work, and Petro, having explored the nearby area, scratches himself a cool place in the shade by a boulder and lies down, used to waiting patiently while Alvin does his work.

"See these arms? I think they're wings. And the head? I think that's a bird head. It's a conflation of bird and human, male and female."

"You ever see anything else like this?" I ask.

"No," he replies. The dust trails of two vehicles pass by on the road, turn around, and return to park. Five people get out and start to walk up to us, two Anglo women, two Indian women, and one older Indian man. Alvin knows the BLM archeologist, and we're introduced to the others, Paiutes down from the Summit Lake and McDermitt Indian Reservations. Alvin doesn't say anything as they approach, but watches their reactions carefully. The older of the two Indian women, as soon as she gets a full view of the figure, shakes her head quietly, and Alvin smiles.

"What do you think?" he asks, still grinning.

"It's not Indian," says the woman, Helen. "It looks kinda like a thunderbird a Navaho would make. I don't think it's real, though."

"Me either," adds Alvin. "I think it's maybe ten years old, maybe less. See how little dirt has blown up against the rocks?"

It's obvious the BLM woman is disappointed. She's doing a survey of the resources of the area for a new management plan, and she's keen to find as many old Indian sites as possible. She asks several questions about the figure. Have they seen anything else around here that looks like it? (No.) Does it have any meaning to them? (No, things that are real usually have something they can "feel.") Can they feel anything here? (No.) Nothing bad, no hex on anybody? (No. It's pointing the wrong way for that.)

She gives up, accepts the consensus for what it is, not a final proof of anything, but the best obtainable likelihood, and relaxes. I take notes, listen to some stories everyone is telling her about local legends. Alvin goes about his business transferring the image of the arranged rocks to the grid of his notebook, and I sit atop the boulder where Petro is lying.

It's odd to me that the grid wasn't accepted by archeologists as the basis for orderly excavation until Mortimer Wheeler, a Britisher, proved its use in the 1930s and '40s. By the 1960s a one-meter standard grid was in widespread use by scientists, usually plotted in conjunction with stratigraphy in layers about two inches deep at a time to catalog the context, or matrix, in which artifacts or bones were recovered. The only vertical displacement Alvin causes today is to lift up a rock to confirm that it's light on the bottom, comparing its protected and unvarnished surface with another stone that is right-side up but unvarnished. If the work was old, everything would be equally covered with patina.

The sun is hot, and I'm regretting that I left my sunscreen in the Jeep, but am too lazy to retrieve it. In the intervals between bursts of conversation the silence rings in my ears, a biofeedback I've come over the years to anticipate, enjoy, and allow to calm me. I once took a Washington, D.C., civil rights attorney who was visiting Reno out to Pyramid Lake in honor of his request that we "go see some desert." Stopping by a large tufa formation on one of the prehistoric shorelines, we got out and sat for a minute on the rocks in the late afternoon of a weekday. No traffic passed by, and a squadron of the white pelicans that roost on Anaho Island glided far below without a sound. Even the wind was still.

He couldn't take it for more than that one minute and asked to leave. He could hear his own blood, probably for the first time in his adult life, and it scared him—it was just too close.

Out here on an edge of the Black Rock the potential for silence is even greater. I'm enjoying the uninterrupted view of brown hills and the distant playa, the horizon that appears anywhere from within twenty miles of us to beyond my ability to estimate distances, though the BLM archeologist and her company chatter in the background. A long string of Western Pacific cars goes by to the north on its way from the East to Oakland, the line put through here in 1906. My thoughts drift back to the grid, to what part the railroad plays in its reach and the politics involved, and what that has to do with art.

UNTANGLING THE GRID AND POLITICS, like the grid and art, is also a daunting task. Not only has the grid been a basis for measured taxation since at least the time of Babylon, but in America it is what the late great cultural geographer J. B. Jackson called "one of the most ambitious schemes in history for the orderly creation of landscapes." The grid in America has its modern roots in eleventh-century Europe, when the irregular and unplanned network of streets outside the city walls grew complicated and confusing enough to impede trade. The grid was imposed outward from the quadrilinear and cruciform walled city in order to ease traffic flow and make available regular plots of land for farming in a flexible and inter-changeable pattern of land usage that, not coincidentally, fit nicely into inheritance laws. Thomas Jefferson, ever the student of Europe, conceived of extending the idea of the grid in order to promulgate democracy across the North American continent by making available equal measures of land, then linking together the townships with a national metagrid of roads.

Both Washington and Jefferson were surveyors hiring other surveyors. As leaders pushing forward the edge of newly created political territory, both were obviously cognizant of the power of maps. Whatever Jefferson's motive—whether as a way to settle taxation disputes, to unify the empire of equality, or to promote science as an enlightened activity in harness with the industrial exploration of the West—he implemented the National Survey, which proceeded to carve up the United States into a recursive grid as strict as that of any Persian garden designer. The more than two-thirds of our country ruled off in this manner is a political manifestation of the grid, and is readily apparent to anyone either flying over the Midwest or hovering over a map of the central and western states.

The grid exercises authority over space by applying a ruler to it in all senses of the word. It stretches out a straight edge across unenclosed space and automatically extends a map to the romantic horizon. A map is noth-ing less than a tightly controlled abstraction of the world in which we are deeply conditioned by our genes and our culture to believe, to accept on faith as an accurate representation of reality. The question always remains, however: Under whose control and to what purpose? As an artificial exten-sion of our egocentric visual triangulation of the world, the grid is auto-matically suspect. Democracy is only one application for the grid, that seductive geometric meme.

The use of the grid to exploit the natural resources of the American wilderness was not only an unavoidable technological evolution, but also the signature of a national mind-set in which we wrestled with the dual nature of what we considered to be our destiny. On the one hand, the immense wilderness, and most emphatically the sublime landscape of the West, was direct evidence of divine order and intent. This was a viewpoint both industry and government, which were sometimes indistinguishable in their actions, promoted with vigor as they sought to encourage the westward emigration of Americans.

Viewers reading the government reports of explorations in the 1800s (reports that cost more to print and distribute than it did to run the expeditions themselves) happily succumbed to colored lithographs that proved the point. The artist William Holmes was probably the most gifted stratigraphic artist the world has ever seen, and his work was featured in several of the expeditionary reports. Viewing his illustrations from the 1870s of the deeply stacked strata of the Grand Canyon—captured with a hyper-fidelity beyond even the capability of contemporary photographic equipment—was like scanning the fossilized and exposed cortex of a universal Mind. The geology of the West, that complex, massive, and obviously ancient stratigraphy of the arid lands, was taken as conclusive proof of order on a cosmological scale, which meant it must be divine.

In fact, maybe it wasn't merely proof, but Order itself. No myth of the gods playing in the garden, a familiar European painting theme, was needed in America for its landscape art. The land itself was the myth. This belief found an expression so compelling in the paintings and photographs of Yellowstone, Yosemite, and the Grand Canyon, by artists such as Thomas Moran, Albert Bierstadt, and W. H. Jackson, that Congress made them national parks, preserving forever the divine evidence, the mythic manifestations for the public edification of all Americans. A good thing, too, as the belief held in the other hand was the biblical exhortation to utilize the land to the exclusive good of the human (and specifically the white) race. Such utilization threatened to destroy, ironically, the very landscape that we held up as proof of divine intent. The agricultural homesteading and industrial subjugation of the West was to be carried forth by what we thought was a divinely inspired geometry, one made manifest by the cartographic grid and its mechanical handmaid, the railroad.

The supreme physical manifestation of the grid actually laid out on the ground in nineteenth-century America was, indeed, the railroad, an industry that almost by default inherited the mission to complete westward expansion across the continental United States. The British, the French, the Spanish, and the Italians had all sought to reach the Far East by sea, thus avoiding the lengthy and complicated overland barriers to trade across the Near East, obstacles that included vast deserts and often impenetrable mountains, ferocious bandits, and enormous tariffs imposed by the Turks. At first they thought that America was the Orient, then perhaps just an island in the way. Once it was determined that it was actually a continent, it was thought the Pacific Ocean might be only a strait separating America from their goal, which is how Mercator portrayed things in his 1569 map of the Western Hemisphere.

For three centuries they sought a polar route around the obstacles, the fabled Northwest Passage that would skirt the northern boundary of the Americas and emerge in Cathay. When that proved unfeasible due to navigational hazards and expense, they looked for the fabled Rio Buenaventura, envisioning yet another waterborne strategy. And when, finally, it was becoming clear that such a river did not in all probability exist, a road had to be invented. A road that was straight and economical, that could be unrolled as ruthlessly as a column could be added up on a piece of paper. The railroad was perfect, a set of steel-ruled lines that receded into the vanishing point of the frontier, and that measured its progress by ties laid out every few feet, a progress that could actually be heard by the passengers as they sat in the dining cars, the click-clacking of the wheels a reassuring metronomic grid. It was a mechanical translation of distance into time, turning "how far" into "how long until we get there," a corollary to the ultimate equation of industry: time is money.

The railroad companies first either directly underwrote or applied enough political pressure in Congress to help make possible the great geological surveys of the midcentury. Their immediate interests were in locating new mineral deposits and thereby expanding the country's industrial base, both of which implied the transportation of large and numerous goods and materials most efficiently handled by rail. In one of those peculiar circles through which our language occasionally wanders, the word from which "grid" is derived is "gridiron," which was first used by the British in the 1850s to describe how the railways had patterned the land.

Sending out the surveyors to map a grid in order to gridiron the country seems almost like a self-reinforcing prophecy.

The railroad companies were also interested in moving people. Although the human race doubled in number during the nineteenth century, America started out in 1800 with a little more than 5 million people living within 868,000 square miles. By 1900 75 million Americans were dispersed over 3 million square miles, an expansion made possible only by the grid—the mapping grid that showed them where to go, and the railroad that, subsequently, took them there. It was not by coincidence that Thomas Moran, who first went west as part of one of those surveys, was later hired directly by the railroads to paint the scenery of the region, particularly the Grand Canyon, in what became a successful effort to promote tourism to the national parks served by the trains.

During that century the railroad was the primary manifestation of the grid because the cities and towns, though for the most part parceled out in rectilinear blocks only occasionally enlivened by other schemes, would remain confined within relatively modest boundaries until well into the twentieth century. The pioneer wagon tracks and stagecoach routes were forced to follow the logic of the land, limited by the power of, at most, a few horses, and contouring wherever possible to save energy. Trains broke through this limitation by applying ever increasing amounts of steam-powered mechanical force that began to level the landscape. Although still constrained to relatively gentle gradients, and therefore obliged to follow somewhat the existing topology, in the main they followed an east-west orientation in order to link the two coasts as directly and quickly as possible, and thereafter established subsidiary lines connecting points to the north and south. In the Great Basin this meant deviating only when necessary to find passes across the east-west, basin-and-range grain of the land in order to meet at Promontory summit for the driving of the Golden Spike in May 1869, but later just following the valleys for the north-south routes.

The railroads were awarded a checkerboard of landownership by the government as it followed the national Jeffersonian pattern, and four-square townships sprang up at regular intervals to fuel the train with coal and, just as important, water. The virtuous civic squares replicated outward into the surrounding fields not only in the great flatlands of America, but also virtually wherever the railroad passed through valleys in the mountainous West.

The grid even metastasized underground. Follow a tunnel into one of the old silver mines in Virginia City and it's like crawling inside the railroad of a higher dimension, the miniaturized track for the ore cars bracketed by square forms every few feet on both sides and above your head, the grid undergirding the very earth. It was a three-dimensional grid plotted at right angles to intersect the wandering veins of gold and silver, and the most advanced mining engineering in the world for its time. It was also mathematics yoked to the extraction of raw currency, science molded by utilitarianism in order to fully use (and use up) the land, transforming the basic material of the planet into that exalted representation of wealth that bears the geometric symbol we most associate throughout history with heaven, the Egyptian pyramid on the back of the dollar bill.

The transportation grid of the railroads began a process that only accelerated upon the arrival of the gasoline-powered automobile, which exercised a much higher and more mobile ratio of power to weight. Able to climb up and then brake downward on much steeper grades, this allowed the highway engineers to simply blast straight through contour lines on the map without having to remove the entire elevation down to the level of the valleys. Eventually, the automobile made imperative the supergrids of the megalopolis, there being no other way to channel workers in their cars as cost-effectively from home to work.

The national highway system often followed the line of attack the railroads had already established, which quickly evolved into dense interstate utility corridors. Behind the trains and telegraph trailed the telephone wires, then high-voltage and fiber-optic lines, and even the wireless microwave transmission towers. It was simply the easiest way to go, abetted by a predictable pattern of existing access roads. Roads and streets, of which there are now an estimated 4 million miles in America, more than one linear mile per square mile of land, are in turn also the reason for the largest distribution of maps in the history of civilization, more than 200 million road maps being distributed to the American public each year. Maps create roads create maps in a spiraling proliferation, which evolutionary theorists such as Richard Dawkins say is typical of the hypothetical meme.

Just as curves were added deliberately to towns and cities to provide residential relief from the rigid grid of the downtown world of work, so were national parks designed to preserve a sense of the divinely ordained order of the natural world. Some of this balance was derived from urban European models, whether it was the romantic wanderings of the French parks provided as a relief to Parisians from Baron Hausmann's rigorously radial street grid designed to facilitate crowd control after the Revolution of 1848—or the Dutch tulip gardens with their round beds as a visual antidote to the monotonous agricultural handkerchiefs ruled out on artificial lands forced outward into the sea. Central Park, laid out by Frederick Law Olmsted in the 1850s, though tightly hemmed in by one of the most photographed grids on the planet, the streets and skyscrapers of Manhattan, is not a classical Italian garden with geometric hedges mirroring the rigid organization of the city, but a romantic English collection of meandering paths and organic interior borders formed by ponds.

Olmsted also chaired the California Parks Commission, submitting a recommendation to that body in 1865 on how the meanders and roads of Yosemite should be shaped in order to accommodate what he predicted would be millions of visitors annually in the future. His report was squelched by private interests holding the rights to a toll road, but he went on to design the public approaches to Niagara Falls and left behind a body of work both on the ground and in books that directly or indirectly influenced plans for many of the public parks in America.

The national parks of the West, often sitting perilously close to the industrial grid—or sometimes bisected by it, as is the Painted Desert with Interstate 40 in eastern Arizona—have likewise followed the romantic tradition. Their trails, even when paved over by asphalt to protect them from heavy foot traffic, follow the contours of the land, bending and dipping in a way calculated to evoke some sense of being more natural and organic than not. *Contour* is the key word, whether it is on the land or in the design of parks. Varying the elevation of a footpath helps us play off the grid. It lets the designer and the mind of the visitor escape the mathematical flatland into something that, if not exactly replicating, then at least echoes irregular nature. If Frémont templated the West by bringing the grid to bear on it, which the Mormons reinforced in Salt Lake City and then attempted to spread throughout the Great Basin, he also brought his primitive altimeter, recording elevations and tracing contour lines, thus facilitating the spread of the modern topographical map as we see it today.

What Frémont found in the Great Basin was exactly the opposite of what he had hoped to discover, a landlocked void instead of a channel to the sea. Instead of finding a way to compress time and hasten the journey west, he defined a place where time could hardly be seen to progress at all. It was a region in which you could lose track of all time and distance, not to mention yourself. As such, it was perceived as a waste of time and space, a desperate place for people to traverse as hurriedly as possible on their way to California out of a desire both to minimize the travel hazards and to avoid the visual boredom and cognitive dissonance of the desert. The grid, manifested in maps and the railroad, was a way of marking our passage. We could visualize our passage and overcome with sheer speed our inability to perceive a region that is a hiatus in our expectations of industrial time and space, a lacuna in the otherwise increasingly rapid pathways of international finance.

The last map of the Great Basin produced by Preuss, before the depressive cartographer committed suicide a few years later, appeared in 1848 and was based partially on Frémont's description of another foray into the region after Preuss and he had parted company. It's hard to say, therefore, why the Preuss map turned out the way it did—whether it was because he was not along to argue topography with Frémont and Kit Carson, or whether it was just the meme of the grid poking its head up out of the unconscious—but the map shows the Great Basin surrounded by four mountain ranges forming a square in alignment with the orientation of the Jeffersonian continental checkerboard. It's as imaginary a piece of geography as those practiced by cartographers a century earlier.

The northern line of the square is not a perfectly straight line, but humps upward on its western end as it traces that part of the Great Basin through which Preuss had marched in person during late 1843. And, although there is no actual line of mountains demarcating the northern edge of the Great Basin, he did represent at least the location of the watershed fairly accurately. To the south, however, he simply created a fiction, a straight line of mountains completing a square that he envisioned would logically hold in all the waters of the Great Basin. The grid abhors a void. Even the fussy and painstaking Preuss, usually so insistent upon empirical observation and geographical accuracy, was overcome by its demand for symmetrical, rectilinear closure.

ALVIN LOOKS LIKE he's about finished with his survey, and the BLM woman is organizing lunch for her Indian guests. We retreat to the Jeep and the last of our tortilla chips.

"I think it's a Burning Man deal," I venture out loud as we start back over the furious washboard, which seems even worse in this direction. "I think one of the artists from Burning Man came up here a few years ago, looking for a place to do something personal."

Alvin hesitates. "Maybe."

Whatever it is, the survey by Alvin, the attention from the BLM, the opinions of the Paiutes, and my writing about the figure all legitimize the geoglyph. At one level, it doesn't matter whether it's aboriginal work or a contemporary installation by a sculptor. It exists on the desert and proposes a human relationship with the void, one that doesn't depend upon the grid.

One of the earliest public artworks of the Black Rock that I have been able to locate is a lithograph from a Pacific Railroad survey volume published in 1861, a copy of which Alvin has at home. Folding out of the book is a long panorama titled *Valley of the Mud Lakes* drawn by C. Schumann from cartography by the Prussian cartographer and artist F. W. von Egloffstein on the 1854 survey of the thirty-eighth parallel. Assuming a viewpoint from one of the Selenite peaks just north of Mount Limbo, it scans the entire western horizon from the southern end of the Smoke Creek Desert to where the Black Rock rolls over the horizon to the north. The panorama is a literal transcription of the void, and even the nine-thousand-foot summit of the Granite Range is reduced by the breadth of its view to nothing more than a single consonant in a very long sentence. In the lower center of the picture stands a figure, perhaps the leader of the expedition, Lt. E. G. Beckwith, with his horse. It's a typical nineteenth-century convention, inserting figures to emphasize the terrifying scale of the land in our imagination, but in this case the figures were insufficient to relieve the uninterrupted flow of vision. Schumann was forced to add a flight of birds in the sky to frame our attention downward, to keep us reading the picture from left to right. Without the birds the eye naturally lifts by the time it reaches the center of the foldout, and then simply falls upward into empty sky, unable to maintain visual concentration. Beckwith was looking for a direct central route for the transcontinental railroad, and the line he laid on the grid is the one followed by the train that I saw earlier in the day.

Now the BLM staff wanders the countryside looking for significant artifacts, carrying with them handheld monitors that receive triangulation signals from the twenty-six satellites of the Global Positioning System (GPS). The grid, which the Greeks first borrowed from their astronomers mapping the sky in order to systemize their understanding of geography, is still being determined by points in the heavens. Instead of divining guidance from the constellations, however, we're listening to radio waves that are capable of pinpointing our position to within a few centimeters. The GPS was first developed by the military as a warfare navigational system, and is run from the Falcon Air Force Base in Colorado. The system went operational in 1993 and is already used by the drivers of expensive cars to plot routes around traffic jams and by golfers to estimate the distance of their shots between greens. The Pythagoreans of ancient Greece would be thrilled that their hallowed celestial mathematics now surround every square inch of the globe, even if its uses are sometimes frivolous.

The grid has allowed our species to so transform the planet that there is almost no land left that we have not explored, mapped, drilled, mined, paved over, or otherwise landscaped. When we look at a space, our neural system begins to abstract it, filtering out most visual information "in order" for us to perceive it coherently, to locate ourselves within it. Our nervous system (an organic network that we currently imitate in the grid of the computer) then begins to make a cognitive picture of it, a mental map, "in order" to remember how to get around in the space. If it's a map we need to share or remember for future reference, we externalize it, make a written or electronic image of it, a map we can share with others in a more or less commonly accepted fashion. This requires an immense suppression of data and a very high degree of abstraction.

Maps are then used to scribe lines across the landscape itself: wagon trails, power lines, railroads, farm roads and streets, motorcycle tracks, bicycle paths—to move from industrial to recreation uses. At that stage of development where we gain any vertical perspective above the landscape, imagined or reproduced, it becomes a page in front of us, and we think of ourselves as reading a map. The land becomes landscape becomes map. At that point we're so distant from land itself that it becomes merely a surface to be manipulated—to be inscribed, erased, written over, which is exactly what happened in America once we had even just begun to fully overlay the cartographic grid upon the West.

You can, if you wish, make a case that the grid made possible industrialization, which in turn led to the greenhouse effect, which means we've changed the climate, thus making it impossible to be anywhere on earth and escape civilization. Some authors argue there is, therefore, no such thing left as nature; others, though, claim the dichotomy between land and altered landscape is a spurious one.

Because human beings are part of nature, I tend personally to consider the differences between land and landscape, between unmitigated nature and urban landscape, a continuum of process. In some places man is currently apparent, in others not, though we may have been there before, even left enduring traces of our presence that have since been subsumed by the undergrowth. But wherever we are, the grid is pervasive and impossible to escape, a perceptual mechanism that guides us to shape the world according to its geometry.

One kind of human activity that can mitigate against the grid, however, that contrasts with and diverts it to purposes other than exploitation of space, is art. I can't speak for the BLM or its employees, but it seems to me that some of the BLM folks, for instance, hope that by locating enough examples of native rock art they can make a case for preserving the desert from further development—or at least channeling the spread of the grid in different directions, perhaps doubling it back toward increased density within existing urban areas.

And I think about Mike Heizer and his sculpture. What *City* does, ultimately, is abstract the mind at work, which is to say the world, at a very deep level. Its geometric forms arise from the void as surely as Nevada's mountain ranges are forced up by tectonic forces far below the surface of the earth. Its berms and out-thrusting trapezoids are the visible structure of force made physical, just as the faces and shoulders of the mountain peaks and ridges hovering above the valley are made to play in the nearly perfect sunlight that is captured and held, day after day, in the Great Basin. The spreading of the gravel and the curvilinear line of the curbing along one side of *City* are arrayed against the right angles, the organic contours a fluid dimension of that same geometry, as if to remind us that to account for the world we must admit more than the sum of straight lines. We must remember the rise and fall of water, the immense evaporative cycle of the atmosphere, the irregular and inconstant interruptions of weather and climate in their own fluid dynamic.

The blank stelae leaning inside the sculpture become unsigned tablets where language has yet to be assigned. Just as the massive berms are uninhabitable form and prearchitectural, so are the stelae silent without the systematic application of gesture to their surfaces. *City* resides at that point in our consciousness where visual image and language are just about to make themselves known to us, surfacing out of our minds from the pressure of our neural tectonics. To walk down into *City* is to place yourself in the midst of that process, the solidifying of a cognitive map all around you. It is not something you can or will forget, so firmly does it place you.

As Alvin and I pull back onto the paved road for the drive into Reno, I'm thinking about those grids carved into the rocks beside Winnemucca Dry Lake by the Paleo-Indians. Were they historical records, hunting instructions, narrative weaving, or sympathetic magic? I also remember an exhortation made by Robert F. Heizer to archeology students in his textbook of field methods, one that instructs them to learn how to locate and use the national section grid so they can correctly plot their excavations and find them again in the future.

My third and final trip for this book, to be taken as soon as I can arrange it, will involve looking at rock art Dr. Heizer actually used to explicate what he thought some of their meanings were. The petroglyphs and pictographs are at a site his son showed him and not far from Mike Heizer's valley. I want to bring together the grid in the void with both the prehistoric rock art and the contemporary sculpture and see what, if anything, the juxtaposition signifies.

& THE SIGN

Instead of listening to the silence, we have shouted into the void. We have tried to make the arid West what it was never meant to be and cannot remain, the Garden of the World and the home of multiple millions.
　　—Wallace Stegner

Many people are afraid to empty their minds lest they may plunge into the Void. They do not know that their own Mind is the void.
　　—Huang Po

If you take the signs away, there is no place.
　　—Robert Venturi, Denise Scott, and Steven Izenour

SEVEN
⊗

THE FIFTY OR SO mourners in Manhattan's Mount Moriah cemetery this March afternoon outnumber the total population of the town. Despite the bright sunshine, the wind blowing up-canyon from the Big Smoky Valley is cold enough that everyone is keeping their elbows pressed tightly to their sides inside parkas. We're at nearly seven thousand feet here, the ceremony for Walter Daniels is half an hour late in getting started, and in order to keep warm Alvin and I start a circuit around the tombstones.

The cemetery is laid out in—what else—a grid, as if the geometry could conquer the ultimate void itself, death. It's not a surprising manifestation of grid versus void; after all, the relatives will know that Walter's ashes can be found along the x and y map coordinates of his burial, six feet deep along the z coordinate of depth, last seen on the temporal line of 2 P.M. on Wednesday, March 18, 1998. And he's not going anywhere soon. That's about as engridded in four dimensions as we can make anything on the planet, though judging from the number of unmarked graves—also outnumbering the current inhabitants of the town—it looks as if entropy will undo both the physical traces and the living memory of his position within a few decades. Even the Egyptians with their immense funerary complexes had trouble preserving the coordinates of their dead. But, traditions die hard. We've been carving out rectilinear cities for our deceased over several millennia, almost as long as we've been building ones for the living.

I never knew Walter, who was a friend of Alvin's and a fellow rock-art enthusiast. Excuse me, "avocationalist." Alvin draws a deep distinction between dilettantes and people who devote their time to serious research, despite their lack of professional degrees. It's appropriate that we're here for Walter's memorial service, though, in deep central Nevada. Alvin had called me last Friday to let me know he was going to be making one of his periodic rock-art recording trips, this time into Heizer territory, and wanted to know if I could scramble fast enough to join him. I jumped at the chance. I'd been out to Mike Heizer's place in February, just a few weeks earlier, hoping to visit the rock art site with him that he had shown his father in the White River Narrows—the site that had subsequently become the subject of that very monograph where Dr. Heizer decried "the efforts of semi-informed amateurs to become the 'code-breakers' of the great mystery of the designs pecked on the rocks" as part of the untrustworthy world of the imagination. (That statement being precisely one of the reasons Alvin insists on the distinction between enthusiast and avocationalist, in fact.)

But it wasn't to be. First, as I drove on the dirt road through the small mountain pass into Heizer's valley, the clouds were so low that they left a gap just large enough for me in the Honda and an F-16 to squeeze through at the same time, an opening that closed shortly thereafter as the clouds lowered and the first of several El Niño snow- and rainstorms moved in. I stayed for four days, watching CNN during the day as we threatened to go bomb Iraq, and trying to call Beth at night on the radio telephone. I had to make the calls early in the evening, the frequencies jammed by the Air Force after eight-thirty or nine P.M. as they practiced overhead for the invasion that, it turned out, was postponed for some other month. I got out before seven on the fifth morning, the only time when the roads were frozen hard enough to drive on, being otherwise deep quagmires of wet clay.

It may have been just as well. While visiting I brought up to Heizer the theory of abstract geometrical petroglyphs being entoptic patterns transferred onto land, versus the version proposed earlier by his father: that the grids were depictions of fences meant to herd animals, both a marker of actual hunting sites and perhaps an attempt to evoke sympathetic magic. Heizer was, to put it mildly, quite skeptical, despite the fact that the primary American writer on the entoptic version, David S. Whitley, holds a Ph.D. in archeology, was the chief archeologist for UCLA, and was one of Robert F. Heizer's students. Nonetheless, I left disappointed not to have visited the site with Mike, and wondering how to finish my book without actually viewing the rock art, which I considered to be traces of the earliest signs in the desert void of the New World.

When Alvin called to say that he was going to meet both BLM and University of Nevada archeologists at the White River Narrows, and that maybe we should go together, I immediately hauled out the family emergency credit card and booked a flight to Reno. So there we were earlier today, back in the blue Jeep with Petro ensconced in his corner, headed southeast through the heart of the state. The trip from Reno through central Nevada had been a classic Great Basin drive, first following the Truckee River east through the mountains outside Reno and then breaking out into the Forty-Mile Desert leading into Fallon.

The route follows the first U.S. Bureau of Reclamation project, a ditch dug in 1903 in order to water crops at the foot of what had been the worst and deadliest stretch of emigrant trail in the arid West. Determined to make the desert bloom at any cost, the federal government has subsidized that particular flow of water for almost a century now, a tiny part of what has since grown into a network of 360 dams feeding fifty thousand miles of canals throughout the country. On the other side of Fallon we stopped briefly to visit Grimes Point, a BLM-administered petroglyph site well known to Dr. Heizer, though when he first viewed it the nearly one thousand embellished boulders were within the borders of the town dump. Across the road from us were the control towers of the Fallon Naval Air Station, home to the Navy's vaunted "Top Gun" aviation school. To the north was the snowcapped Stillwater Range, its highest point, Job Peak, one of the triangulation substations for the Great Arc Survey.

Signs of the void and the grid were all around us with more to come. A few minutes down the highway (and now officially on "The Loneliest Road in America"), we crossed what has always been my favorite playa in the Great Basin, a salt flat deeply incised by narrow runoff channels and polygonal desiccation fractures, a pattern that is just regular enough to tempt one into visualizing a grid. Closer inspection reveals that it's the opposite, a chaotic system, a set of approximate repetitions that revolves around a set of rules, instead of following them as does a grid. The attraction of the desiccation fractures is that they hint at a secret structure, which appeals to our innate mental will to pattern the surface of the world.

At the far northeastern edge of a playa stands the almost mystical Sand Mountain, the largest single dune in the Great Basin. The five-hundred-foot-high scimitar of sand produces deep booming reverberations at irregular intervals, signals generated by the complex harmonics of its crystalline physics, yet another desert structure only partially understood. Both the tortuously replicated polygonal fractures and the great internal echoes of the sand remain mysterious and signature manifestations of the void for me.

Alongside the playa for the last several years various travelers, most of whom seem to be romantically inclined teenagers, have taken to borrowing dark rocks from the roadbed in order to spell out messages. Some of them boldly declare "I love Mary" or "Susan" or "John." Others specify geographical origins, such as "Sam . . . Texas." This, too, is rock art as signage, public assemblages of aesthetically arranged symbols carrying a variety of messages, and a variation on the "newspaper" rocks found throughout the West. One of my favorites is a prominent mesa in New Mexico, El Morro National Monument. At the foot of the sandstone cliffs is a famous watering hole formed by runoff from above, making the tall landform not only an obvious landmark for early travelers, but also a critical resource. It's not surprising that the prow of the sandstone contains an entire stratigraphy of signatures acting as signposts pointing west. Starting with the highest level are petroglyphs of an unknown age, presumably Anasazi, followed by names and dates incised in script by Spanish explorers, then the block letters in English used by U.S. Cavalry officers, and finally the more casual graffiti of emigrants. The march downward of the messages demonstrates the wearing away of the soil at the base of the rock as increasing numbers of travelers passed by.

At the entrance to Sand Mountain, a BLM recreation area, a lone public telephone sat at the bottom of a pole that is topped by a solar panel. No wires led to or from it. It was off the power grid, off the telephone grid, a self-contained radio unit for emergency use. A sign declared it "The Loneliest Phone," which is suitably romantic, another message center in the Big Empty.

We passed over the Sand Springs Range on our way into Dixie Valley, all of the area either an active bombing range or a fly zone thick with military associations. One of only two atomic explosions in Nevada off the Test Site was conducted underground here several decades ago, a place I've visited with my sons, Tarn and Mathew. We ate peanut-butter-and-jelly sandwiches at ground zero while helicopters kept us under surveillance, circling around us every thirty minutes or so. Waving to the pilots, we hoped that the hundreds of feet of dirt under us and filling the shaft to the explosion chamber were as much shielding as we'd need from residual radiation of the small-yield device. It's not a place the public is really supposed to visit, but neither is it technically off-limits. Steve Glotfelty, one of my climbing partners and our Jeep driver that day, had located the place on a USGS topo map: "GZ Canyon," it read, clear as day. Ground Zero Canyon.

After driving through Dixie Valley, with its bomb targets neatly arranged by yardage out on the desert floor, and its sign for the United States Navy "Centroid" Facility, part of the world's largest electronic warfare center, we turned off toward Gabbs. I spent a couple of weeks in Gabbs during the early 1970s as a poet-in-residence for the Nevada State Arts Council, and it looked like it had definitely gotten quieter than it had been even then. Home to a large magnesium mine since World War II, when the mineral first came into demand to make lightweight alloys for aircraft, and then later for missiles and rockets, it had seen the mine's level of production slowly wind down over the years. What's left behind is a devolving collection of buildings and businesses, and the monumental terraces of an open-pit operation.

Although you can't observe completely the progressively bermed terrain of the massive gold mines in operation along the Carlin trend unless you fly over them, the magnesium operation that's stripped away part of the mountain east of Gabbs is in your face and horrifyingly beautiful. It's one of the few places where you can actually witness the destruction of a landscape— not just a reshuffling of land, mind you, but a place that's actually been blown up and thoroughly addled. The remnants are stately and, like Mike Heizer's *City,* evoke monuments from ruined civilizations. This nineteenth-century convention of viewing a tortured landscape as romantic ruins is so pervasive in the West that it doesn't matter if the landform is the Grand Canyon or a mine, just as long as it's big. The magnesium mine is more compact than the cyanide-leaching gold mines, but you wouldn't know it unless they were side by side. Viewing through binoculars the quiet benches that for years were blasted daily out of the mountainside made me feel like I was cruising down the Nile past the Pyramids.

By eleven-thirty we had turned off the state highway onto Pole Line Road, a clean and level manifestation of the grid's proclivity to overturn sagebrush with the blade of a grader. We threaded our way through what used to be an unsigned maze of dirt roads cutting across the basin and range toward Manhattan, population forty. Maximum.

"What? What's this?" Alvin yelped. "Since when did they start putting up signs?" I didn't see anything but a BLM sign pointing toward Peavine Campground, still out of sight over a mountain range. Alvin was indignant. "Now anybody can find their way around out here!" That's the point, I thought, even though there was no sign directly naming Manhattan and you still had to know from experience or friends that the Peavine Campground cutoff leads to the highway in Big Smoky Valley. Alvin, though, is used to memory being the key to navigating in the void, the topo maps in my lap notwithstanding. Externalizing personal memories by erecting signs anyone can read, that's dirty pool. But where the grid goes, so goes signage. Just as the grid hates a void, so a sign hates an unlabeled intersection, or even a stretch of the grid that remains mute for too long. Hence rock messages from teenagers, carved inscriptions in prominent landmarks, and road signs—and perhaps, I think, petroglyphs and their painted counterparts, pictographs. Even Frémont and Kit Carson carved their names on rocks and trees as they went west.

The dirt road rose slowly toward the sky, mirages of a mountain peak and a lake floating ahead of us, the boundary between the superheated air just above the ground and the cooler air above bending light rays into apparently recognizable forms. Alvin and I puzzled over first the water then the peak, trying to guess if either was real. Mirages are usually an obvious game in our cognitive dissonance with the desert, their images wavering slightly in the instability of the optical boundary. The small lake appeared to tilt toward us, as if to spill its contents across the desert floor; the peak shifted left and right, daring us to pin it down. We decided the water was an illusion, the peak actually a nearby hill. Our road crested the divide between valleys, and the lake turned out to be a stockman's reservoir just to our left. The hill resolved itself into a reflection of a large peak more than fifty miles to the north. So much for our ability to winnow reality from mirage.

MANHATTAN IS A TOWN I've wanted to visit for years. First, and in the way of general principles, it's in the Toquima Range, just east across the Big Smoky Valley from the Toiyabe Range. The two parallel ranges rise to more than eleven thousand feet, more than sixty-five hundred feet above the valley floor, forming the deepest and most dramatic basin-and-range in central Nevada. When driving between Reno and Las Vegas, the rest of the state sere and bone dry, snow on these peaks beckons the eye upward on imaginary hikes. And midway up the valley sit the Wild Granites, a legendary band of thousand-foot-high granite cliffs first climbed by Alvin in the 1960s. Stretching for more than a mile along the eastern flank of the Toiyabes, they are a talismanic wilderness destination for climbers bold enough to venture beyond the indoor gym and small sport cliffs of established areas. In fact, all of the geography around here is highly desirable for those of us who relish the Big Void.

Just one basin farther to the east is Monitor Valley, the floor of which runs from roughly six thousand up to sixty-eight hundred feet. That's the highest valley elevation in the Great Basin, the apex of the hypothetical dome underlying the region. In theory, the slowly uplifting dome is the result of the North American tectonic plate sliding over the Pacific plate. The subsequent rising of the curved earth's crust is stretching the region apart, a movement that, according to John McPhee in *Basin and Range*, has moved the sites of Reno and Salt Lake City away from each other by some fifty feet. It's the same geological phenomenon that's stretching the ground under Yucca Mountain on the Nevada Test Site some 1.7 millimeters annually. Doesn't sound like much, but it's a symptom of tectonic restlessness. Nevada is the second most geologically active state in the country, surpassed only by California, a fact that is increasingly giving more than a few scientists qualms about storing spent reactor fuel rods inside the Yucca Mountain Nuclear Waste Repository.

Manhattan is the settlement that served the nearby Toquima gold mines discovered in 1906. As we came into town we passed the radically deformed hillocks that had been eroded and sterilized by runoff from what was once the largest gold-dredge operation in the lower forty-eight. The mine produced $10 million in gold over its forty-year run, and the line of its tailings still reaches out into the valley below. By contrast, the immense contemporary leaching operation at Round Mountain just up the road in the Big Smoky, the tailings for which were visible as we entered the valley, produced more than $75 million in gold in 1990 alone. Open-pit mining is an activity especially poignant in the Great Basin as the holes it leaves behind cruelly mimic the void surrounding them. On a human scale the mines are sublimely large, entire mountains torn down into a pit that is then surrounded by tailing berms as high as foothills. The first big pit was the Bingham Canyon copper mine in Utah. Started in 1904, it's now two and one-half miles across by a half-mile deep; 5 *billion* tons of earth have been removed there. By the end of this decade the modern gold mines of Nevada will leave behind three dozen pits running as large as three miles long by a mile wide by a half-mile deep. Each of those operations will have removed between one and one and a half cubic miles of earth, enormous man-made voids filled with highly acidic lakes. The once lionized but now abandoned operations in Manhattan appear quaint by comparison.

The mine is in the lower part of town, while the upper part contains the remaining civic buildings, two bars, and a few dozen houses, most of them wood with corrugated metal roofs, some of them snug and handsome and hidden back in the piñon-juniper forest. The cemetery is on the outskirts below the mine. Now standing just inside its entrance is Bob Bottom, the man who organized the memorial service for Walter Daniels and is now eulogizing the dearly departed's numerous accomplishments.

Although Walter had moved to Manhattan from Virginia City only five years ago, apparently he'd been a vocal presence in town for the establishment of a local museum and cleaning up the historical buildings. Bob is clear that sometimes Walter's enthusiasm escalated into sheer gadflyism, but he's also genuinely choked up. While a deputy helps Bob lower the urn containing the deceased's ashes, two sheriffs fire off three volleys into a sky that is without clouds from horizon to horizon. Shovels appear and several of the men step forward to quickly fill the grave, Alvin among them.

I pace out the cemetery one more time. Many of the graves are bordered by rectangular cement curbs laid out in rows, each bearing small metal frames on stakes planted in the ground. The frames are empty, the intersections of life with death left unsigned.

The grid unrolled westward from Mesopotamia like a carpet welcoming the arrival of civilization. It enabled people to establish an order they understood all along their route, an order that captured the existing local relationships with topology and subverted them to the flow of expansion. It also helped subdue their fears of the unknown. When possible, the grid was internalized as maps, first copied by hand and passed from person to person, and then printed to colonize the imaginations of the citizenry. Along with the Bible, maps were the most frequently carried printed materials of imperial colonialism.

By the time the grid reached America, exploration was poised on the brink of a cartographic technology that would soon enable it to extend its triangulation into any territory we would care to explore, and then to endlessly reproduce the results so every wandering eye could own a copy. In the mid-nineteenth century the grid exploded across the West with the Great Surveys, one of which had a triangulation station atop Arc Dome just across Big Smoky Valley, a location within sight as I pick my way from grave to grave. The division of terrain by surveys and railroads dissolved almost all preexisting bonds with the land. Only the lands underneath the feet of a few Native Americans and Spanish colonialists retained even a semblance of their natural order, principally in the well-established pueblos and towns of New Mexico, because they had been there long enough to develop a substantial, resilient, and appropriately scaled geometry of their own, one based more on the paths of local irrigation than on the quadrilinear divisions of capitalism. For everyone else, the message was coexist with the Jeffersonian grid or get out of Dodge.

Because the West was settled so fast, a feat made possible by the grid and its technological partner, the railroad, the region has retained the habit of migration, a restlessness fueled by the boom-and-bust extractions of gold and oil and coal. People still move along the grid in droves, often not settling down long enough to build more than the shallowest of memories, thus for the most part failing to convert space into place. That's the path Walter Daniels was following, moving from Virginia City to Manhattan, from one old boomtown to another. And that was his adopted cause, attempting to preserve the thin layer of history left behind in the tailings and fragile buildings.

The overriding fact of the West is space, and without slow demographic growth there is no hope for a climax population with a deep and stable geographic imagination. Space will remain merely a barrier to be overcome. The grid is our most efficient tool for the task, given that our species has evolved with it. So, we plant our feet on a baseline that's hooked to the national grid, level a survey at the nearest horizon, and set out a square plot. And then another and another, tiling away one yard at a time ahead of the developers who follow behind us. We either ignore or make only minimal concessions to the contour lines of the land, essentially insisting on a flatland of impoverished imagination.

In desert cities such as Los Angeles, we push the grid beyond the limits of public safety, building up to and then straight into floodplains below the San Gabriels, the steepest mountains on the continent. As John McPhee pointed out in his essay "Los Angeles against the Mountains," even though massive debris flows there come crashing down the mountains and through peoples' homes on a regular basis, the collective memory we allow ourselves is so short that we just keep on carving terraces out of the mountain faces. We build geometrically subdivided housing units right on top of the largest earthquake fault we can find, perch homes over unstable mud slopes, and then straighten out the rivers with concrete in order to drain the local land as fast as possible—a practice that only accelerates and deepens the floods downstream. The mindless repetition of the grid replaces memory.

I use Los Angeles as an example because it is the ultimate American prototype for all the other desert cities on the continent, such as Phoenix and Las Vegas, all aggregated bedrooms laid out on the grid. Even Salt Lake City has fallen prey to a variation on the theme, a modest and workable rectilinear pattern of irrigation that has metastasized north and south all along the front of the Wasatch into a look-alike checkerboard of strip malls, fast food restaurants, gas stations, and suburbs to accommodate a religion that, like many other desert monotheisms, traditionally encourages overpopulation in order to conquer the void.

Because the desert retains the ability to dissociate our perceptions from our expectations, a reality check of the severest nature starts promptly where the concrete ends, the juxtaposition a rampant surrealism. This branch of twentieth-century aesthetics, which specializes in throwing radically dissimilar objects together in close proximity, underlies much of what passes for comedy, irony, art, and politics at the turn of the millennium. All of which, by the way, goes a long way toward explaining why Las Vegas is built on the edge of the Great Basin, equipoised in the nowhere. It is a city of signs, and much of what they promise is implicitly about the fantasy pleasures of the grid juxtaposed to the genuine rigors of the void. "Stop here," the neon commands. "Don't bother to go farther—there's nothing out there. Why risk yourself in the desert when you can stay at our oasis? Our rooms are cheap, the girls pretty, the drinks for free." But the sybaritic humidity of the oasis ends abruptly in the sand.

The inhospitability of the western deserts has long been noted. In 1819 the Topographical Bureau of the U.S. Corps of Engineers sent out Maj. Stephen H. Long, who was charged with compiling a report regarding the headwaters of various rivers that might breach the Rockies. By all accounts he was a somewhat geographically challenged leader, constantly confusing the various and variable rivers of the arid lands with one another. But he made at least one correct, if slightly overstated, deduction from his travels in the lands west of the hundredth meridian. He defined the region as the "Great American Desert," a place "wholly unfit for cultivation" and "uninhabitable for a people depending upon agriculture for their subsistence." He was lambasted for that perception by boosters and boomers throughout the nineteenth century, but he had it right. Agriculture has blossomed across the region for almost a century and a half, but it has been enabled to do so only through prodigious irrigation that has diverted and dammed up nearly every river in the West, as well as used up the prehistoric waters of the aquifers, waters that cannot be replaced within the lifetimes of our foreseeable descendants.

Although land promoters succeeded in drowning out his warning through an extensive public advertising campaign, Long's perception was backed up by almost every topographer who succeeded him. Frémont stated that, even on the front range of the Wasatch, irrigation would be needed to grow crops, and Lt. William Emory in 1846 described the territory from Colorado to California as being one where settlement would be forced to limit itself to the land around naturally occurring surface waters. This was an organic pattern of settlement formally proposed to Congress by John Wesley Powell thirty-two years later in his official report on the arid lands. His recommendations were, however, in direct opposition to both the geographical and the intellectual expansionism of the century—complementary developments founded upon the use of rectilinear measurements overlaid upon nature. Powell's recommendations were ignored.

The grid simply ran over reality with its obsessive mathematics. In 1896 George Wheeler began what he proposed to be a survey of the entire West from the hundredth meridian to the Pacific Ocean, in his first year doing groundwork over twenty-four thousand square miles of Nevada. His baseline on the desert outside Sutro in west-central Nevada is a good example of how exacting was the grid work. Using a twenty-foot wooden rod, his crew laid it out 1,181 times over twelve days for a four-and-a-half-mile baseline, then promptly turned around and repeated the process in the opposite direction within eight days—and came up with a measurement only .003 of an inch off the first one!

Wheeler's map extended east from what is now the San Bernardino County line in California and across the Colorado River into Utah and Arizona, and as far north as Elko. During 1877 Wheeler was running forty-six people in Colorado, Nevada, and Utah on his survey crews, and in one seven-month season in the field set out five baselines, established 106 main and 264 subsidiary triangulation stations (such as the ones on Troy Peak above Railroad Valley, Job Peak in the Stillwaters, and Arc Dome), and measured 10,800 miles with an odometer wheel.

Wheeler was unable to complete his goal, a general topographical map of the West, a region of some 1.4 million square miles, but it was a critical step in the nationwide effort that would follow. The work of the topographical engineers, and the ambitions of later army surveyors such as Wheeler, was recast as the mission of the United States Geological Service in 1879, which began to produce unified contour maps of the entire country.

Simultaneously, the survey of lands within the public-held federal domain was being extended by the General Land Office. By 1865 the GLO grid was in Carson City, the capital of Nevada; one of its maps from the following year shows the state marked off with nine counties and the mostly rectilinear spaces of twenty-eight mining districts with gold and silver deposits. Shortly after the turn of the century the entire state was divided, at least on paper if not verified exactly on the ground, by the Jeffersonian grid. The surveyors might have known that the lands they were crossing and recrossing with their equipment were unfit for general settlement, but by 1889 newspapers in the eastern and southern regions were calling for the use of the arid lands as a home for the increasing population of America.

The grid, whether projected as squares onto a map or as perspective into a painting, helps us shrink the world to our size. Just as our vision ruthlessly pares down the massive amounts of information it receives per second through a steep hierarchy into vastly simplified boundary recognition, the grid divides the world into equal measures to which we can relate and then manipulate. Maps are often said to be the triumph of geometry over geography, a rational system imposed over the irrational, organic, chaotic world. As cartography moved from guesswork to measurement, from art that represented imagined or desired or feared places, it became a science the primary purpose of which was the commensurate extension of the grid. As Werner Heisenberg, the formulator of the Principle of Uncertainty, put it: "The transition from the 'possible' to the actual takes place during measurement." He then added, of course, his famous dictum that to measure something, inevitably, was to alter it.

As humans, we tend not to consider a place truly discovered until we have mapped it so that we can reach it again; we think we possess the world by measuring it. In the nineteenth century we assumed, as the supposed pinnacle of evolution, our inheritance to be the natural world, which we could claim only by mapping it. This cartographic imperative took the world, especially that of Western Europeans, out of the theoretical province of a divine inheritance and placed it firmly within our measured grasp, available whenever we wanted it, as if nature were a place hung on a pegboard in the garage. Descartes is often credited with being an important thinker in the Western history of man's deliberate divorce from nature, primarily because he facilitated the rise of dualism in philosophy: man or nature, the rational or the irrational. The Cartesian grid, the rectilinear intersection of an x and a y axis, became the grid whereupon we plotted out the progress of rationality, mathematical proof that we could lift ourselves above our animal nature through the application of reason.

The grid, no matter its form, allows us to shift consciously from being an experiencing subject to a dispassionate observer of objects that we experience, thus divorcing us from nature, our algebraic trajectory out of Eden. The grid of perspective places us outside the picture, and we find ourselves mere viewers gazing through a window back into the world. The grid of the map lifts us cognitively off the ground and into the air.

Despite all the advantages offered us by the grid—such as, paradoxically, allowing us to navigate through, travel around, and thus see more of the world—we nonetheless expend enormous amounts of energy trying to regain the ground and entrance to the garden, whether through prayer on rugs, or the synthesis of the grid with complexity theory. We pray for unification with the natural world, whether we expect to find it in heaven, or to rediscover it here on earth through higher and higher orders of mathematics that, finally, branch so far out into thin air that they come to resemble the endlessly recursive and fractal outlines they describe, from the structure of the seashore to weather systems.

We also hedge our bets. If we can't achieve what is probably and only a hypothetical unity with nature through understanding it, we can at least be aware of how we have mediated it. That is, we are still and always animals and thus part of nature, which we define as the world before we arose as a species with the ability to change it (or, in religious terms, corrupt it). But we also now can't forget the fact that we change the world, often in unpredictable ways that end up being harmful to ourselves and every other species around us. So, while we attempt to pray and calculate ourselves back into the good graces, we also seek to become more aware of the praying and the calculating, to reconcile the grid to the void, to expand the frame of our awareness so that we are simultaneously still in the picture but aware of it—which is exactly what I'm attempting while walking through the Mount Moriah cemetery.

The grave is topped off with the last shovelful of dirt and tamped down with the stomping of feet. It's time to retire to the bar, the "upper bar," actually, of the two in town. The vehicles all head out back toward the road, most of them four-wheel-drive pickups. There are still two-foot snowdrifts under the trees in town, and people had talked before the ceremony about the impossibility of getting into Monitor Valley for several weeks yet. The runoff from the 200-percent-of-normal snowpack this year was proving formidable, and though they thought the highway crews might be able to keep Big Smoky open with enough ad hoc drainage ditches, Monitor Valley would just have to wait until things dried out.

Inside the bar a ferocious pall of cigarette smoke hovers overhead, but the pool table in a small room to one side has been set aside for a potluck buffet. Never shy about a free meal, Alvin and I are right behind the sheriffs with our plates. It's a high-carbohydrate feast suited to the rigors of desert life at seven thousand feet; I go easy on the breads and pastas. Alvin's appetite, however, remains as amazing as his overall level of fitness, and he puts away multiple plates of food without a whimper. While he's finishing off a separate plate of desserts, I continue to check out the guests. The crowd veers from mechanics in overalls to bikers in their leathers, from Mormon families to two Marines in dress uniform. One of the virtues of the grid is that it allows the most diverse populations imaginable to assemble in remote places.

"Well, that ought to hold me until Tonopah," announces Alvin, patting his stomach. Because Tonopah is only forty-five minutes down the highway, a slight diversion off our route in order to pick up our friend Courtney Smith, I figure he's telling the truth. We say our good-byes, and I nod to the marines on the way out. Petro is curled nervously in the back of the Jeep, not at all happy about the volley of rifle shots fired earlier. He hates the sound of gunshots, a basic survival strategy for a dog in the Great Basin.

We're in Tonopah at three-thirty and find Courtney parked outside the town's one strip mall. Out of the handful of towns in the west-central part of the state that might outlast the cycles of mining boom and bust, Tonopah is probably the only one. Although the town of Round Mountain was swallowed by the ever growing maw of its open pit, which also literally ate its namesake landform, and Manhattan might simply fade into the company of those other five hundred towns in Nevada that have come and gone in the last century, Tonopah sits almost exactly halfway along the north-south highway from Reno to Las Vegas. The grid has actually provided the town with a perfect location for refueling along that route, and in addition to the inevitable gas stations with their convenience stores, it now boasts a McDonald's, a sure sign of ongoing commercial viability.

We leave Courtney's sport-utility vehicle parked at the house of a friend and transfer his gear into the Jeep, then head out on Highway 6 to hook up with State Route 375, officially designated by the State of Nevada as the "Extraterrestrial Highway." This is the route most native Nevadans consider to be the real "loneliest road in America," and not that pretender passing through Fallon to the north, Highway 50. True to form, for the next two hours we see only three other vehicles.

Courtney sits in the back seat adding commentary to the drive. Thirty-four years old, deeply freckled, brown hair a random thatch seldom under even the illusion of control, Courtney first showed up in our lives as a teenage friend and climbing partner of Alvin's son, Aaron. Although he's since wandered over a fair portion of the globe, he settled in Bishop, the de facto capital of the eastern Sierra about four hours south of Reno and almost directly west of Tonopah. He works mostly seasonal jobs for the Forest Service and the BLM, has fought forest fires and measured daily the air quality of the Owens Valley, but spends as much time as possible climbing, hiking, and skiing. And, increasingly since 1990, looking for rock art. Like me, he jumped at a chance to go out with Alvin, knowing that he would see sites/sights he hadn't visited before. He hasn't exactly registered with the BLM or anyone else all the rock art sites he'll take us to, plus Courtney figures he has a better chance of finding new sites with Alvin than on his own.

Alvin McLane has the deepest topographical intelligence of anyone we know, not only memorizing the contours and coordinates of most places he's ever been, but also constantly correlating one site to another, whether it's a rock climb, a panel of petroglyphs, or a coffee shop. As if to illustrate my point, just now we turn off from 6 and onto 375 at a junction called Warm Springs. Alvin recalls for us not only the names of the rancher and his wife who own the place, but what the structures were that have since been torn down, where the nearest petroglyph is on the property, and what he ate for dinner last time he visited. This kind of intelligence, part personal memory and part professional hyper-file, enables Alvin to look at a rock and tell whether a crack in the face is climbable, what kind of moves it will allow, and how long it might take—or to squint his eyes up a valley and estimate the probability of a rock art site based on the types of rocks present, the location of water, and the flow of the terrain.

It's almost as if Alvin retains two kinds of maps in his head, one based on the conventional grid of Western civilization, but another one rooted in pretechnological times that demands other scales of measurement. Don Long, a writer and old friend living in New Zealand, recently wrote me about how the Maori reacted to initial requests from Europeans to draw maps of their country. What they produced were extremely accurate and detailed charts of their territory, but utterly out of scale with the European maps. Where the seafarers had brought with them maps based on equal and regular units of distance—the grid—the Maori drew maps according to time, to how long it would take to walk from one place to another. "What was the point," as Don put it, "of drawing two places close together if the country in between was impossible, and took a bloody long time to cross?" Alvin remembers not only where places fall on the topo sheets, but how long it took to walk from one point to another. His map knowledge is in context with the terrain, a point that will prove crucial to our search for sites over the next several days.

We curve gently around the northern end of the Reveille Range and drop down into the southern end of Railroad Valley, almost connecting to the route Beth and I took with Heizer through the huge basin a few months ago. Across from us are the Quinn Canyon and Grant Ranges, both now snow covered. Alvin points out that we're crossing Frémont's trail of his fifth and last exploration of the Great Basin. The state has 253 official historical markers along Nevada's byways, several of which we've passed today, but nothing commemorates these intersections of wandering geography other than the small flags I place in my notes.

There is, however, no lack of signs as we come up on Rachel, the unofficial UFO Central of the Extraterrestrial Highway. Our road is nearly touching the far northeast corner of Nellis Air Force Base, that military preserve containing the Nevada Test Site and America's most famous secret military base, the eighty-nine-thousand-square-acre Area 51 also known as the Groom Lake Weapons Testing Facility, Dreamland, the Ranch, the Box, Watertown Strip . . . all names for the base with the world's longest airstrip from which the Air Force launches its ultrasecret "black budget" aircraft. Despite clandestinely snapped photographs of Area 51 published for years in numerous books and newspapers around the world, the Pentagon continues to deny its existence, a policy that seems deliberately designed to fuel speculations of the most outrageous kind. We're just more than a hundred road miles east of Tonopah, and Rachel exhorts us with signs to visit "The Little A'Le' Inn," the local tavern that serves not only a pretty good cheeseburger, but also a world-class collection of UFO enthusiasts. Or maybe they're avocationalists. They certainly take their work seriously enough.

When I was a kid Reno hosted an annual UFO convention sponsored by the owner of Miguel's, which was then the largest Mexican restaurant in town. I attended one of the gatherings in the 1960s out of curiosity, and found myself in the back room of the restaurant sitting on a red vinyl chair in a small crowd of middle-aged men and women, all of us watching scratchy home movies of what looked liked flying dinnerware. Nowadays the image quality and special effects are better, and instead of flying saucers visiting us from Mars it's allegedly our own military that's doing the flying as they attempt to reverse-engineer a collection of captured UFOs kept at, where else, Area 51. The military's steadfast refusal to even admit that the Groom Lake facility exists, much less that they continue to develop experimental aircraft there, has simply changed the operative premise of the UFO-ologists: somewhere in the desert, at a location kept secret from us by our own government, there are aliens. The void of outer space has met the void of the desert and the Other walks among us.

We don't stop at Rachel this time, Alvin still full from the potluck in Manhattan, and continue on into Tikaboo Valley. The most infamous sign in all of UFO-dom sits on our right about halfway down the valley, the "black mailbox" where many an experienced watcher has spotted strange lights in the night sky, and dark shapes that hover over Groom Range just to our west, then zoom away at unaccountably high speeds. UFO watchers from all over the world come to this valley to recline during the nights on lawn chairs. Wrapped in sleeping bags and blankets to keep warm during the frigid desert nights, many of them swear they have witnessed alien aircraft flying through the sky. Multiple sonic booms and unearthly whirring noises sometimes accompany the sightings. We pass what is, in reality, rancher Steve Medlin's large postbox, and note with grins that, once again, he's painted it white in a vain attempt to return his driveway to anonymity.

The military knew it had its hands on a good thing when it carved Nellis out of the Great Basin. The base was larger than all of Connecticut, yet empty of anyone but military personnel and the few civilian contractors carefully escorted on and off the base at periodic intervals. Where else in the country could be found a more secure location in which to test nuclear weapons, nerve gas, laser beams, rockets, unmanned drones, and the newest in supersonic and hypersonic aircraft? When people say they've seen strange things flying through the night sky, there's no reason to doubt them. Unmanned computer-controlled aircraft, for instance, can perform almost any maneuver you can imagine, and some you couldn't if you tried. There are both credible witnesses and videotapes to prove it. And if you've never before seen a Stealth fighter, its frontal profile with landing gear retracted can look remarkably like a flying saucer, which Glenn Campbell illustrates in his entertaining and useful *"Area 51" Viewer's Guide.* "No such things as flying saucers," is what Heizer continues to assert, and I believe him. What we see out here at night when strange shapes ghost silently in front of the Milky Way is ourselves in Halloween drag practicing for trick-or-treat with other sovereign powers.

Shortly after dark we reach the tiny town of Ash Springs in the well-watered Pahranagat Valley and unlock the gate to the property where we're staying. The air smells like wet ditches and orchards about to bud, a slightly delirious mixture after the aridity of crossing the state. After stumbling around with flashlights for an hour, trying to figure out how to hook up the electricity and water for the trailer loaned to us by another acquaintance of Alvin's, Clayton Wadsworth, we conclude that the necessary extension cords and hoses must be stored somewhere else. Back in the Jeep we drive the few miles south to Alamo and the Del Pueblo Mexican-American Restaurant. I've heard rumors about the doubtful quality of the food, but Alvin swears it's OK. And it is.

SEVEN A.M. and back in the Jeep. Well, I actually never left the Jeep. Although Alvin and Courtney opted to sleep inside the trailer, I chose to fold down the rear seat and crash in the back of the vehicle. Despite the road dust and Petro hair, and the slightly curled profile I have to adopt in order to fit, it's actually roomier than the space left over on the trailer floor. There's a faucet outside with running water, the stars are amazingly clear, and I can stay up reading and writing out notes as late as I want without disturbing the other guys. And it makes for a quick transition from sleeping to driving, which Alvin encourages.

Today we're supposedly looking for rock art on the southeast corner of Timber Mountain, a sighting passed along by a trapper to a fellow researcher from Ball State University in Indiana, thence to Alvin. I find it more than coincidental that the peak is the highest in the Seaman Range, and that Alvin is only barely able to contain his excitement at the prospect of climbing to a high vantage point. I point out that the possibility of rock art seems more like just a ruse for a climb, and Alvin allows that I might want to stay down low, unaccustomed as I am to the elevation. Courtney, who's nursing himself out of a cold, isn't sure what he wants to do.

Ash Springs and Alamo, Timber Mountain, the White River Narrows—all places in which we'll spend the next few days—are part of the White River and Pahranagat Wash drainages that lead south through Moapa and Overton, eventually emptying into the northwestern arm of Lake Mead on the Colorado River. Even the underground water here, a prehistoric flow system that may reach as far north as the Ruby Mountains and one that Las Vegas would like to capture, ends up feeding Lake Mead. This means we're technically not in the Great Basin that drains only inward; if you look at a hydrological map of the region, we're standing at the tip of a finger reaching deeply upward and north from the Colorado River Basin.

We are still, however and somewhat confusingly, in the geological, biotic, and ethnographic Great Basin. The landforms, plants, animals, and both prehistoric and historical Indians here are all classified as Great Basin types, and from looking around you'd have no idea that you were anywhere else. Once away from the numerous springs bubbling up into the Pahranagat Valley, the land resumes its pallid countenance. The Hiko Mountains to the east are dry colonnades shrouded in morning shadows, while the desert around us transitions through the creosote typical of the Mojave's influence on the southern Great Basin into the sagebrush that dominates its more northern reaches.

What we're attempting is a circumlocution for rock art throughout what is, essentially, Heizer territory. Not only are we only a few valleys away from Michael Heizer's, but the White River Narrows site that Mike took his father to in the spring of 1973 is less than thirty miles north of our trailer camp. The petroglyphs were first referred to in newspapers as early as 1925, and recorded by the Desert Research Institute in 1967, but not really examined until Dr. Heizer and his colleague, Thomas R. Hester, documented and analyzed the rock art. The subsequent attention, plus its immediate proximity to the road, led to placement on the Register of National Historical Places. But we're saving the Narrows until Saturday, when we'll meet a host of others also traveling here to examine the rock art.

By seven-thirty we're on a decently graded dirt road heading more or less directly toward our objective for today, Timber Mountain, which even at only eighty-four-hundred-plus feet has snow resting on half its elevation. Alvin takes a turn to the right, climbs up a steep hillside, and suddenly we're in piñon-juniper woodlands, the land becoming less arid as we gain altitude. Rhyolite cliffs break up the long ridges running down from the peak, and across a small canyon jut numerous spires and towers. We stop at sixty-four hundred feet where the road disappears under a snowbank too deep for us to force our way through. Just steps away from the Jeep are rock rings and chert cores in a light lithic scatter, promising signs for our search. Rhyolite is a rock that readily acquires the deep patina favored by petroglyph carvers, and traces of habitation and hunting obviously indicate the earlier presence of Indians. After checking out the nearest band of rock with no luck, we turn our attention to the steep ridge above us.

"You might just want to stay down here, poke around those cliffs across the way," Alvin suggests.

"Well, I'll at least start up with you guys. You know how it is, once you get going . . ." I respond.

"Peak fever!" Courtney nods. His ears are stuffed up from the cold, and I give him one of my ever handy over-the-counter decongestants. If the pills were good enough for the astronauts, as once advertised, they ought to be good enough for a minor ascent in Nevada.

The ridge quickly steepens into a major slope of sharp-edged talus, and each of us retreats into the silence typical of mountain climbing, a camaraderie of quietude as each member of the party constantly checks visually on the others, but saves his breath for the work underfoot. It's a strenuous mode of locomotion that Edward Abbey professed to hate, yet continued to practice his entire life, and one I miss more than I can say in the wilds of Los Angeles. The only hiking I've been able to do this winter was in the Santa Monica Mountains just before the storms hit. Walking for an hour on a relatively level trail through head-high chaparral, only to turn around and see the tall office buildings of Century City—that's an activity I can compare to mountain hiking in the Great Basin only by strenuously exercising my imagination.

The ridge grows steeper, and we're soon using handholds for a thousand-foot session of third-class scrambling. It's nothing that requires a rope, but it's not a place you'd care to fall. Petro has no trouble with any of the moves, springing easily up on various combinations of his four paws. We reach an outcropping on the ridge, pull over it, and sit for a breather. In front of us and to the south are the Virgin Mountains on the border of Arizona down by Lake Mead, and what we think are the Spring Mountains west of Las Vegas. Behind our ridge is the snowy summit of Wheeler Peak in the Great Basin National Park. The seventy-five-mile radius of our view will only grow as we climb, an incentive that pulls us back up on our feet.

The altitude is definitely slowing me down, Alvin and Courtney soon far ahead of me. We've all been climbing together for so many years that we know we're each comfortable alone on the peak, and I enjoy the sense of soloing each of the progressively higher knobs along the ridge. Near the top I descend through knee-deep snow to a saddle, then walk slowly up to the final ridge, traversing left to gain the small summit at a few minutes past noon. My companions are finishing their lunch as I arrive; Petro is ensconced happily in a depression in the snow he's dug out for himself.

Gazing through 360 degrees of Great Basin, I can see into Nellis Air Force Range and the Test Site, the valley where Heizer sits with *City*, all of the Pahranagat drainage, and the immensely long valleys to the east leading up to the national park. The world disappears over multiple ranks of high mountains in all directions. No wind, no clouds, no voices, no grid. Just the void, the winding empty maze of basin and range. This is the way to reset my mental parameters before casting about for signs, I think to myself. Place yourself in the void, get slow and quiet. Then go looking.

The descent takes half as long as the trudge up, though we find ourselves floundering in waist-deep snow on the north side of the ridge. Petro apparently has just large enough feet that he can stay on top of the crust, but all three of us humans are continually breaking through. Alvin doesn't seem to mind, just keeps heading down. Courtney and I give up, sit on our butts and do some serious glissading downward for fifteen hundred feet, stopping every now and then to work our way around clumps of rocks and trees, and even patches of prickly pear. Snow and cactus, the hallmark of a high desert peak. By the time we reach the creek bed at the bottom we're thoroughly tired and soaked. Courtney seems to be almost over his cold, or maybe it's just the decongestant at work; I, on the other hand, suspect the exertion will manifest itself in my body by a cold of my own within a few days. It's a side effect of physical stress I know all too well.

By three o'clock we're almost back to the Jeep when Alvin calls a time-out to recheck some boulders he looked at last year. Something in his memory of them is bothersome. By all rights there should be rock art here, he thinks, though he didn't see any this morning. I'm sitting and wringing the water out of my socks when I hear a "Whoop!" from behind the nearest boulder. Sure enough, petroglyphs; not many, but they're there. Snow has recently fallen off the top of the boulder and broken off a piñon branch next to the rock, uncovering a few symbols. A minute later, encouraged by the one find, there's another "Whoop!"—a muffled one this time. Alvin has his head stuck under a low rock shelter. He's found a rarer pictograph, and directs us to get on our bellies, let our eyes adjust to the darkness, and find the meter-and-a-half-long ocher line with finger marks drawn on the ceiling. Overall it's a modest find, but as Alvin goes about photographing the site, it's obvious that he's pleased to confirm both the trapper's story and his own intuition. The southeast corner of the mountain does, indeed, hold rock art.

We walk the final few minutes back to our vehicle and pile in. I'm so tired that I don't even notice we're not heading back to the trailer, but instead turning off to the east to explore another possibility, this time a lead from Mark Henderson, the resident BLM archeologist in Ely, who has told Alvin of a site nearby. We end up driving along what is essentially another creek bed, this one with heavily patined rocks to our left. We don't see any obvious petroglyphs, so park in order to poke around. I'm amazed my legs are still working. In fact, I don't feel all that bad. Alvin and Court work their way up to the nearest rocks, while I follow the canyon for a couple of hundred yards in order to pick a different line up the hill. As I work up-slope through the small rocks, I see that there's an extensive boulder field still ahead of me, and above that a steep cliff probably a hundred feet high that's not even marked on the topo maps. Alvin's excited yelps of discovery start bouncing off the rocks, and I gather that whatever it is he's found, it must be spectacular.

The afternoon sun is warm on my shoulders and already sunburned neck as I pick my way through the boulders in the direction of the shouting. Snakes, I tell myself. Rattlesnakes. This is their kind of weather, and it's almost that time of year when they come out to sun. Nevertheless, I pick my way as quickly as I can through the Volkswagen-sized rocks, which end at the edge of a grassy trough about three yards wide running under the cliff. It's a hidden garden with panel after panel of petroglyphs rising above the long grasses. There are spirals and grids, several of the inevitable mountain sheep found carved into rocks throughout the Great Basin, a rare deer, and an unusual anthropomorph with its arms raised to form a circle around its head. Alvin is taking pictures while Courtney examines a series of what appear to be masks, each scoriated with several horizontal lines across their faces and surmounted with horns or antennae.

It's a major site and one hardly ever visited. We count off twenty-six separate panels running for hundreds of feet. Alvin notes the presence of a long horizontal line with short vertical tick marks drawn down from it. Although Dr. Heizer apparently never saw this particular collection of panels—it's so spectacular he surely would have recorded it—the line is one he would have classified as a "fence," which he proposed as a representation of brush diversions erected by Indians to channel game, particularly deer and mountain sheep, into a constricted area for killing. Alvin, on the other hand, points to the nearest sharp vertical arête of rhyolite and says no, it's a calendrical glyph. "See how the shadow of the rock will fall along the line at midday? Too bad we're not here at noon on Saturday. That's spring equinox. I bet we'd see the edge of the shadow hit the center of the line right at noon." This is a discussion that will frame the rest of the trip: what, if anything we can decipher, the rock art means.

The two guys finish taking their photographs, and Alvin puts away his notebook. Even he's tired and hungry from the climb, and the sun is getting low in the sky. Our trip back out is uneventful; both Court and I fall asleep once we hit pavement. We don't stop at the trailer, just pass through Ash Springs and go directly to the bathroom at Del Pueblo where we wash up with cold water. I order a Negro Modelo beer and a cheeseburger, while Alvin and Courtney go for the shredded beef enchiladas I had last night. Before the food has a chance to arrive, Alvin is shaking hands with several people who have just come in the door: Sharon Graf and her friend Mike, both from Las Vegas, and Sherrie Chambers, a local resident who helps manage the town's only motel.

All of them are rock art people, know Alvin, and are anxious to hear what he's been looking at. As the person who's recorded more rock art sites in Nevada than anyone else, Alvin is known to almost everyone who spends much time in the Great Basin looking for glyphs, probably having read his bibliography for rock art in the region. Sharon's a painter who specializes in watercolors of rock art, which she sells through galleries and the gift shops in national parks. Mike works as her framer, and is also a photographer, while Sherrie is an avid rock art person who has led Alvin to some sites she's found on her own.

As we're going to be seeing all three of these people tomorrow, I check out of the conversation and go call Beth. It's a relief to be on a regular phone and not be interrupted by the Air Force jamming from Nellis over-flights. She's more interested to hear that we made it up a peak today than she is in the rock art, which remains an abstraction for her, a set of signs that she associates more with our time spent in New Mexico than here. Her memory of petroglyphs centers around Tsankawi near Los Alamos, a low mesa where you can sit inside an Anasazi rock shelter while looking at a radio telescope, one of the better examples of surrealism in America. She tells me that she can hear the tiredness in my voice and to get a good rest. After saying goodnight I walk outside to wait for everyone.

It's cooling down rapidly, and by the time we get in the Jeep I'm ready for bed. Back at the trailer we empty out our gear from the day. I fold down the seat, unstuff my down bag, and crack a window for some ventilation of the still wet socks I hang from one of the overhead handles. Taking notes and reading until ten, about an hour later, I fall quickly into an untroubled sleep once turning off the light. A little sore from the climb, I wake up later and turn over on my back, wedging my feet between the tipped-up back of the seat and a door. It's oddly comfortable, at least for the moment, and I roll down the window just a bit more. The headlights and noise from traffic pass-ing by earlier on the highway, an equal mixture of passenger cars and big rigs, has disappeared, and I'm enjoying the silence when suddenly a hollow roar from above pervades the atmosphere and then just as quickly disappears.

I lie very still. What I've just heard isn't your normal aircraft noise, but a sound most of us haven't experienced before, the telltale trace of something cloaked that flies down a cold tunnel and swallows its own tongue. I try to analyze it. It lasted less than a second and left the impression that it was moving from south to north, and I find the words *powerful, fast,* and *invisible* coming to mind. I venture a guess that I've just witnessed the midnight flyby of a post-Stealth aircraft from Dreamland.

I readjust my position and relax, knowing that I'm probably never going to know what it was. I think about Court examining the masks we saw today, a strange assemblage of unknown meaning just spooky enough that you wouldn't want to get too close to it, never mind the protocols warning one to never touch a piece of rock art. Aliens everywhere, I mutter to myself as I fall back asleep.

EIGHT
❧

" IN THE 1920s, the San Francisco newspapers paid Alan LeBaron to come into the Great Basin to go digging. He claimed the Garden of Eden was in Nevada, up near Yerington, and that the petroglyphs were actually Asian in origin."

"What?" I'm distracted by a yellow sign on our right.

"Oh, Bill's gotta see this!" Courtney exclaims. "Back up." Alvin puts the Jeep in reverse. It's just after eight A.M. the next morning, and we're on the dirt road for the Mount Irish Petroglyph District.

DANGER

ROCKETS MAY LAND IN THIS AREA DURING TESTS

NO TESTS TODAY: ROAD IS OPEN IN CASE OF EMERGENCY

CALL _____ OR _____

"They haven't used this area for tests since, oh, I dunno, the 1960s I think," Alvin comments. "They used to try and round up everybody off the area when they were firing rockets over at the Tonopah Test Range. They weren't aiming anything toward here, but sometimes things, you know . . . went wrong." I wonder to myself if there were ever any phone numbers provided; it doesn't look like it. He puts the Jeep in forward when I'm finished writing. "Anyway, LeBaron, he came up with all sorts of crazy stories. We can look it up when we get back to Reno."

In 1993 Alvin published what is, to my knowledge, still the only bibliography compiled of literature on rock art in Nevada and the Great Basin. The earliest among its more than nine hundred entries is for an article about a petroglyph site near Parowan in Utah circa 1861; the first one listed for here in Lincoln County appeared in 1881. Scattered throughout are numerous examples of fanciful interpretations. In 1908 an article in a small Nevada newspaper, the *Humboldt Star* in Winnemucca, claimed that rock art in Death Valley had been created by a people related to the builders of the Egyptian pyramids; the symbols appeared to the writer to be hieroglyphic in origin. In 1924 it was Aztec or Babylonian script, or Chinese characters written three thousand years ago; in that same year LeBaron stated in the *San Francisco Examiner* that the world's oldest irrigation system was still visible near Fallon. The next year he described nearby rock art as "Mongolian carvings." Even as late as 1982 the Great Basin glyphs were being described as remnants of a language left behind by Nordics who ruled America in 1900 B.C., and in 1983 they were described as marks from an Egyptian funeral ritual, a return to the 1908 interpretation. No wonder both the Heizers, father and son, have been so steadfast in their insistence on empirical data to support interpretations.

"How many rock art sites are there in Nevada?" I ask Alvin. He purses his lips, squint, shrugs.

"The Nevada State Museum and UNLV keep records; they're the central collection points for all the registrations. There's a few hundred petroglyph sites listed for Nevada right now. But Nye County alone, because of the Test Site being federal property and having to survey everything before any construction, it has twelve thousand known archeological sites. But that includes rock rings, art, lithic scatters . . ." He pauses, looks sideways at me. "And of course, there's a lot of sites I've recorded that are unregistered." He laughs. There are sites the BLM and other agencies try to play down, or even keep the public unaware of without actually hiding anything, but there are some sites Alvin doesn't even want anyone else to investigate just yet, much less put on the public record.

At eight-forty we enter the boundaries of the Mount Irish site, 640 acres set aside by the BLM in 1970 as a protected area. Now the sign on our right reads: "Indian rock art is often interpreted as having a magical or religious significance. However, the precise purpose of the art remains a mystery." Only the collective intelligence of a government committee could construct such a massive understatement. Within five minutes Alvin parks, and we step out into a classic desert wonderland of huge rounded rock outcrops and small cliffs interspersed with bright green areas fed by nearby snowmelt, as well as by spring runoff from the mountains above. We're at the bottom of a pass, a throughway from Tikaboo Valley to the west into the White River drainage. The rock is welded tuff, a volcanic ash deposit that is deeper here than anywhere else in the world. Single outpourings of the stuff more than 40 million years ago ran as thick as six hundred feet and covered areas the size of Massachusetts. It was so hot it welded itself into rock. If it had cooled any faster than it did it would have solidified as volcanic glass, otherwise known as obsidian. The rocks are whitish with a deep-brown patina and full of shallow caves ideal for use as rock shelters. It's prime rock art geography.

The first petroglyph we find is a horizontal line more than thirty feet long; vertical lines drop down from it and section off groups of spirals and bighorn sheep. The panel is dense with intent, though totally inscrutable to my untrained eyes. I have trouble even focusing on it or seeing the individual elements, much less being able to venture a guess as to the engraved meanings. I'm still overloaded with images from the multipanel site we stumbled across yesterday afternoon, which Alvin has decided to name Hidden Cove. I look away, then crane my head back at the sky to clear my vision. Overhead an olive-drab fighter-bomber flies by headed east, a dull roar tailing behind it, while to our right a helicopter chugs its way up-valley toward the top of Mount Irish where there's a large electronic installation. I wonder what a Paleo-Indian would have made of a rocket that dropped screaming out of the sky to land nearby. Hell, I wonder what I would make of it.

We get back in the car and continue up the road to Shaman Hill and my introduction to the Pahranagat Man, an initiation Alvin and Courtney are relishing.

"Man?" I ask.

"Pahranagat figures," Courtney adds. "They're mostly men, but there are what appear to be some pregnant women, too, though they're rare." Once again we stop. "Killer pace, huh?" Court is only half jesting. "It goes like this all day. Drive, walk, drive, walk. It gets tiring, though it doesn't seem like it should."

We walk around a stoop-shouldered boulder to a flat face on the other side. An oblong figure looks out at us, its potato-shaped body pecked out of the rock with only the eyes left untouched. Light-colored body, dark eyes.

"Casper the Ghost," says Alvin. "That's what we call them, this style. Then there are the patterned-body anthropomorphs that are called 'blanket men.'"

Pahranagat Man. Men, actually. Several of them. Unlike the petroglyph anthropomorphs found elsewhere, which tend to have skinny bodies and outsized limbs and digits, these have distinctively large bodies that seem to hover on the face of the rock and stare out at you. They have a presence that's much less ritualistic to our culture, appearing more as if they were a different species than a stylized human.

Alvin and Petro have disappeared, wandering off to one side and toward the back of the rocks. Suddenly Alvin's face appears over the top. He's grinning. "Water. A *tinaja*. See, I told you! Wherever there's a Pahranagat figure, there's water. He's either staring at it or it's right on top of him." Courtney and I look at each other, lift our eyebrows, then follow Alvin up the rock. He's standing on top taking pictures that include both the *tinaja*, which is Spanish for a natural water tank, and the surrounding countryside. He gestures around him.

"I always tell everybody you have to look at the landscape. It's all in context. You can't just study a single petroglyph, or a single panel. You have to see what's around it, look at the setting and the resources. Come look at this."

Court and I peer into the small basin, the kind of eroded pocket that you often find on desert rocks where wind, sun, and frost have conspired to carve out cavities that trap rainwater. This one is four feet across and about three feet deep, filled with clear water. I've seen these for years when hiking and climbing in the desert, and like everyone else found them intriguing and good places to rest while contemplating the surroundings. But I've never assigned much meaning to them.

"These would be important sources of water," Alvin continues. "Sometimes you even find them with rock lids. The tuff is light and strong enough that one person can lift a piece large enough to cover this. And I've seen places on the Nevada Test Site where they set timbers across really big *tinajas* to hold up several rocks for covers to prevent evaporation."

For the next hour or so we make our way from rock to rock visiting petroglyphs that Alvin has seen before. Often our first clue to a Pahranagat figure is Petro, who appears soaking wet on top of an outcrop where he's taken a dip in a *tinaja*. During one of our breaks I bring up interpretation.

"So Heizer said that some of this was related to hunting magic?"

"He did," Alvin affirms. "He said the long lines were depictions of fences showing animals being herded into a trap for killing. And the bighorn sheep with spears in their sides were prayers for successful hunts. But that was a theory based on turn-of-the-century European interpretations of cave art, and it's since been disproven. Whitley's shown that the lines and other geometric petroglyphs are the results of hallucinations, and that the dead sheep are actually part of a rain ceremony. They're symbols used by shamans, and not about hunting."

Courtney nods, picking up the explanation. "There's this business about the sacred realm, which is the obverse of reality. The surface of the rock is actually also the surface of the other realm, and the petroglyphs represent interactions with or entrance into a different reality."

"So you guys don't think some of this might even be depictions of actual events, like hunts or specific history, or maps?"

"Why?" asks Courtney. "It was an oral culture. Why make a picture when you could tell a story, or draw maps when directions were passed on verbally?"

Alvin and Courtney are patient, taking me from panel to panel and tracing out different figures to demonstrate some of Whitley's interpretations, which Alvin and I had first talked about on our way out to the Black Rock Desert. Since that trip in the fall I've been doing some reading of my own, though, and it's clear that the matter is far from settled.

Heizer, along with his colleagues Baumhoff, Hester, and other mid-twentieth-century anthropologists, based their hunting magic theory on the realities of the Great Basin for the last ten thousand years since the Pleistocene and the retreat of the last ice age. It's a dry region with a harsh climate, they reasoned, and by far the most important and time-consuming activity must have been hunting. They also figured that pecking out rock figures was so energy-intensive that it could have been related only to the major survival activity of the people. Furthermore, it appeared as if the rock art was not found near habitation sites, but only in places where it was logical for game trails to have existed. It didn't hurt the theory any that Heizer, growing up as a boy in Lovelock to the north, had been told by his boyhood Indian friends and their parents that the petroglyphs were about hunting. So the theory is based on common sense, context in the environment, and local ethnographic testimony. It was also an analysis that dovetailed with European theories, based on what anthropologists had discovered earlier in the century in another arid region of the world, the central deserts of Australia.

People arguing against the theory note that now that so many more sites have been discovered in the last twenty years, rock art does indeed occur near or in habitation sites. Experiments have been conducted demonstrating that petroglyphs can be pecked out in a matter of minutes using a hammer-and-chisel technique with sharp rocks. Whitley's alternative explanation proposes that the abstract geometric designs are manifestations of hallucinations during the first stage in shamanistic trances. In the second stage the visions produce various animal figures, such as stylized sheep and deer; in the third and final stage the shaman becomes a participant in the vision and sometimes merges with the animals, producing transformational figures such as the patterned-body anthropomorphs, including the Pahranagat figures.

One objection to the vision-quest business brought up by Mike Heizer is that there are no hallucinogenics native to the Great Basin. However, jimsonweed, a hallucinogen widely used by Indians and also called the sacred datura, grows next door in the Mojave. Prehistoric trade in everything from shells to obsidian is a well-established fact in this part of the West. Why not also an ancient drug trade? Even more compelling, however, are many examples of trance inducement through other means still practiced by various tribes around the world. You can daydream, dance, or reputedly even masturbate yourself into a trance. Alaskan natives practice repetitive motion to enter a trance, such as rock grinding, and there are grinding sites next to *tinajas,* or even in the basins themselves, that would seem to have no practical purpose other than for such an activity.

All of these theories and others—such as the original "art-for-art's-sake" theory of the late nineteenth century, those concerning cosmological beliefs, clan boundaries, fertility magic, and even simple pornography for the realistic vulvas found carved in rocks around the world—have been debated for years in Europe where rock art and its study have much longer histories. Because the North American Indians are believed to have migrated over the Bering land bridge from Europe and Asia since at least twelve thousand years ago, and possibly up to forty thousand years ago, and because American anthropology has a long tradition of following European trends, I consider cave art research relevant. Either the rock art of North America is related to European examples in the far past, or our theories are based on the work of European theorists, or both.

Paul Bahn is an international authority on prehistoric rock art who obtained his doctorate from Cambridge in the 1970s. He specialized in the prehistory of the Pyrenees, where the first examples of cave art began to attract widespread attention in the 1860s, though its origin wasn't accepted by the academics as Paleolithic until almost the end of the century. Bahn often arouses the ire of other rock art experts, professionals and avocationalists alike, because he so clearly and persuasively traces the history of rock art interpretations as they relate to current intellectual fashions. So Bahn is an expert not only on rock art, but also on the study of rock art, and that makes him entirely too well informed for many people.

The oldest known example of rock art may be a small red stone that appears to be worn by weather and water into the resemblance of a human face. It was found in a South African cave in 1925, and the archeology suggests that it was carried there from at least twenty miles away by one of our australopithecine ancestors about 3 million years ago. It has no meaning obvious to us other than possibly self-representation, a geofact that might have had aesthetic and mystical appeal.

Numerous Old World sites contain direct and indirect evidence of various kinds of art—which is to say, a variety of carved and painted nonutilitarian objects, markings, and the materials to make them—that range in age from several hundred thousand years old to almost a million years old, examples being found in Europe, India, Israel, and elsewhere. The more we look, the more we find. Traces of artistic activity have now been pushed so thoroughly far back into time that it's not unreasonable to argue that it's a fundamental human trait. By at least the end of the Pleistocene art was spread worldwide, though some research at the end of the 1990s is already pushing back tentatively the arrival of art into California from 11,500 years to around 19,000 years.

Robert Heizer suggested that the first phase of rock art study, of locating and cataloging examples, was over by the 1950s, and that it was time to begin to build very carefully and empirically toward theories of interpretation; but, it's important to remember that every time he mentioned hunting magic in a publication he also qualified his views with statements such as "We have no direct evidence," or "The meaning of the majority of rock art may never be known." Dr. Heizer appears to have been a prolific but prudent writer on the topic.

When Heizer was a young anthropologist, rock art research consisted of locating, recording, and describing sites and their contents. Petroglyphs were often documented by his colleagues taking rubbings directly off the rock surface, or chalking in the incised lines in order to enhance contrast for photographs, both practices guaranteed to contaminate the art for further study, and in some cases destroying it outright. Most theories that had been advanced about the origins and meaning of the art were based more on academic supposition. Heizer's contribution was to attempt an empirical explanation that placed the art in a larger anthropological and environmental context.

As Bahn points out, the hunting magic theory was originally advanced by a Frenchman in 1887, then proposed again during 1906 in studies about modern rock art made by the Arunta in Australia, who painted animals on rocks in a ritualistic endeavor to guarantee successful hunts. Based on interviews with living people, the interpretation gained a high level of credence. Because the stone tools of the Aborigines were considered by scientists of the day as "primitive," the people and their art were considered equivalent to Paleolithic "Stone Age" people, a leap in logic that most anthropologists now would abhor. Heizer took an existing European theory and applied it to the rock art in North America, seeking to understand the art as part of the nomadic hunting and gathering life in the Great Basin. Researchers working today may dismiss the hunting magic theory put forth by Heizer and his colleagues, but most subsequent interpretations accepted by academics owe their basis to similar insights and methodology. Whitley's shamanistic theory, for example, is based on ethnographic evidence, as was Heizer's, and also aims to place the rock art in the context of conditions specific to the Great Basin.

So how about Whitley and his followers? His vision-quest interpretations are based on ethnographic research conducted on the Bushmen of southern Africa. If you're going to dismiss Heizer's ethnographic evidence from Indians in the Great Basin—questioning the relevance, perhaps, of what twentieth-century Indians have to say about art left behind eight millennia ago by a people who may not even have been their ancestors—then why would it be valid to connect petroglyphs in Nevada to shamans in Africa? You can't have it both ways. Ever the skeptic, Bahn reminds us that there's no ethnographic evidence linking rock art with either trances or the activities of shamans. American neurophysiologists, who have made statistical analyses of the frequency of repetition in petroglyph images, further insist that hallucinations are too narrow and of too specific a state of mind to have produced the variety of rock art present in the Great Basin.

And so it goes. The three of us continue tramping around the rocks, up gullies and over low ridges, around outcrops and into rock shelters. We take a break for lunch and debate some more Heizer versus Whitley interpretations. In the afternoon Alvin and Court give up trying to convince me of anything and stick to pointing out each new site. We lose track of Alvin for a minute as he disappears around the northwest corner of an outcrop, when suddenly we hear him calling. Court and I find him crouched in silence before a truly astonishing panel. What looks like a blanket covers the entire wall. Long horizontal lines define the upper and lower edges, while both straight and squiggly verticals weave a complex pattern in between. A petite sheep figure slightly smaller than my hand walks across the top line.

We look at each other as if to say: "What do we make of this?" It's not so much a question as our unspoken acknowledgment that there's simply no telling. Is this a pretextile design after which blankets were later patterned? Or the reverse? Or is it the work of a person joyously combining visual elements into a rhythmic composition? Whatever the purpose, it's mesmerizing. I sit counting lines and sketching long after my friends have gotten up and walked off to the next site. Heizer never said he could account for most of the rock art symbols in the region, and Bahn says flat out that we should be content, at one level, to just admire an art that was never meant for us and that we will never be able to interpret with any certainty. All I can fall back upon is my predisposition to view geometry laid across the desert as an attempt to strengthen our cognitive abilities in the face of the existential void. I finally rise up, shake my head at the blanket petroglyph, and walk away.

WE DRIVE TO another portion of the district, cresting a rise to find a Dodge pickup and a Ford Explorer parked in the middle of the Jeep trail. I fumble with my notes for a few minutes, then hurry to catch up with Courtney as he's plunging up a short wash and over the nearest ridge to the north, following Alvin into what they call the Big Sheep site. Court talks to me over his shoulder.

"The shamans identified with animals, and the rain shaman had the bighorn sheep as his spiritual helper. The animals moved between the natural and the supernatural worlds. A dead sheep shows the shaman entering the spirit world as a kind of sacrifice for rain. Did you notice that all the sheep have their tails pointing up? That's what they do when they die."

Bahn dismisses this take as a Western academic construct, but I keep my mouth shut, preoccupied with trying to walk and take notes at the same time while avoiding the prickly pear, miniature barrel cactus, and the numerous Spanish bayonet plants with their two-foot-long needles aimed at my shins. Courtney is wearing a pair of khaki *bombachas,* the outsized pants worn by Argentinean cowboys, which are accompanied by a brilliantly colored cotton sport shirt manufactured to his specifications in Bali while on a trip. His ensemble is completed by an old, almost respectable sports jacket of indeterminate origin and color. Thus armed against the vagaries of desert vegetation he plunges steadily uphill as I, dressed in shorts and a T-shirt, carefully maneuver my notebook, pen, and binoculars around the spiny obstacle course.

We pass over the ridge, and down below Alvin is standing to the side of a large boulder and talking to two strangers, a Mutt-and-Jeff pair of men from New Mexico, one of whom Courtney recognizes as the well-known author of a recent authoritative study of the Kokopelli petroglyph, or hunchbacked flute player, a figure found in Anasazi sites around the Southwest. A hundred yards farther on I spy Sharon Graf and Mike above a streambed, Sharon sketching and Mike taking pictures. Sherrie, dressed in pants and carrying a walkie-talkie, is walking toward us with the bemused posture that rock art people automatically adopt when out in the field. Eyes cast down while scanning the ground, Sherrie is concentrating not so much on where she's stepping as on what pottery shards or worked flakes she might come across. The desire to find a piece of human narrative is so compelling that at times it reduces our gait to an awkward lurching.

"It's a regular convention," I observe.

"Weird," Courtney confirms. "You never see other people when you're out here." He walks up to the group and introduces himself. Alvin peers at me over his glasses.

"Turn around." Swiveling left I find myself next to the largest single figure of any petroglyph known in the region, an almost life-size sheep pecked out over nearly the entire surface of the boulder next to us. Everyone laughs at my double take, including me. All the sheep figures we've encountered the last two days have been no larger than a sheet of paper, most of them roughly hand-sized or smaller. While I examine the giant figure the others compare notes on various local sites. It turns out that the New Mexico visitors have been here before and have visited most of the better-known panels, though not the Hidden Cove area we found yesterday. Within a few minutes Sharon and Mike join us, and a consensus emerges to follow Sherrie to a site none of the others has yet visited.

Before making our way back over to the Jeep we take a quick circuit around the little valley to a relatively rare petroglyph usually described as a birthing scene, an anthropomorph with a smaller figure inside its swollen belly. Alvin notes that female figures have been interpreted to mean bad luck, and that the vulvas we've seen incised here and there were considered especially dangerous. I'm not sure I follow the reasoning, remembering that Whitley, for instance, claims that the vulvas marked sacred openings to the spirit world. I shake my head and sigh, speculating as I write about the possible gender prejudices of the mostly male anthropologists—who mostly claim rock art was made by men.

By the time we get back to the Jeep I've seen too much and am in overload mode, taking only minimal notes. Even Petro is tired, still recovering from the climb up Timber Mountain. As we drive back down toward the highway the helicopter passes us, apparently finished with its business on the peak. It's a civilian aircraft, probably ferrying up a private contractor to work inside what looks through the binoculars to be a huge metal box atop the mountain.

THE LAST SITE for the day is a modest natural amphitheater above Alamo. The sun is low over Mount Irish, directly across the Pahranagat Valley, and sunlight glints off the White River as if it were pooled mercury. Below us the tall sign winks on for "R-Place," the gas station and minimart a couple of hundred yards north of our trailer. Down there the trees are in full bud, the grass is green, and it looks like any good farm country ought to in the spring. Up here, less than a thousand feet above the valley floor, it's a different story. The ground is stony, the vegetation low and sparse. The tall palisades of the Hiko Range to the north flare redly under a huge cloud of virga, the orographic rain that falls but never hits the ground, instead evaporating into the hyperarid air. The single dark-gray cloud covers what Alvin and I estimate to be an area of at least twenty by twenty miles. That's four hundred square miles of desert aching for the moisture suspended just above it. It's a sight that for the moment makes the rain shaman a more likable theory.

All eight of us prowl through the site at our leisure, everyone taking pictures and chatting. A rancher has stuck a length of large-diameter black plastic hose deep into the sand by a nearby spring. Shotgun shells, broken beer bottles, and the head of an African American doll are scattered about, the site too close to town to remain undisturbed for long. It's as good a camping place now as several millennia ago, a fact obviously not lost on the local teenagers. Two BLM placards are mounted on three-foot-tall flat metal posts set into the ground, one warning visitors that the rock art is protected by the Archeological Resources Protection Act of 1979 and the Federal Land Policy and Management Act of 1976, the other asking people not to touch the panels.

"What do you think of our signs?" Mike asks Alvin. A volunteer who has helped the Nevada Archeological Association and the BLM put up warning signs at petroglyph sites, Mike is obviously enjoying the change in his life since retiring a few years ago as a homicide detective with the downtown division of the Los Angeles Police Department. The only sign of his previous occupation is the holstered snub-nose he carries on his belt, and perhaps a penchant for visible law and order.

"Well . . ." Alvin begins. "I guess I'd try to move them out of sight." Mike frowns, arms folded across his chest. "They attract too much attention where they are. I'd put them down so only people who got out to take a look would see them."

Mike tenses for a second, then relaxes as the paradox of attracting people to something you're trying to protect sinks in. "Yeah, I see what you mean, but we had to put them there. There's solid rock two inches under the dirt everywhere else." Now it's Alvin's turn to nod, knowing there's probably a way to figure it out but that it's not worth a discussion that will, after all, not result in the signs being moved, bureaucracy being what it is.

The party breaks up, and we all agree to meet at Del Pueblo later. On the way back to town I ask Alvin about the role of the BLM. Growing up in Nevada, I always understood the role of the agency as one helping ranchers and farmers succeed in an environment basically hostile to their efforts, a paternalistic hangover from the last century. Many of the dirt roads that we've been driving on, for instance, were created by the BLM to aid ranchers in moving livestock, part of the twenty-thousand-mile network they maintain. And most of the waterworks in the desert, such as the piping of spring water to communal tanks, were BLM jobs.

"The agency's really changed in the last twenty years, but BLM archeologists used to have a pretty hard time there. The agency was supposed to be the rancher's best friend, and suddenly they were told to go back to their original mission, managing the land for multiple use. That's their original purpose, but it was a hard change to make. Now they're pretty good about the archeological resources."

I ponder this. So the signs were put up by an agency conflicted over helping ranchers use the land for grazing, but also trying to preserve it for campers and hikers, hunters and drive-by tourists. They end up installing signs where they will draw attention to the rock art, but telling people to not touch it, which of course just makes it irresistible. The signs give the titles and dates of congressional acts, summarizing the results of political and legal battles associated with our increasing consciousness of limited natural resources and fragile prehistorical ones. These are signs I know how to read. I have no reason to believe that a single petroglyph panel represents anything less complex.

Later that night I wake up in the back of the Jeep and check my watch. It's almost two-thirty A.M. Overhead there's a deep but low whistle of tortured atmosphere riding over a surface so sharp and fast that it's almost a scream. That sounds more like a Stealth, I say to myself as I fall back asleep, wondering if I'm just happening to wake up when the planes are flying, or they're so frequent every night that I can't help but hear them.

I'M UP AT SIX with the sun. It's Saturday morning, the big day when we're planning to visit the White River Narrows and check out the petroglyphs that Mike Heizer showed his father just more than twenty-five years ago. This is a piece of narrative symmetry I've been waiting for the last six months to complete, a chance to tie together the lives of the two Heizers and frame the metaphors of the void, the grid, & the sign within localized history. Or so I hope.

Alvin emerges first from the trailer, then Courtney, Petro coming out last with very little enthusiasm for arising so early. We're at "R-Place" before seven, gassing up, buying coffee and muffins, and using a bathroom for the last time until our return. By seven-twenty we're at the lower entrance to the Narrows, a high-walled gorge that once carried a river during the Pleistocene, but now runs with water only during cloudbursts.

Heizer and Hester noted in their 1974 report on the Narrows that the area had been mentioned as a petroglyph site in the 1920s, studied by a researcher from the University of California, Berkeley, in 1968, and even surveyed by Don Fowler from the University of Nevada, Reno, a year or two earlier. But no one had attempted to record as many of the petroglyphs in as much detail as had Heizer and Hester.

We turn off the highway onto a dirt track, what remains of the original road that has since been relocated out of the lower gorge to accommodate faster traffic and the big rigs that, even this early on a Saturday morning, are already on their way from Las Vegas to Ely and back. A side road, in turn, is blocked a few hundred yards ahead by a pile of large boulders. We get out and start walking to what is now called Cane Site A. We're no farther away from the Jeep than a hundred yards when I hear the telltale roar of an approaching jet. Turning, I find an F-16 coming at me about a hundred feet above the Jeep at what seems like two hundred miles an hour, its nose aimed slightly down and at the center of my chest. The lethal gray jet passes, banks slightly left to accommodate the curve of the gorge, then pops up over the rim and is gone before I can open my mouth.

Courtney makes a nervous wisecrack, but Alvin hasn't even lifted his head. The only aircraft he pays much attention to are the Blackhawk helicopters that have the disconcerting habit of approaching silently behind, leapfrogging over your head, and then turning around to hover only a few feet off the ground in front of you until they're satisfied you're harmless. Or not. To the jets, however, you're target practice. Their pilots are not interested in your identity, only the imaginary kill. I don't know if the one this morning was targeting the blue Jeep or my bright-red pile jacket, but I decide to take off the garment as soon as it's warm enough.

The site, when we reach it, contains several panels of abstract and representational art. What's unusual about it are the sheep figures, some only two inches long, which are quite a contrast from the enormous sheep I saw yesterday at Mount Irish.

The next petroglyph, farther up the valley, is a classic Heizer "fence," a slightly uneven horizontal line several feet long with more than sixty tick marks extending vertically upward a few inches from the baseline. The panel also contains a Pahranagat figure, three sheep, and a wriggly line that could be water or a rattlesnake, or both, snakes often being found near water. Alvin is busy scanning the cliffs on either side.

"Look at this," he says, pointing to the sharp arête of rhyolite to our left. "The shadow from this edge is going to cut right across the tick marks at summer solstice. Fowler and the classically trained archeologists won't accept these lines as calendrical because the Indians first found here in the last century were preagricultural. And they figured why do you need a calendar if you're not planting crops. But you can't tell me that people who lived in the outdoors for thousands of years didn't notice the sun changing direction at the vernal equinox, and that they didn't want to celebrate the coming of spring with the extra food and warmth it would bring! And they could tell when the sun was standing still at solstice midway through a season. They looked at these mountains every day; they knew where the sun was coming up and which way it was going!"

I crane my head to peer up at the cliffs. It seems plausible to me. But I also remember Heizer's words, that petroglyphs often tend to run along canyons and appear under perches convenient for shooting down on deer and sheep. Several such ledges and gaps are handy to both sides of us. "I dunno," I reply.

I also remember, just to be self-contrarian, reading recent articles in several science magazines pointing out that agriculture is now known to have been practiced in the New World thousands of years earlier than previously thought.

Back in the Jeep we proceed to our next stop, a site that Heizer apparently skipped over, perhaps because it's not along the main track of the gorge. It's still too cold to take off my jacket, the ground frozen in the shade. The panel we reach at eight-thirty is small but eerie, fully justifying its name, Martian Home. Eight faces or, perhaps more accurately, masks stare straight out at us. Named in the 1980s by its discoverer, a woman named Jean Stevens from Preston, a town near Ely, the site evokes definite alien fantasies. The roughly life-size ovoid heads are crossed by a series of horizontal stripes and are crowned with antennae, appearing almost insectoidal. If it weren't for the fact that the "Blanket Men" Pahranagat figures and other patterned-body anthropomorphs were so common, you'd be tempted to label these as extraterrestrials carved by teenagers from Rachel.

While Alvin and Court take several photographs, I notice that the glyphs have been chalked in sometime in the last year or so. Although a rainstorm blowing in from the right direction will clean off the chalk, it amazes me that people are still messing with the rock art. It takes only one such chalking to contaminate the site for potential dating, and only a few touches before the rock can discolor and the marks begin to erode. Left alone the rock art can last for thousands of years before fading; touched too often it can begin to disappear within a generation.

Before leaving we spot another panel of masks on a tier above a ledge high over our heads. I count six of the facial glyphs through the binoculars, and Court climbs up to examine them. Much larger than the ones at ground level, these float over the valley with a peculiar kind of visual restlessness, as if only tethered to the rock, a trick of foreshortening achieved by their elevated position. Making the glyphs would have taken balance, a long arm, and a good head for heights. Alvin hollers at Courtney to stand to the right, using him to provide some scale in the photograph. Pictures of pictures, I realize.

The next site we move on to is the big one, Heizer's Locality #2. The granddaddy of all assembled petroglyphs in the region, its thirty-two panels extend for roughly six hundred feet in an amphitheater that's now been

184

bisected by the highway. Although cars and trucks rumble by at sixty to seventy miles an hour within two hundred yards of us, there is thankfully little feeling of interaction with the traffic. The rock art isn't readily discernible from the roadway, and stopping alongside the road there would be dangerous; to approach the petroglyphs you have to come in the way we did, following the dirt road around the curves in the bottom of the Narrows. Nevertheless, given the prominence and size of the site, the BLM has planted more of its markers—which are visible from the highway—these citing the Antiquities Act of 1906 for their legal authority.

We park the Jeep in the sun, then walk across frozen mud to the cliff that is still deep in shadow. A very long line with vertical tick marks, another "fence," runs for more than forty feet. Underneath it are deer and sheep figures, paw- and footprints, spirals, rakes, and a series of stacked cubes Heizer labeled "ladders," as well as assorted anthropomorphs and unrecognizable zoomorphs. Above the line is scratched a graffiti: NO HORSES. On one panel "Carl Williams, Sept 18, 1926" lets us know he's been here. Another part of the rock between panels hosts a crudely grooved circular target with bullet holes in and around it. "R. Halsey, 1986, 18/9" proclaims the accompanying graffiti, a tally of his nine shots hitting inside the target out of the total of eighteen holes in the rock.

Courtney shows me a figure that seems to be that of a woman trapped inside a man, and points out several vulviforms mostly down near ground level, a location that reinforces the interpretation that the vagina sign represented an entrance to the spiritual underworld. In fact, several petroglyphs look as if they're emerging from up out of the ground, and Alvin remarks that flash floods have both deposited soil and taken it out. I'm reminded of El Morro in New Mexico with its descending layers of language carved on the sandstone, and wonder how many layers here might lie beneath the ground and have never been excavated.

As we're examining the site we're joined by Bill White, an archeologist from the Harry Reid Center for Environmental Studies at the University of Nevada, Las Vegas, and one of his colleagues, David Smee. Then Mark Henderson, the BLM archeologist from Ely, shows up in his blue pickup with a white camper perched on top. Bill and Dave are dressed in bush pants and casual shirts. Mark's in full BLM garb and looking very official, but he's brought along Yolanda, his wife, who's talking to a very handsome and self-possessed green parrot caged in the back. It's only nine-thirty and already we're up to seven people, which has set Courtney to once again shaking his head.

"Some of it's planned, of course, Alvin meeting these guys out here because they had called to tell him they'd be out here. But I think he just attracts people whenever he's out in the field. They hear he's going to be someplace and they come out of the woodwork."

"Or rocks, as the case may be," I reply.

Mark and Bill have wandered off to one side and are simultaneously looking for any signs of paint in the petroglyphs and debating what kind of samples the archeologist can take, and what, if any, visible impact there might be. Mark's territory covers the 10 million acres of the Ely District, which includes some of the largest roadless areas in America. He's here to decide whether or not the UNLV guys will be allowed to sample the rock art. Bill and Dave are under contract to survey Airfield Canyon, a remote location on the Nellis Air Force Base. Apparently the government is planning some construction there. Although we're curious, we all know better than to ask what it might be. Archeologists hired to work on the base or its subset, the Test Site, are notoriously tight-lipped about the details. What seems to be going on here, though, is an attempt to compare dates between comparable rock art in Lincoln County with that on the base in Nye County.

The dating of rock art is still, despite all the scientific advances of the twentieth century, not much of a sure thing. Experts can attempt to put the rock art in context of geological conditions, nearby tool assemblages, and associated organic materials, such as the carbonized remains of fires. But because they often don't know when the various cultures that lived in the area produced what art, it's hard to tie a style to a time period, assuming they even know which elements went into which style group. Attempts have been made to date the repatination of the rocks, but the rates vary enormously. The patina on various kinds of rocks under variable climatic conditions, and facing the sun in any one of several directions, reacts differently to each individual circumstance. Cation-ratio, as the technique is known, is getting better, but it's dicey.

Part of the study Bill and Dave are starting will compare carbon-14 dating of paints from pictographs with cation-ratio estimates for associated petroglyphs made by other archeologists, a sort of blind-trial experiment to see how accurate are some of the repatination datings. And just now, much to their delight, Alvin leads them to a small panel of petroglyphs with traces of ocher actually in the art. Painted petroglyphs, as opposed to the merely painted surface of pictographs, are rare, and they immediately ask Alvin if he knows of any other examples. He tilts back his head, and I can see him start to rifle through his mental card catalog.

In the meantime Courtney is telling me about Mark Henderson's nephew, Cody, a playwright from Los Angeles who is going to be visiting the area today with his director. They're here to absorb a little atmosphere in preparation for an upcoming production involving archeology and will camp up at Mount Irish tonight with Mark and Yolanda. We're not going to be able to get together, but I wonder how a different kind of writer would approach this scene. The possibility of my writing about a writer, who is writing about people taking pictures of pictures, is a nice metaphorical parallel to the layers of images on the wall, some of the petroglyphs having been pecked over older ones and then graffiti applied on top.

Bill and Dave want to visit the rest of the sites in the area, so we form a caravan with the vehicles and drive back out the dirt road to the highway, figuring we'll start with the Heizer and Hester Locality #6 at the north end of the Narrows, then work our way back toward Hiko and Ash Springs. So it goes for the rest of the morning, stopping alongside the road for a guided tour with Mark, each site with similar images yet completely different in appearance.

The first stop features an animal enmeshed in a grid, as if trapped. The next site has pitchforks and a cross, numerous initials and a swastika surrounding the spirals, snakes, and sheep. In 1991 the BLM blasted off the motto "JESUS LOVE YOU" and a heart on the rock with a hydraulic paint removal system. Mark admits they were perhaps just a little too aggressive with the scrubbing, the rock looking as if it had undergone a radical facial peel in Beverly Hills. Clair Whipple, the daughter of a local rancher, inscribed her name and the year, 1924, which leads Bill to wonder if they could date some of the repatination on names left behind by nineteenth-century ranchers.

"Maybe," says Mark. "You have to remember, though, that some of the ranchers carved their names in the rocks with false dates in order to establish claim to the land." Somehow this shocks me more than the simple graffiti. It's not bad enough that you can't trust everything you read in the papers, but even things carved in stone might not be true. As if to compound my discomfort, at the next site we're greeted by what reads like a joke, a carving of a farmer leading a bull by a rope and pouring onto the ground what might be milk from a pail. Milk from a bull? Nobody has any ideas about that one.

Just before noon we pull off to park and hike to the last site we'll visit in the Narrows, a Pahranagat figure high up on a hill to one side of the watershed that leads, eventually, up to the Hidden Cove site on the flanks of Timber Mountain. Two more people join us, friends of Mark's from Ely who do a little contractual work for him documenting sites. Older retired folks with portly figures in matching safari vests, they nonetheless prove nimble enough as we make our way up the hill.

When we find the figure, Alvin disappears up the rock; sure enough, there's a *tinaja* up top. Mark and I measure it, a rough oval of sixteen by twenty-four by six inches, large enough to hold a few gallons of water. Courtney points out two flat slabs of tuff nearby that fit over the top. Bill's never heard Alvin's theory about the "P-men" looking at or standing under water, and he starts to bring up specific examples to test the theory. Alvin provides the location of the water to every figure Bill mentions.

"Damn. Now I'm going to have to go back and look at all those again." Bill's expression is pained.

"Look at the landscape," Alvin chants. "I keep telling you guys that. It's important."

I leave everyone behind debating Alvin's theory, and circle down off the rocks and back toward the Jeep, hoping to wolf down a peanut-butter-and-jelly sandwich before we start moving again. To the west lenticular clouds are building over the Grant and Quinn Canyon Ranges, and there's a faint circle around the sun. Its circumference is large so the amount of moisture in the upper atmosphere isn't very dense yet—the smaller the circle the closer the precipitation—but it's obvious there's a change in the weather coming within the next day or two.

THE CANYON we drive up after lunch is not far from the Narrows but has no name on the USGS topo map, a fact we keep checking in disbelief. Red tuff walls more than 150 feet high narrow down to almost touch the sides of the Jeep. The depth of the gorge isn't as impressive as that of High Rock Canyon, nor did any famous explorers pass through here that we know of, but it's much narrower here. The gorge has as much presence as any I've seen outside of slickrock country in Utah and is a location that by all rights should bear a fitting name. Although the place is pretty obscure, the dirt road we're on was bladed by or for ranchers, so it's hardly unknown. Alvin makes a mental note to try and track down any local name that might exist.

We're looking for rock art, and that's the other mystery: none is visible and we can't figure out why. Sherrie and other hopefuls have been up here looking and never found any, which has Alvin puzzled. Beautiful blank rock faces are covered with a rich patina awaiting inscription. There's water, and although it's a box canyon for all vehicular intents and purposes, it's a perfectly walkable wrinkle and therefore a route from valley to valley through the mountains. It's even an obvious place to hunt game.

I'm riding in back, so my view is limited by the rear window. Courtney watches out the passenger side of the road while Alvin simultaneously drives and scans the cliffs. No matter how many times I've watched him do this, it still amazes me that we don't end up high-centered on a boulder or deep in the sagebrush. As worrisome a habit as it is here, though, at least our speed is under fifteen miles an hour. It's a little scarier when he does it on the highway, which is why some people refuse to ride with Alvin after their first and only experience riding shotgun in the Jeep.

"Wow!" Alvin brings us to an abrupt halt in a cloud of dust. "Do you see that? Look up there on the walls. Where are the binoculars?"

Alvin is already out of the Jeep before Court and I can even get our seat belts unfastened. I can't see anything, and for a moment neither does Courtney, then he, too, starts to hoot enthusiastically. I hand Alvin the binos and shade my eyes while peering upward. Faint at first, then growing stronger as my eyes adjust, what emerges is a series of horizontal red lines painted on the rocks. Long rows of tick marks alternate with solid lines, and I count nine in all when it's my turn with the glasses. To the right is a large complicated pattern of intersecting diagonals that looks like a diagram of some kind. It's no wonder that no one has found this site before. Not only is it relatively faint red paint on red rock, it's at almost sixty feet above us. Alvin and Courtney start to scramble up, but are stopped by a slick rounded face a good ten feet before reaching a ledge underneath the pictograph.

"I gotta come back with my gear," hollers down Alvin. "At least a rope and my shoes." I can tell he's disgusted at not being able to reach the art, but he's wearing J. C. Penney work boots that, though inexpensive and practical for desert hiking, are about as useful for rock climbing as a pair of ice skates.

Back on the floor of the canyon he checks out the immediate surroundings. It seems like the lines climb up the wall far above the height of a person, but there's a crack off to the left that's climbable. The artist(s) either used the crack to hang from with one arm and then paint with his (or her) right hand, or hauled a ladder up to the ledge.

"Maybe a test of manhood?" Courtney guesses.

"Look at the sun and arête," Alvin says, pointing to the rock left of the crack. "The sun must move that shadow right across the tick marks. Looks to me like it measures off the spring equinox. Too bad we weren't here at noon."

At this point I give up. Site after site we've visited with the lines and tick marks—they're all oriented to take advantage of a specific solar interaction with their locales, to catch the shadow of a rock pointer at the right time of year. I haven't been completely convinced until now, agreeing with writers such as the art critic David Bourdon, an expert on earthworks, who states in *Designing the Earth* that archeo-astronomy proponents take enigmatic ancient sites and turn them into "crypto-utilitarian ocular devices appropriate to today's aerospace era," a viewpoint also endorsed by Paul Bahn. But what other explanation, I wonder, could there be for marks in such deliberately difficult spots placed time and time again on the precise receiving end of shadows during the solstice and equinox of the four seasons?

The Nobel Prize–winning physicist Murray Gell-Mann once said that to see patterns that aren't there is superstition, but to ignore patterns that are is denial. That's an elegant formulation that covers the dilemma of interpreting rock art in the Great Basin, and one of which I think even Dr. Heizer would have approved.

Back in the Jeep we continue up-canyon, meeting Bill and Dave who have driven in from another site to the north. Alvin tells them about the site, which we've decided to name the Red Edge, and they're excited to check it out on their way back. More paint to examine. After they leave Alvin looks at me in the mirror. "Feels pretty good to find a new site, doesn't it?" I admit it's exciting. I had asked Alvin earlier about why he cares about rock art—other than the fact that it's a logical pastime for an aging rock climber—and at first he'd given me an answer that's appeared before in interviews with him: "Because it's disappearing and ought to be documented."

Fine and dandy, I said, but why? He couldn't pin down any specific reason, and didn't bother to repeat the official government line about preserving knowledge of ourselves. Instead, he offered: "It's something you can do where you can actually discover something. There aren't many ways to do that anymore." And that made sense to me. Alvin has fashioned a life that has supported his quest to climb new peaks, to plumb new caves, to ski new slopes no one else has tried before. It's his way of understanding the world, of ordering the universe. It's his religion, his science, his art, to orient himself bodily in places that reveal new views. Rock art sites provide him the opportunity to stand where others long past have been, and to see what they've seen in a time less obscured by civilization.

Although most people who study rock art, professionals and avocationalists alike, haven't dedicated their lifestyle as thoroughly to exploration as has Alvin, I think their motives are similar. Like English tourists visiting Roman ruins in Europe, which gave them a chance to marvel at time passing and our place in it, or German archeologists methodically following the remnants of ancient cultures in order to trace the diaspora of the human race, Americans wander the Southwest looking for rock art as evidence that our world has not only spatial frontiers, but temporal ones as well. Robert F. Heizer's fascination with the manipulation of rock from Egyptian tombs to Olmec stelae to archaic Nevada rock art makes sense as an intelligent and coherent exploration of a medium in which people have set forth a record of their deepest beliefs about the world. And I'm not so sure that Michael Heizer's work on *City* is anything less than just as profound an effort to query and interact with the cosmos, one conducted through a systematic sculptural ordering of elements derived from antiquity.

All this musing about the signs we leave behind us is cut short a bit later in the afternoon when Alvin unexpectedly turns east off the highway into Ash Springs and onto what appears to be less a Jeep trail than a set of cattle tracks through the sagebrush leading up the ramparts of the Hiko Mountains.

"Doesn't look like anyone's come through since I was here last year," he ventures, pleased at the thought. He actually puts the vehicle into four-wheel drive, a rare mode of transportation he usually reserves for quicksand and frozen lakes. I grab a handle in the roof and hang on. Sure enough, I endure fifteen minutes of involuntary massage provided by various parts of the Jeep before we stop. In front of us is a steep mountainside proceeding upward for more than a thousand feet. Alvin points.

"We'll just walk up there for a bit and turn at that rock band on the right. If you lose sight of us, just keep going up and right and you'll find us." Court, Alvin, and Petro take off at a good clip. I lapse into the slow pace that has earned me the reputation of being a turtle, but that, if nothing else, affords me contemplation of the ground I'm walking on. Layers of tuff, limestone, and sandstone stack one atop the other, evidence of prehistoric mega-volcanoes, vast oceans, and inland seas, the rubble of abrupt and violent interruptions folded into a bewildering accumulation of geological time. There's no one simple story to the land here, no orderly progression or single cataclysm that characterizes how the land appears to us. Instead, we're presented with many categories of events from subterranean tectonic upheaval to surface erosion.

One rock especially catches my eye, a small whitish piece of sandstone that lies tilted downhill along the slope of the ground. What appears to be a huge dark skeletal hand floats on its surface. I stop and bend closer, see that the articulated bones and joints of the hand are composed of desert varnish, an almost blue-black patina that has resisted weathering, while the rock around and underneath it has been worn away by countless winter storms and summer cloudbursts, by the incessant winds that scour the surface of the desert, and by the relentless forty-degree-plus diurnal temperature swings—the same forces that had blasted apart the top of the hill that I walked up as Heizer and Jennifer cut down the juniper last summer.

The fingers by my feet in the late afternoon sun taper to a wrist, a form created by the downward tilt of the rock directing the erosion. In a century or two even these few remaining "digits" will be gone. It's a geofact that only appears to mimic a human hand, yet so close in its visual approximation that I find it difficult to not take it as a handy metaphor for the inscrutable length of presence humans have had in the area. I also take it as a cautionary sign: Don't believe everything you see, or think you see.

I continue slogging up the mountainside, thinking about more conflicts implicit in every interpretation of the rock art. Who says petroglyphs can be about only magic? Why can't a supposedly preliterate culture have both an oral tradition to hand down stories full of critical survival information, such as where to find water and set diversion fences for deer, and a record hammered into the rock walls? And who says that oral cultures are so static, anyway, that the use and meaning of symbols wouldn't drift over millennia, or that certain talented individuals wouldn't adapt them for new purposes as time went on? I find myself resisting the idea that any one interpretation is valid over another—Whitley insisting that his vision quests supersede Heizer's hunting magic, for example—and wondering whether they are all possible, or even likely.

I veer around the ridge and find Alvin and Court snapping away at several panels of petroglyphs that are traced out on horizontal boulders in the same patina as I'd seen on the "hand" below. This is what Alvin calls "the lone cowboy and the lieutenant" site after two unique anthropomorphs boasting features that look like a cowboy hat and shoulder epaulets. In fact, that's exactly how they appear, the two figures on separate boulders many yards apart, but apparently in the same constellation of petroglyphs. Alvin's name is both visually accurate and ironic, openly acknowledging how biased are our interpretations. We can see the glyphs only in terms of our own time and culture. As our beliefs shift, so do our interpretations, and we move from earth-mother goddesses in the 1960s to interspecies communication in the 1990s, from one archetype underlying a pop culture trend to another. The academic professionals are just as susceptible to interpretative drift as are the tabloid-reading, landscape-shredding pot hunters riding around in their trucks ripping off the rock art for sale in the underground antiquities market.

Alvin hasn't told the BLM where this site is, and Courtney and I are the only other people he's brought up here. We're honored and take turns shading the art for each other's photographs. How much rock art has been lost to erosion? I wonder. Unlike Europe, where Paleolithic art has been well preserved in caves closed off by geological accidents, most of the art here is totally exposed. Cave paintings in both Europe and Australia have been dated tentatively as being more than thirty thousand years old. The most optimistic dating, not to mention the most controversial and one that Alvin thinks far too early, sets rock art in the western United States at only nineteen thousand years old. If people migrated over the Bering land bridge starting forty thousand years ago, why don't we have rock art at least as old as that in the Old World? Is it because older examples have simply weathered away? I think of the soft tufa boulders on the highway by the desiccated Winnemucca Lake, and how they're disintegrating almost in front of our eyes.

The sun is behind Mount Irish by the time we get back to the Jeep. Once again we're so tired and thirsty we drive straight to Del Pueblo and wash our faces in the bathroom sink. We're sunburned, our hair sticks out at every conceivable angle, and we feel every inch the intrepid explorers who have brought back a new discovery. Tonight there's a party of three people sitting at the next table who have driven in from St. George a couple of hours away and across the border in Utah. We can't help but overhear them talking about rock art sites, and Alvin thinks he recognizes one of the two women as a well-known river guide who works the Grand Canyon and is an expert on the rock art there that the Park Service attempts to keep supersecret. After dinner he turns around in his seat to ask her if her name is Mary Kay. Not only is that who she is, but it turns out that they're in town to meet Sherrie in the morning, who's volunteered to bring them to meet Alvin and accompany us on our last day in search of rock art.

Courtney pushes his glasses up on his forehead and passes a hand wearily over his eyes. Then he looks at me. "Unbelievable," he says in a tone that both accepts only grudgingly the inevitable result of Alvin's notoriety and slightly revels in the presence of it. Then he turns to join the conversation while I go to make my nightly call to Beth.

NINE
୧୭

T HE RATTLESNAKE IS, not to put too fine a point on it, pissed. Coiled underneath a green ephedra, or Mormon tea bush, he's almost invisible, though the sound of his buzzing tail is loud enough to force Courtney to keep his distance out on the rock ledge. He's now trapped twenty feet above the three patterned-body blanket men anthropomorphs below. I was about to follow him out onto the rounded shoulder of tuff to look for a *tinaja* when he suddenly turned. "There's a buzz-tail there. Watch it!" We're separated by the snake that, though not pursuing us, is not keen to let us pass, either.

"Let's see if we can bluff him out of the way," Courtney suggests, and I comply by slowly approaching. The snake, a two- or three-foot Great Basin rattler, shifts his ground and retreats partially under a rock at his back. I'm guessing at his length, unable to see all of him, and in fact able to make out only the light-and-dark geometrical pattern of his scales by squinting my eyes and concentrating. It's like watching one of the petroglyph patterns come alive, a zigzag motif that reveals itself for a moment, then self-conceals its own meaning by becoming part of the environment.

He's still shaking his rattles, but at a less furious clip. Court risks the crossing and makes it back off the ledge without suffering a strike. We exhale, grin, and climb back down the rocks to join the others. Great Basin rattlesnakes are the only venomous reptiles in the region. Although they can grow up to five feet long, are seldom aggressive and maybe not as poisonous as their neighbors, the Mojave green rattlesnakes, they are one reason Alvin favors hiking in high-top work boots rather than the low-cut walking shoes Court and I prefer.

"A snake? Did you see a rattler?" Sherrie is clearly excited. Amazingly enough, in all her years hunting rock art out here she's never run across one, so Courtney takes her up for a look. I wander off with my pad and pen to find Mary Kay and her two companions, Gail, a paralegal secretary also from St. George, and Connie, a fit young guy from Namibia who's visiting Gail. Working as a tour guide in Botswana and Zimbabwe, Connie's home desert is the Sand Sea of the Namib, an immense and rainless desert stretching for more than thirty-two hundred miles along the South Atlantic coast of Africa. He lives in a seaport from which massive sand dunes as high as twelve hundred feet stretch inland for six hundred miles. The best we can muster in America are the Eureka Sand Dunes just north of Death Valley, which top out at eight hundred feet. And where we are this morning, a typical Nevada basin just northeast of Ash Springs, isn't even desert to him. After all, there's stuff growing here and there's a paved highway only twenty miles away.

Rock art isn't something Connie's ever paid much attention to, and he's with us this morning simply because it's Gail's passion. On the other hand, when Courtney rejoins us and tells Connie that he's been to some rock art sites in Africa, they launch into a lengthy discussion about the relative merits of various sites around the continent. For a person who professes not to care much about the subject, Connie obviously knows far more about the prehistory of his land than the average American tour guide would about the Anasazi.

Part of the world's fascination with Africa is based on our understanding of it as the birthplace of our species, as well as one of the cradles of civilization. Tourists who go to African countries expect their guides to know at least a smattering about the discoveries of the Leakeys, the building of the Pyramids, or whatever the prehistory of the particular area may be. It's only natural that Connie would keep handy some of that knowledge. But his easy familiarity with prehistory also bespeaks the fact that he's a minority settler in a land of natives, and thus resides within a radically positioned context. Born in Africa, he's nonetheless a European beholden to and under the spell of a foreign land, one where ancient rituals and folkways remain very visible, though increasingly buried under layers of imported jeans, rock 'n roll, and reruns of American sitcoms. The prehistorical roots of Africa's cultures are still considered by Europeans to be more integrated into contemporary life there, a continental attitude that can express itself variously as a long-standing disdain for the "primitive natives," a source of inspiration for artists, an opportunity to exploit cheap labor, and sometimes all three.

How we regard our own American West, and most particularly the desert, is deeply preconditioned by European relationships with Africa. For instance, American scientists in the eighteenth and nineteenth centuries desperately wanted to prove that Native American cultures were as old as those in Africa, or perhaps even older, a sort of nationalistic competition for the oldest possible dates that still crops up occasionally. Witness the comparison of Great Basin petroglyphs with hieroglyphs. Writers have compared the deserts of the Southwest to the Sahara and the Kalahari, and have spoken of the mysterious Great Basin as if it were a similar void that could be crossed only with almost superhuman effort. The parallels drawn between the deserts of Africa and North America are still marketed to great effect by Las Vegas, where hotels such as the Sahara, the Dunes, and the Desert Inn have presented themselves as libidinous oases deep within the parched wastelands.

Having Connie with us is a reminder that the void of the Great Basin is just one of many around the world, and neither the largest, nor the oldest, nor the most impenetrable. For instance, the Sahara, a name that has been translated from the Arabic as "the brown void," is the largest desert on the planet at 3.3 million square miles; the Great Australian Desert is approximately 1.3 million square miles, the Arabian Desert a million. The Great Basin at 208,500 square miles is only one-sixteenth the size of the Sahara.

This morning we're working our way through several valleys east of the Pahranagat drainage, prowling among a large area of spheroid tuff boulders that form a series of interconnected alcoves. Known as Petroglyph Village, it's part of an expansive region of rocky outcrops that seems to us to be as extensive as Joshua Tree National Park in the Mojave to the southwest of us. The rock here is volcanic ash and the Joshua Tree crags a nasty variety of granite known worldwide to climbers for its tendency to shred fingertips. That means the climbing here would be different: fewer cracks to follow, but more pockets for handholds and desert varnish for small edging on your toes. If this area were as close as Joshua Tree is to an urban center the size of Los Angeles, however, it would be overrun with campers and climbers every weekend. Out here, the isolation protects both the petroglyphs and our ability to savor their presence.

At noon the small caravan of four-wheel-drive vehicles leaves Petroglyph Village for a reconnaissance into the foothills of the Pahroc Range. We can see a dirt road that runs uphill to what looks like a spring, as always a likely site for rock art, and Alvin is keen to locate the petroglyph called "Sheep on a Line" that's rumored to reside up there. Maybe because it's my last day to be out in the desert for a while, I'm anxious for a little solitude this morning and ask Alvin if he'll pick me up on the way back. He looks at me from beneath the bill of his cap and nods, recognizing the feeling. I shoulder my pack and begin to circumnavigate the outcrop of the Village.

My path is a looping one, proceeding counterclockwise and turning left into each alcove as I come to it, almost as if I were proceeding around the perimeter of a cathedral and visiting each of the chapels. And, in fact, some anthropologists have proposed that rock art alcoves were ritual sites, the natural precursors to churches. They imagine that a shaman would crouch in the *tinaja* and then stand up above those assembled below, a mystical figure of power appearing suddenly atop a rock pulpit. The Pahranagat figure, thus, would signal not just water but also where to assemble for worship, an understandable conflation in the desert.

Like all of the other rock art theories, I find this one neither absolutely persuasive nor to be dismissed. As a climber and hiker I've always found rock alcoves a natural architecture that compels interest and respect. In combination with rock arches, yet another category of features that Alvin has been cataloging around the state, such rooms attain a mystical solemnity for me, matching that of the most glorious of Gothic cathedrals. Walking under several hundred tons of rock suspended between sky and earth to enter a sanctuary open to the sky is to immediately reconfigure the relationship of one's body to the earth, to be both enfolded within it yet offered up to the sky. Finding petroglyphs and pictographs in such places is so logical that it's disappointing when you don't find them there, as if a church were lacking stained-glass windows.

As I loop in and out of the alcoves I flush a number of rabbits, not the large jackrabbits of the region, but bunnies with round white tails, perfect prey for the rattlesnakes. It's still a little too chilly for many of the snakes to be out; they prefer it when the temperature sits between eighty and ninety degrees—but I keep a close eye on the ground where the boulders are configured to provide what are in essence reflecting ovens hotter than the rest of the terrain, anticipating the heat of summer. Within only a few weeks the entire area will be roiling with patterned-body reptiles.

Leaving the Village I follow a huge spine of outcrops stretching to the north and find numerous rock shelters, some so large that cattle have obviously used them as protection from the weather. The overall topography is immensely complicated by these ancient eroded volcanic eruptives. What's more, the cartographic grid on the map covers only half the sheet, much of the quadrant being unsurveyed; the squares on the other half are traced in dotted lines, indicating only provisional information. This is part of the Great Basin that's been mapped from the air with only sporadic confirmation on the ground, and it lacks the section corners that we found up north.

The sketchiness of the map signals how carefully we have to move around here. The terrain is harsh, providing cover, water, and the biology necessary to support only those humans clever enough to take advantage of every resource. It's also the kind of fractal landscape in which I could become hidden all too easily. I keep an eye on the tallest rock in the Petroglyph Village group, as well as a peak in the Pahrocs, points off which I can take a backbearing to rendezvous with my companions.

After I've walked for a half hour I find an easy pinnacle to climb, set out my water and sandwich, and savor a slow lunch while listening to my heartbeat. Alvin and I will drive back to Reno tomorrow in time for me to catch a plane for Los Angeles, and I'm half dreading the return. I'm eager to be home with Beth, and to sit at the computer to write through my thinking—the letters on the screen yet another system of symbols reeling along in front of me—but the frustration of leaving behind so much unexplored physical ground is only just balanced by knowing I'll be covering new mental territory.

THE FIRST PLACE we had visited this morning, a site not yet officially named, is one of the few where I've had an emotional as well as an intellectual response to what I was seeing, which only increases the sharpness of my feelings today. Set within a group of spheroid tuff boulders enclosing a protected space was a large rock undermined by a hemispheric tunnel. The passage underneath was just large enough to sidle through while lying on our backs, and we took turns wiggling our way inside to see the ocher anthropomorphs and zigzags. Two feet in front of our noses, hidden from all but determined eyes, the pictographs are touched directly by sunlight only at dawn on the summer solstice, when, for just a few minutes once a year, the sun rises through a gap in the mountains and sends light streaming narrowly onto the figures.

Unlike viewing rock art when standing up in the open air, lying on your back both literally increases your contact with the earth, with the place, and makes you vulnerable to the gaze of the figures. You are constrained by a lack of space in which to move, and your limbs are separated, spread-eagled on the ground in the only position possible to witness the art. The ancient marks were, therefore, much more with me—or I with them—than at the other sites. It was unnerving and exhilarating, an intimate version of the emotional state I experience in the larger architecture of alcove and arch. And it was a spectacular example of rock art positioned for a solar interaction, a site of such deliberation it would be almost impossible to deny its intent. Maybe the figures have other meanings as well, from hunting magic to vision quest, but to deny the obvious and specific extension of this geometry from ground to sky would be the most unscientific attitude of all.

Later in the morning we had spread out across Six Mile Flat by foot to find the "Many Circles" site. On the way we stumbled upon a unique piece of geology, the sort of unlikely occurrence that's led people through the ages to refer to their favorite supernatural deity as an architect. In front of a large rock shelter formed by a hanging roof was a natural rock arch; access to the shelter meant passing under the arch and climbing behind it up from the first floor of the shelter to the second, where the top of the arch then became a balcony. To me, a twentieth-century city dweller, it evoked a town-house condominium complete with a formal entrance. The only dweller in recent times, though, seemed to have been a packrat, who had left behind an extensive midden composed of sticks, bones, stones, and other debris found in the near vicinity.

"See the amberat," Alvin called out to me, pointing to the hard yellow coating anchoring the rodent's nest to the rock. I nodded, but Connie frowned.

"What's that? A mineral?"

"No, crystallized packrat urine. It helps hold the nest together. Packrats carry stuff back to their nests from within a radius of no more than about two hundred yards, then they pee on it and the whole thing hardens. Some middens, if they're protected from the rain like this one, are so old they can't be dated by radiocarbon, which means they're older than forty thousand years. The seeds and pollen preserved in the midden can be analyzed and show the spread of plants during the Pleistocene, so they've become important scientific resources."

As Alvin explained this to Connie, I thought back to a project Michael Heizer has been working on for years, photographing the middens in and around this part of the Great Basin. The nests, which contain on average about twenty cubic feet of material, can range more than five feet high and two feet wide, their tunnels maintaining an even temperature in the high eighties during the summer, even when the ground outside is frying at more than 160 degrees. The rodents, which can grow to as long as eighteen inches, are actually more closely related to mice than rats, and will collect everything from cactus spines to coins, cow pies to dentures. Fascinated by the complicated assemblages, Heizer's photos demonstrate that either packrats exercise aesthetics in choosing and placing materials or people can't help themselves from perceiving artful organization in the most haphazard imaginable collection of detritus.

Looking at the packrat midden with Alvin and Connie, I find myself speculating about why this stick here, that bone there. Packrats, when carrying something in their mouths back to the midden, often will drop what they're carrying in order to pick up something they like even better, most especially anything that's shiny. Unlike other animals, which either curl up under a bush or go to ground in order to cope with the weather, packrats actually build shelter. Ascertaining their genetic motives for this behavior might be possible, but untangling their individual choice of materials would be, no doubt, about as difficult as deciphering petroglyphs.

Rock arches and alcoves, tunnels and middens: they are all about the enclosure and the definition of discrete empty spaces. The natural features counter the larger void, become sanctuaries where time is measured and intent recorded. The packrats of the Great Basin build their walls and tunnels in sheltered spots and so do humans. Leaving behind a record of millennial botany, the packrat goes about its business, the motives for its behavior coded deep in its evolutionary response to the environment. Indian peoples built rock walls behind which to camp, and crawled into caves and crevices in order to paint and peck out a systemized iconography. Alvin and Bill White suspect their symbols may be part of a larger western archaic desert tradition, given the symbols found in common among sites from Oregon in the north and clear south to Baja California. Wherever there are people they eventually end up making signs, part of the human genetic makeup that Steven Pinker at MIT has labeled "the language instinct." I suspect the occasional and, as Mike has pointed out, wrongheaded temptation to read packrat middens as architecture is another example of the human will to pattern, to assume that nature is a systematic language we can read. I'm further tempted to remember the range of the packrat as being coextensive with the desert rock art, both being shelters and symbols specific to the Great Basin, but even as I write this suspect it's just my mind erecting yet another pattern.

The geometry and juxtaposition of forms constructed by humans is likewise part of our evolutionary response to the environment, but is genuinely a vocabulary we have systemized over time to signify much more than shelter. Walking down into Mike Heizer's *City,* for instance, is to participate in one of the oldest architectural traditions known to humankind, negative space carved out of the earth traditionally being a gesture meant to increase spiritual energy. You are enclosed and worshipful of the effort such a massive work entails; the void is defined, and your presence completes an obscure circuit of perception. Shivers run up and down your spine, an ancient neural message.

Here, too, and even in the midday sun, I shiver, another kind of environmental "re-cognition" setting in. From my lunch perch I count the kinds of plants I can identify, among them cholla, prickly pear, Spanish bayonet, two kinds of sagebrush, Mormon tea, junipers, and the tiny wild fuchsia geranium commonly called filaree. This is an environment in which I can name many of the inhabitants and know their habits, including the clouds. The lenticular masses, which yesterday were stacking up toward the White Mountains on the border with California, have spread to the north by Wheeler Peak. The ring around the sun today is smaller than it was yesterday.

Moisture is increasing at several levels in the atmosphere, and I can affirm with some reliability my prediction that the weather will proceed to worsen over the next day or so. Naming names and reading these signs—and being aware that I know how to read these signs—this is how I know I'm at home here.

AFTER AN HOUR of solitude the three vehicles return, bringing with them the smell of burning sagebrush. Small branches get caught between the skid plates and undercarriage of four-wheel-drive vehicles, slowly cooking there for hours, a warm fragrance we associate with Great Basin overland driving. It's a common-enough occurrence that some desert drivers carry fire extinguishers; only last year Sherrie used hers to put out a small brushfire started by an escaping ember. I climb into the back seat of the Jeep, and we're off, trailing behind us the misleading odor of a campfire.

The "Sheep on a Line" site had been disappointing, apparently, nowhere near as interesting as the other sites, but that's just a harbinger of things to come for the rest of the afternoon as we cross, recross, and crisscross the valley looking for more rock art. Despite the hundreds of outcrops and dozens of what seem to us to be likely sites, we find nothing. It's not dismaying for Alvin, Courtney, and myself—we've had our fill of rock images over the last several days—but the visitors from Utah are disappointed, and by midafternoon it's time for them to head back. We escort them to a dirt road that will return them to the highway, Mary Kay and Gail offering to take us around to their local rock art sites if we're ever in St. George, and then they're off in the proverbial cloud of dust. After a brief consultation Alvin decides there's one more place he'd like to try to find, a "picture rock" that's on the way back to Ash Springs.

Alvin leads the way, recalling out loud a description of the site provided him by an informant. Courtney counts off landmarks on the map as we drive by each fence line and outcrop, Alvin countering with his memories of when he first saw them. The recitation is like a Great Basin version of an Australian Aboriginal songline, but instead of recounting tribal myths of origin and geographical lore, it's a combination of natural and human history woven into memory. The circumstances are different, but I think by only degree, not kind, and the intent seems identical. Both are oral correlations of passage through space and time, highly developed skills necessary for navigating the void. The Aborigines are aided in their travels by a variety of signs, including rock art; we use road and topo maps.

It's four-thirty by the time we reach a barbed-wire fence alongside which is neatly arrayed a series of isolated boulders. The rock art is lined up with the fence line, which is itself set along the right-angled standards of the grid. The road, of course, follows the fence and takes us from rock to rock. We stop, admire the petroglyphs, and are satisfied that we have successfully located one final site as a way of ending the exploration.

Alvin, Courtney, and I circle the last boulder and put our hands on those surfaces absent of petroglyphs. We're testing the friction coefficient of the rock and the integrity of the patina on its twelve-foot faces to see if it will hold our weight. Old rock climbing habits, again. We catch each others' eyes, grin, and put down our cameras, pads, pens, and pencils. I'm the first on top, Alvin second, Court third. Petro whines at us, unable to follow. We downclimb, still a little stiff from too much time in the car, climb up a second time a little more smoothly, then spread out around the rock to find other routes, three in all. Sherrie insists we gather on top so she can take our picture, and this, too, becomes part of the story that someone else will tell when they drive out here, part of the memory of place that Sherrie will insert into local lore.

As for us, Alvin in his sixties, me approaching fifty, Court in his thirties, all of us figuratively tied together through years of sharing ropes on steep rock, it feels as if we're taking an oath of allegiance to the trip. By physically participating in a moment of shared play we divert our attention away from the rock art and acknowledge how the last few days fit into the larger pattern of our lives. We bind this trip into a chain of travels handed from one generation down to the next, a constant shuttling back and forth through the Great Basin picking up the pieces of geographical memory, sometimes just as they're about to be lost by one or the other of us. It occurs to me, sitting atop the boulder and watching its rusty sheen turn iridescent in the last glow of the day, that Alvin is handing off his sites to Courtney. He knows that the younger man is a good candidate to both preserve the localized memories and hold quietly to himself those sites that need the extra protection of obscurity.

Eventually, all the petroglyph panels will be found by other people. The drive to discover something new, even if it is recovering something once known in the past but forgotten for a few millennia, is perhaps yet another genetically embedded behavior. It may take a while, though, for people to blindly stumble across all of the rock art that Alvin's recorded. After all, even though the Great Basin is small compared to the Sahara, it still covers almost a quarter-million square miles. At best only 1 to 2 percent of it has been surveyed for archeology. Only the ground adjacent to the grid, those lands next to roads and thus the most easily accessed, has been looked at with any consistency.

Alvin will spend the rest of his years tracing down the lesser-traveled lines of the grid, those that cross the most remote corners of the void. Along the way he'll go off that rectilinear pattern to search out the old contours of passage that follow the watercourses. He'll log the sites he finds in these interstices of the grid, sharing them with others according to the degree of confidence he holds in them. His notes will go to the Nevada State Museum; archeologists and other scientists will scrutinize them, slowly backtracking his explorations.

Out of curiosity, I count up the combined years of exploration between the three of us. I start with Alvin wandering the backwoods of West Virginia as a schoolchild, when he would walk off so far that he couldn't return home before nightfall. He would just find a depression to sleep in overnight, pulling leaves over him for a blanket. Since then he's banged around mountains from South America to Bhutan. Courtney has poked around Mexico, Africa, Southeast Asia, and Micronesia, often looking for rock art. I've hiked through Europe, climbed in New Zealand, guided in Nepal, worked on movies in the mountains of Greece. Ending with this trip, between us there is almost a century of trying to find the most remote places we could. We've hiked around or climbed peaks on every continent except Antarctica, walked cross-country through deserts, jungles, rain forests, swamps, and even in volcanoes about to erupt. None of us have any illusions that we've found any land that's not been traveled by others before; almost without exception someone was there before us.

The depth of human interaction with the earth is so extensive it cannot be measured anymore. We have left behind signs of wandering over and rearranging the land, our most basic activity, everywhere we can look, from the eight hundred miles of lines scuffed in the desert pavement of Nazca to the bark carvings of Basque sheepherders in the aspen groves of Nevada. It's a long story and one that I cannot help but feel we must try to read, even if only in pieces, for the sake of our survival. Patiently sifting through the remains of Mesopotamian and Anasazi civilizations, for instance, we decipher the failure of hydraulic societies overtaxing their use of water. Underlying the hubris of those waterworks is a visual geometry that shows how we both celebrate the natural world and attempt to master it. The patterned prayers of ancient rugs and pottery display our faith that we can alter the course of the world through worship, as if we had a telephone line to a universal control room; the straight edges of our roads and irrigation canals have for centuries proposed that we can overrule local conditions. If we couldn't find a pattern in nature, we created one.

And yet, and yet . . . where the world is most visible to us, where without trees and intervening landforms we can catch the long view of the void, we find ourselves on the edge of a nature that is patently larger than us. One value of the desert is that we need an empty space in which to stretch our arms and take a deep breath, a place where the lack of things in the middle ground allows the muscles in our eyes to relax, thus inculcating a meditative state. But another value, I think, is its ability to threaten us.

If the overarching fact of the West is space, then that is a planet-bound analog to the greater void that surrounds this and every other body in the universe. If we posit aliens in the desert, so then should we be reminded that the void here on earth is simply reminding us of the void out there. Regardless of whether we think that the earth is the only planet with life in the universe or just one of many, the difference between those viewpoints, when compared against the larger void, is so statistically trivial as to be meaningless. Deserts remind us of our place.

I climb down off the boulder, and my shoulders feel light, as if a weight has been lifted from them. It's a feeling I re-create every time I climb to the top of a rock, and not one I can duplicate when climbing inside on a gym wall. The movements are almost the same, but only the deliberate placement of body on a higher point of ground-under-sky, whether it's a twelve-foot boulder or a nineteen-thousand-foot peak, is an act of worship for me, a striving to see a bit more of the emptiness I seek. Sherrie is shaking her head, saying, "It must be a boy thing." All she sees, of course, is the physical leveraging up a face, and not the psychological lift.

"Yeah," I reply, "except girls make better climbers, and there are more of them every year. It's like climbing trees: everyone does it when they're a kid. It's a human thing." She flaps a hand at me in good-natured dismissal and gets into her truck. We drive back out through the wire and down into the valley where the dark has begun to gather together the trees along the river.

MONDAY MORNING and time to drive back to Reno. We're once again on the road by seven o'clock, a milky sky overhead, the head cold that I've been anticipating since the slog up and down Timber Mountain now finally in residence. We retrace our passage over the Extraterrestrial Highway, seeing only three other cars, one road crew, and a herd of wild horses stretched out over both sides of the pavement. By nine-thirty we've reached Tonopah and drop Courtney back at his truck. It's been a long time since I've seen him, and it might be a long time again, depending on what work he finds this next year. I'm already thinking maybe we three should try to make this an annual event.

Alvin and I turn north on 95, the highway from Las Vegas to Reno, and drive straight into a windstorm that grows more intense the farther north we go. Storm clouds are stacked up on both the White Mountains and the Sierra; each playa we cross is giving up its surface to the dust clouds now covering most of the state. Petro goes to sleep in the back, obviously disappointed by the lack of a view.

We drive north through the valleys, turn west at Fallon, and follow the Truckee River Canyon back into Reno on that coast-to-coast flow of goods we call "the interstate." To our left the long dark rails of the Union Pacific parallel our course. Because explorers couldn't find the Rio San Buenaventura flowing as a watercourse, we subsequently created its equivalents in steel and concrete, laying first rails and then roads, mixing together millions of tons of sand, water, and lime to do so. If there were no natural contours matching the lines of our national grid, a pattern of rivers and trails that we could follow in order to complete our westward destiny, well, then, by God we would just build them ourselves.

It's only midafternoon when we reenter the Truckee Meadows, so there's time for a shower at Alvin's, as well as a quick shuffle through some of his library. While I take notes from the files about sites we visited, Alvin retrieves his phone messages. The annual international conference on rock art will be taking place soon in the desert just north of Los Angeles, close to the most extensive petroglyph site in North America, a series of small canyons protected from vandals only by the fact that they're located within the China Lake Naval Reserve. People are calling to find out if Alvin's going to attend, present a paper, or visit the local sites. There's also an invitation to speak in Las Vegas next month, and someone inquiring if he's available to do some fieldwork.

Petro watches me as I repack my briefcase, obviously ready to jump back in the Jeep for another trip, and I apologize to him for offering only a short ride to the airport. I'm unplugging from a closely knit society of scribes dedicated to preserving a vast network of prehistoric mystery, and there's that sense of discontinuity any writer has when leaving a community of believers.

Most of the people I've met in the last few days have been levelheaded and not at all wild-eyed worshipers of prehistoric conspiracies. But, rock art people are intensely protective of the ancient images, an attitude that derives from the very indecipherability of their subject. The images come out of the void of time past, a reality we cannot recover but only speculate over. The petroglyphs and pictographs are, therefore, a language of the Other, and we cannot help but be attracted, wondering what's there that we don't know: perhaps some set of arcana that will unlock the universe.

Dr. Heizer was right when he linked the attraction exercised by UFOs and rock art upon the popular imagination, and it's easy to understand his frustration over the speculations of "code-breakers." The careful recording of rock art and its methodical analyses within the context of anthropology are all too easily overwhelmed by sensationalistic theories about ancient astronauts, the same kind of cultural fantasy that leads the enthusiasts camped on the edge of Area 51 to declare Mike Heizer's *City* a landing area for UFOs.

It's difficult enough to keep classical physics and the medically proved facts of neurophysiology in mind when walking through the desert, fighting our inevitable cognitive dissonance in such a large and empty space. When confronted with something in the desert that is mysterious, whether a light moving oddly in the sky or a prehistoric grid deeply incised into a boulder, our first reflex is to try and place it within comprehension. Either we start to analyze it, ruthlessly proposing theory after theory until we construct one that is consistent with every test we can bring to bear on the observed phenomenon—or we weave a story that ignores facets of external reality in favor of answering an inner need, usually a reassurance that we're not alone in the void, that the Big Empty is not really devoid of intent. Most of us aren't trained as scientists, and Carl Sagan once noted that one in every five Americans believes they've been abducted by aliens. Scientists, whether studying rock art or astrophysics, are rowing upstream against the tide of popular belief, which apparently finds it much easier to flow downhill toward science fiction.

People are information-gathering animals. The way we maneuver through and survive amongst the prodigious input our senses bring to us is by making patterns, some of which are relatively true to the facts, some not. A few scientists even state that it doesn't matter whether the patterns have any basis in the physical world. If they work, they work. The constellations we draw in the sky don't exist as actual groups of stars located next to one another, but are visual associations we pull together from our viewpoint on Earth. Yet, the visual fictions served the needs of seagoing navigators for millennia. We are, however, also a species given to excess, tending to overdo a good thing. Extending our belief in star patterns to astrological signs that supposedly govern our daily actions has little genuine application to our individual personalities—although, once again, it serves as reassurance against the threatening void of the night sky.

Heizer and McLane know their constellations; neither believes in astrology, and both have the ability to discern among patterns. They may disagree about the meanings of rock art, but it's startling to see how many of the same sorts of books are on their shelves, and even identical individual titles. Both men insist that any interpretation of rock art be founded upon scientific research and not naive speculation. I can't help but wonder, as I snap shut my bag, if such rigor doesn't derive at least in some degree from living in the desert, versus just visiting. Both men are comfortable with the void and don't need much in the way of metaphysical assurances. They know which way to walk for water, so to speak.

Despite what threatens to be a major late-spring snowstorm, dense waves of cloud pouring down into Reno from the direction of Donner Pass, my plane takes off on time. Climbing to twenty-seven thousand feet we pass through the wind and clouds onto a smooth gray twilight deck stretching inland from the Pacific to somewhere over Utah. Our route, one that I have memorized over the years and is clearly visible in my mind despite the rising darkness and cloud cover, takes us down to Mono Lake, crosses the Sierra south of Yosemite, turns left through the Central Valley, and brings us in over L.A. from the east.

The air held within the basin formed by the San Bernardino and San Gabriel Mountains is clear tonight, and the great grid of 17 million inhabitants stretches all around us, virtually unbroken up and down the coast from Tijuana to Santa Barbara. It's magnificent, a seemingly infinite constellation of streetlights and headlamps, the flaring orange waste gas above the refineries in Long Beach balanced with the turquoise of swimming pools illuminated in thousands of backyards. It's a beautiful pattern, but a dangerous one.

I've been told that Los Angeles is the second largest desert city in the world, following Cairo. Looking at satellite images of the Egyptian city, as well as those of other cities around the world, you can see how they at first followed the contours and watercourses, but then lapsed predictably into the more easily managed rectilinear grid as population pressures overwhelmed slower and more organic development. The grid of Los Angeles is immense, ten thousand miles of streets within just its own city limits. All of the desert cities of the world, from Cairo to Mexico City, from Phoenix to Ridayh in Saudi Arabia, are now paved grids. And all of them are suspended over the void on the rigid and unyielding geometry of progress, ignoring the signs that we're living beyond our means.

It doesn't have to be this way, I remind myself. The grid is something we can't run away from; the way we organize the world is given to us by our stereoscopic vision and height, the result of a genetically bred triangulation. The grid runs across time and cultures, representing everything from the Milky Way in petroglyphs to the Cartesian ground across which the stock market fluctuates. We throw a visual net over the world, to be sure, but how we use it is our choice. Instead of the insolent sprawl of Los Angeles, that ultimate urban apocalypse standing at the terminus of western expansion, its grid a land-use pattern prodigiously wasting land and water, we could just as easily harness the grid to concentrate our populations and leave open those spaces of the void needed to recharge our aquifers and our minds.

"Signs," I mutter to myself. The business-suited woman next to me who has the window seat, and who for the duration of the flight has tolerated my gazing silently past her out over the leading edge of the wing, gives me a hard look, then turns her back and obliterates the view. Not that I can blame her. I'm dressed in slightly less than reputable clothes and carrying all my belongings in a climbing pack draped with ice-axe and crampon loops, hardly the accouterments of a civilized man of my age. I am in her eyes, no doubt, some kind of desert rat, one of the eccentric unwashed captivated more by the lure of the next sand dune than a good meal in Beverly Hills. She has it just about right.

Signs. The intersections of the grid over the void, evidence of the need to control our ancestral fright of the dark and the empty. How we read signs is part of the solution, how we cope with our cognitive dissonance that otherwise leads us to so misjudge our environment. We sneak up to the edge of the void, titillated to be so near the limits of our senses, but when forced to actually deal with the Big Empty, to cross the desert of our understanding, we throw the grid over it, a safety net allowing us passage in our climate-controlled cars and airplanes, which further disconnects us from the environment and its consequences.

We erect buildings at the intersections—gas stations, motels, casinos— at first adorning them with signs, then turning the buildings themselves into signs. And it's at that moment, when a black mailbox becomes a signifier for the Other, or when a Las Vegas motel turns into the faux pyramid of a hotel-casino, it's right then that we have a chance to recapture an awareness of what we're doing. We provide ourselves an opportunity to reconnect our senses and cognition with the world, to resonate with it instead of vibrating noisily in dissonance against it.

What rescues us is metaphor, that pivotal ability hardwired into our brains enabling us to compare one reality with another. The will to metaphor may be the only cognitive trait humans possess that distinguishes us from other primates, and one that some scientists argue is the basis for both art and science. E. O. Wilson, the preeminent sociobiologist, is one of them, noting that new comparisons, or analogies, are what innovators in both disciplines seek, and that when several previously unrelated elements are brought together in a synthesis that allows us to perceive a hitherto hidden objective relation, we have metaphor. We have an elegant equation, for example, that allows us to see how matter translates into energy, which in turn becomes a meme we apply to describing everything from warfare to lovemaking.

Look at a map—first as a system of symbols representing the land, then as a picture of how we have landscaped the territory. What was an objective document becomes a metaphor of human ambition, a piece of art. Or, compare petroglyphs with the signs in Las Vegas. The next time I look at the neon figure of Vegas Vic, a cowboy waving his arm in the night on Fremont Street, I will inevitably think of the Lone Cowboy petroglyph discovered by Alvin. Knowing that the two figures are separated in time by thousands of years, I'll nonetheless tie them together as figures in the arid environment. Instead of just nodding my head at the obvious ironies produced by this conflation of two signs, both will have become metaphors evoking how we relate to the one world we inhabit.

When Las Vegas pushes the envelope of urban fantasy—literally to the edge of its physical valley and figuratively to the limits of building technology—that's when we start to realize how estranged we've become from the place in which the city resides. And make no mistake about it, there was a place there before the city. It wasn't empty space. People were establishing trails around the springs and carving glyphs into the rocks there for thousands of years before Los Angeles ever sent an architect to stack up cement blocks around a slot machine.

Look long and carefully enough at the petroglyphs and you can't help but connect them back to the environment in which they reside. There's no way to even begin to make sense out of them otherwise, no matter if the interpretation is hunting deer, locating water, or praying to the night sky. Walk at night among the signs of Las Vegas and Reno, of Jackpot and Wendover, all the border stations ringing the heart of the Great Basin, and after the dazzle wears off all you can see is how abrupt the transition is to the great empty that waits just outside the lights. Seen within their bleak context, we read the signs as metaphors for desire.

It's at those moments of recognition, of recapturing cognition, that we start to understand the difference between signs as reality and signs as metaphor. We read into them more than they were meant to say on the surface. We look at the glyphs and are led to ask what kind of cosmology did their makers envision, which is an opportunity to understand that their constellations can tell us something about how the human mind works. The glyphs won't unlock any conspiracy theories, but they can help us better know the nature of our own minds, a secret of the universe to which we have direct access.

When we assign names to the petroglyph sites and then erect warnings, piling signs on top of signs, we multiply the possibilities of this process, but the densest possible accumulation tends to occur when the article provoking our consideration is art. That is, after all, part of the reason we create art: to embody metaphor. Early sacred architecture was built to imitate nearby mountains, which were held to be the homes of the gods. The shapes of both the mountains and the temples, from Teotihuacán in Mexico to Uruk in Mesopotamia, were governed by gravity. Heizer is not a landscape artist and *City* not a deistic homage, but by adopting the early architectural forms of the sacred for his artistic vocabulary, he taps directly into a natural geometry adopted by humans for millennia to signify human order impressed upon chaos, consciousness over the void. He's putting old forms in new contexts, making a new analogy, creating a metaphor for the void, the grid, and the sign. Once again we're led back to how we think.

The lady next to me swivels to face forward as our plane makes its last turn and initiates the final drop toward the runway, the grid rising up to meet us. I have always loved flying at night, rushing over the empty black desert and following the roads below from town to town, the miniature carpet of their streets lit up along the great net we have stretched around the globe and projected into the sky. It's an act of willful dissociation that allows me to imagine the earth as mind, a metaphor for the cognition that we strive to make visible.

After finding the last picture rock yesterday, Courtney and I were reminiscing about our favorite mountaineering books, the literature that had urged us to seek high places when we were younger. Making a pun off one of the most widely admired titles ever written, Courtney had declared us "Conquistadors of the Obscure"—friends who would follow the map and then fall off it in search of new metaphors to describe ourselves and our place in the world.

That's the thought I carry with me as we land, the pilot aiming us between two straight and parallel rows of light that narrow and then join somewhere ahead of us, a vanishing point in the dark.

As far as the word *desert* is concerned, what fascinates me is to see how far the metaphor of the void, from being used so much, has permeated the whole word. The word itself has become a metaphor. To give it back its strength, one has therefore to return to the real desert which is indeed exemplary emptiness—but emptiness with its own, very real dust. Think also about the word *book*. The book, where everything seems possible through a language that one thinks one can master and that finally turns out to be but the very place of its bankruptcy. All the metaphors the word can inspire lie between these two extremes. None of them really gets to the heart of it, but between this all and this nothing, the unfathomable opening takes place, which in the end is what every writer and every reader is confronted with.

—Edmond Jabés

POSTSCRIPTS

ॐ

MICHAEL HEIZER has received a large grant to complete the first phase of *City*, and by the end of summer 1999 had substantially finished work on *Complexes One, Two,* and *Three*. The first element was refaced and repairs made to its concrete elements, the stelae were finished, and the concrete curbing outlining the complexes was touched up. In the meantime, Heizer has been building clay models for what *City* might someday look like. Stretching out for roughly a mile, draft plans include placing a large version of his sculpture *45° 90° 180°* at the far end as *Complex Five*. A nonprofit, tax-exempt corporation has been formed with the eventual purpose of allowing limited public access to the work once it is finished. Heizer remains adamant, however, about his privacy, and severely limits photographs of the work in progress to placement only in his archives.

TWO WEEKS AFTER we visited the Black Rock, Andy Green broke the sound barrier and set a new world land-speed record. On Wednesday morning, October 15, 1997, the Thrust SSC went through its measured mile at 759.333 mph on the first run and 766.609 on the second, establishing its official speed at 763.035 mph. Officials calculated the speed of sound that day, given weather and altitude, was 748.11 mph. Observers reported only a muffled sonic boom, but were able to actually see the shock waves as he broke through the barrier. Craig Breedlove remained in the area for a few more days, but was unable to match or break Green's record.

ALVIN MCLANE continued to refine his analysis of the "wounded elephant" petroglyph, and in his final survey report noted that one of the cadastral surveyors from the General Land Office, who sectioned off the surrounding region in 1919, could have been the artist—as well as anyone using the old road that passes through the canyon and is now almost obliterated.

A month after being bitten by the black widow, I still had a red mark on the inside of my arm, as well as dreams that I was growing a red hourglass-shaped stigmata on my back. Both the mark and the dreams faded, and there seem to be no other side effects.

ALVIN AND I remain in disagreement about when people may have first crossed the Bering land bridge, and how to date the earliest petroglyphs found on the continent. He is much more comfortable sticking with the figure of 12,500 years ago for entrance into the New World, for instance, whereby I find enough credible scientists citing 35,000–40,000 years ago as a possibility that I'm willing to take their word for it. I suspect Dr. Robert F. Heizer would have sided with Alvin.

DESPITE RUMORS that Area 51 has been abandoned by the military and its operations dispersed to other installations within the Great Basin, most notably to chemical- and biological-weapons development centers in order to discourage unauthorized visitors, no evidence exists to support such a move. Several observers of Area 51 have, in fact, claimed the rumors are simply disinformation efforts.

SOURCES

❧

I am a happy wanderer among many sources of information in books and underfoot. But, because I am neither a cognitive scientist nor an anthropologist, I owe it to the authors listed below to absolve them of any responsibility for my speculations about the void, the grid, and the sign. Their works have provided the ground upon which I have erected my speculations, and I can only hope I have quoted their facts correctly. My inferences and conclusions are entirely my own, however, and in some cases may actually contradict those of the authors listed below.

In General

Basso, Keith. *Wisdom Sits in Places.* Albuquerque: University of New Mexico Press, 1996. Retelling and analysis of Western Apache use of place-names as stories by an unusually lucid and humane anthropologist.

Bloomer, Kent C., and Charles W. Moore. *Body, Memory, and Architecture.* New Haven: Yale University Press, 1977. A useful primer on body-space orientation, haptic systems, place, and the role of memory in the built environment.

Chris, Bruce. *The Myth of the West.* Seattle: Henry Art Gallery, 1990.

Cronin, William. *Uncommon Ground: Rethinking the Human Place in Nature.* New York: W. W. Norton, 1995. Excellent anthology examining simulated nature and natural simulations; see specifically chapters by K. R. Olwig and the always provocative N. Katherine Hayles.

Goetzmann, William H. *Army Exploration in the American West, 1803–1863.* New Haven: Yale University Press, 1959.

———. *Exploration and Empire: The Explorer and the Scientist in the Winning of the American West.* New York: History Book Club, 1966.

———. *New Lands, New Men.* New York: Viking Penguin, 1986. This is the final volume in a classic trilogy, an indispensable and readable reference work that starts with a relatively narrow focus on the role of the U.S. Army Corps of Topographical Engineers in western exploration, widens to include the entire history of the opening of the West, and concludes in this third volume by placing that history within the larger sequence of worldwide exploration.

Lopez, Barry. *Desert Notes.* 1976. Reprint, New York: Avon Books, 1981.

————. *Arctic Dreams.* New York: Charles Scribner's Sons, 1986. One of the masterpieces of modern nature writing, though about a different kind of desert; source of valuable insights on the nature of exploration and mapping, Eskimo cognition, and a geography relevant to the idea of void.

McNamee, Gregory, ed. *The Sierra Club Desert Reader.* San Francisco: Sierra Club Books, 1995. An all-too-short international anthology.

Novak, Barbara. *Nature and Culture: American Landscape and Painting, 1825–1875.* Rev. ed. New York: Oxford University Press, 1995. A breathtaking study about art during the American century of westward expansionism that underlies virtually everyone's treatment of the subject; instructive to read in conjunction with Goetzmann and Pyne.

Pyne, Steven. *How the Canyon Became Grand.* New York: Viking Penguin, 1998. A short yet profound discussion of the most metaphorical void of all, the Grand Canyon, by a student of Goetzmann, a MacArthur Foundation fellow.

Reith, Charles C., and Bruce M. Thompson, eds. *Deserts as Dumps?* Albuquerque: University of New Mexico Press, 1992. Scientists explain why they consider arid lands best suited for disposal of radioactive and hazardous wastes.

Ryden, Kent. *Mapping the Invisible Landscape.* Iowa City: University of Iowa Press, 1993. A generous account of how story and folklore form place.

Stegner, Wallace. *The American West as Living Space.* Ann Arbor: University of Michigan Press, 1987. A concise and biting explanation of how we misunderstand, and thus mistreat, the West.

Tuan, Yi-Fu. *Space and Place: The Perspective of Experience.* Minneapolis: University of Minnesota Press, 1977. The definitive, much cited, and groundbreaking study of the subject.

Turner, Frederick. *Beyond Geography.* New York: Viking Penguin, 1980. A broad-ranging history of western expansionism.

My thoughts on the cognitive basis for our perception of the desert, our deployment of the grid in transforming land into landscape, and the formation of signs within the grid were guided in particular by the following:

Jakle, John A. *The Visual Elements of Landscape.* Amherst: University of Massachusetts Press, 1987.

Johnson, George. *Fire in the Mind: Science, Faith, and the Search for Order.* New York: Alfred A. Knopf, 1995. An eccentric and engaging search for patterns in postquantum physics and complexity counterpointed with studies in contemporary neurobiology and the belief systems of the Pueblo Indians of New Mexico; the source of the Murray Gell-Mann quote in chapter 9, which neatly encapsulates the book's fundamental concern.

Mithen, Steven. *The Prehistory of the Mind: The Cognitive Origins of Art and Science.* London: Thames and Hudson, 1996. An archeologist seeks physical evidence for the evolution of human intelligence in this thorough and provocative book.

Pinker, Steven. *How the Mind Works.* New York: W. W. Norton, 1997. A comprehensive and somewhat controversial overview of cognition and its evolution; the third chapter contains information quoted on evolutionary timetables, the fourth on visual cognition (see also Solso listed below).

Solso, Robert L. *Cognition and the Visual Arts.* Cambridge: MIT Press, 1994. The springboard for many of my speculations on cognitive dissonance.

Wilson, Edward O. *Bibliophilia.* Cambridge: Harvard University Press, 1984. My thanks to Dawn Marano for leading me to the essay "The Poetic Species," wherein Wilson proposes metaphor as the common root of art and science.

———. *Consilience.* New York: Alfred A. Knopf, 1998. Currently the state-of-the-art summation of how our behavior is guided by the mechanics of neurobiology.

The Great Basin

Banham, Reyner. *Scenes in America Deserta.* Layton, Utah: Gibbs M. Smith, 1982. Required inoculation against the Baudrillard cited below.

Baudrillard, Jean. *America.* London: Verso, 1988. French intellectual hyperbole with both interesting insights and some instructive mistakes.

Castleman, Deke. *Nevada Handbook.* 4th ed. Chico, Calif.: Moon Publications, 1995. The single indispensable guide to Nevada.

Cohen, Michael P. *A Garden of Bristlecones.* Reno: University of Nevada Press, 1998. One of the most unusual and enlightening natural history studies arising from the Great Basin.

Duncan, Dayton. *Miles from Nowhere: Tales from America's Contemporary Frontier.* New York: Viking, 1993. Population densities of the West and their histories as told through a travelog.

Durham, Michael S. *Desert between the Mountains.* New York: Henry Holt, 1997. The subtitle reads "Mormons, Miners, Padres, Mountain Men, and the Opening of the Great Basin, 1772–1869."

Fiero, Bill. *Geology of the Great Basin.* Reno: University of Nevada Press, 1986.

Frémont, John Charles. *Report of the Exploring Expeditions to the Rocky Mountains in the Year 1842 and to Oregon and North California in the Years 1843–1844.* Washington, D.C.: United States Senate Expedition document 174, 2d sess., 28th Cong., 1845.

Grayson, Donald K. *The Desert's Past: A Natural Prehistory of the Great Basin.* Washington, D.C.: Smithsonian Institution Press, 1993. The most comprehensive single-source natural prehistory and anthropology of the region.

Hart, John. *Hiking the Great Basin.* Rev. ed. San Francisco: Sierra Club Books, 1991.

Houghton, Samuel G. *A Trace of Desert Waters: The Great Basin Story.* Reno: University of Nevada Press, 1994. The definitive study of water in the inland basins.

Hunt, Charles B. *Natural Regions of the United States and Canada.* San Francisco: W. H. Freeman, 1974.

Hulse, James W. *The Silver State: Nevada's Heritage Reinterpreted.* Reno: University of Nevada Press, 1991.

McCracken, Robert D., and Jeanne Sharp Howerton. *A History of Railroad Valley, Nevada.* Tonopah, Nev.: Central Nevada Historical Society, 1996. Almost all of the facts and figures given about the valley derive from this book, which is a fine example of a thorough and well-written local history.

McLane, Alvin R. *Silent Cordilleras: The Mountain Ranges of Nevada.* Reno: Camp Nevada, 1978. A concise history of the geology and exploration of the Great Basin is followed by an extensively annotated listing of 314 mountain ranges in the state.

McPhee, John. *Basin and Range.* New York: Farrar, Straus, Giroux, 1981. One of the most interesting books about American geology for the layperson written in the twentieth century and an excellent primer on the complications of Nevada's terrain.

Perry, John, and Jane G. Perry. *Sierra Club Guide to the Natural Areas of New Mexico, Arizona and Nevada.* San Francisco: Sierra Club Books, 1985.

Ronald, Ann. "Why Don't They Write about Nevada?" In *Wilderness Tapestry.* Reno: University of Nevada Press, 1992.

———. *Earthtones: A Nevada Album.* Reno: University of Nevada Press, 1995.

Shepperson, Wilbur, ed. *East of Eden, West of Zion.* Reno: University of Nevada Press, 1989.

———. *Mirage-Land: Images of Nevada.* Reno: University of Nevada Press, 1992. A history of rhetoric as applied to the state from John C. Frémont to Jean Baudrillard.

Trimble, Steven. *The Sagebrush Ocean: A Natural History of the Great Basin.* Reno: University of Nevada Press, 1989. An excellent and readable book by one of the most prolific natural history photographers in the region.

The Void

Austin, Mary. *The Land of Little Rain.* New York: Houghton Mifflin, 1903; New York: Penguin Books, 1988.

Bachelard, Gaston. *The Poetics of Space.* Boston: Beacon Press, 1994. Little to say about large spaces, but a few wonderful leads.

Bernal, Ignacia. *The Olmec World.* Trans. Doris Heyden and Fernando Horcasitas. Berkeley and Los Angeles: University of California, 1969. Michael Heizer pulled this book off his shelves and suggested I read it.

Campbell, Glenn. *"Area 51" Viewer's Guide.* N.p., 1995. Amusing and thorough debunking of the activities surrounding this remote corner of the Test Site; includes practical information on how to survive the armed patrols, as well as speculation on sleep hallucinations and other cognitive dissonances that may underlie some of the "observations."

Drucker, Philip, Robert F. Heizer, and Robert J. Squier. *Excavations at La Venta, Tabasco.* Washington, D.C.: Smithsonian Institution Press, Bureau of American Ethnology, 1955. Michael Heizer literally holds this book aloft and calls it his Bible; even a casual perusal will show that it is the source of many of his sculptural forms.

Heizer, Robert F., and Thomas R. Hester. "Two Petroglyph Sites in Lincoln County, Nevada." *Contributions of the University of California Archaeological Research Facility* (May 1974): 20.

Jabés, Edmond. *From the Desert to the Book.* Trans. Pierre Joris. Barrytown, N.Y.: Station Hill Press, 1990.

Jenkins, Olaf P. *The Great Watershed of California.* Monterey, Calif.: Angel Press, 1978. One of the numerous monographs published by Michael Heizer's maternal grandfather.

———. *Early Days: Memoirs.* A privately published book.

Miller, Mary Ann. *The Art of Mesoamerica from Olmec to Aztec.* Rev. ed. London: Thames and Hudson, 1996. On page 26 the author states: "The playa, a 'negative space' seen in the sunken courtyard of La Venta, was as significant as the structure of 'mass' that defined it."

Nevada Bureau of Mines and Geology. *Major Mines of Nevada, 1996.* Reno: University of Nevada Press, 1997. Annual report on mining activity in the state.

Po, Huang. *The Zen Teaching of Huang Po: On the Transmission of Mind.* New York: Grove Press, 1958. An instructive source in the Buddhist literature of void.

Titus, A. Constantine. *Bombs in the Backyard: Atomic Testing and Nevada Politics.* Reno: University of Nevada Press, 1986. A concise history of the country's atomic weapons program and the Nevada Test Site.

Michael Heizer

Beardsley, John. *Earthworks and Beyond.* New York: Abbeville Press, 1989.

Celant, Germano. *Michael Heizer.* Milan: Fondazione Prada, 1997. The largest and most profusely illustrated book about the artist.

Brown, Julia, ed. *Michael Heizer: Sculpture in Reverse*. Los Angeles: Museum of Contemporary Art, 1984. The most substantive discussion of the artist with an extensive and invaluable interview conducted in late 1983.

Heizer, Michael. *Effigy Tumuli*. New York: Abrams, 1990. The essay by Douglas C. McGill is not always factually accurate, but the photographs are the most complete view of these sculptures available to the public.

———. *Double Negative: Sculpture in the Land*. New York: Rizzoli, 1991.

Kastner, Jeffrey, and Brian Wallis, eds. *Land and Environmental Art*. London: Phaidon Press, 1998. A massive and very useful compendium of images and source documents about Heizer and his contemporaries, as well as the historical context of their work.

Sonfist, Alan, ed. *Art in the Land: A Critical Anthology of Environmental Art*. New York: E. P. Dutton, 1983.

Taylor, Mark. *Disfiguring*. Chicago: University of Chicago Press, 1992. Chapter 8, "Desertion," investigates the physical and philosophical voids of and subsequent implications for Heizer's sculpture *Double Negative*.

The Grid

Bartlett, Richard A. *The Great Surveys of the American West*. Norman: University of Oklahoma Press, 1962.

Corner, James, with photography by Alex S. MacLean. *Taking Measure across the American Landscape*. New Haven: Yale University Press, 1996. Stunning aerial documentation of how we have used the grid to transform nature into culture, plus intelligent essays and speculative drawings.

Gandelsonas, Mario. *The Urban Text*. Cambridge: MIT Press, 1991. Graphic representation of the interpenetration of architecture, landscape, and power as expressed through the grid.

Hall, Stephen S. *Mapping the Next Millennium*. New York: Random House, 1992.

Heizer, Robert F., and Martin A. Baumhoff. *Prehistoric Rock Art of Nevada and Eastern California*. Berkeley and Los Angeles: University of California Press, 1962.

Hester, Thomas R., Robert F. Heizer, and John A. Graham. *A Guide to Archaeological Field Methods*. 3d ed. Palo Alto, Calif.: National Press, 1965. One of the textbooks for which Dr. Heizer was famous.

Jackson, J. B. *The Necessity for Ruins*. Amherst: University of Massachusetts Press, 1980. An indispensable book by the now, sadly, deceased grand theorist of the vernacular landscape.

———. *Discovering the Vernacular Landscape*. New Haven: Yale University Press, 1984.

Jellicoe, Geoffrey, and Susan Jellicoe. *The Landscape of Man*. 3d ed. London: Thames and Hudson, 1975. The standard textbook on the intersecting evolution of landscape design and architecture; heavily illustrated with photographs.

Kinsey, Joni Louise. *Thomas Moran and the Surveying of the American West*. Washington, D.C.: Smithsonian Institution Press, 1992. A thorough investigation into the intersection of economics, railroads, cartography, and art.

Kostof, Spiro. *American by Design*. New York: Oxford University Press, 1987. The print version of the PBS series; its fifth and final chapter summarizes the origins and growth of the national grid.

Lawlor, Robert. *Sacred Geometry*. London: Thames and Hudson, 1982. Well-illustrated popular history of the golden section, the progressive Fibonnaci series, and attempts to square the circle.

Lippard, Lucy. *Overlay: Contemporary Art and the Art of Prehistory*. New York: Pantheon, 1983. Although the anthropology underlying the book is dated, Lippard's encyclopedic methodology and numerous photographs of both ancient and contemporary works executed on the landscape, as well as map-derived art, are useful.

Makower, John, ed. *The Map Catalog*. New York: Vintage Books, 1986.

McLaughlin, Glen. *The Mapping of California as an Island*. San Francisco: California Map Society, 1995.

Moore, Charles, et al. *The Poetics of Gardens*. Cambridge: MIT Press, 1988. A singularly interesting book on the history and theory of gardens in landscape design.

Moreland, Carl, and David Bannister. *Antique Maps*. London: Phaidon Press, 1993.

Murbarger, Nell. "High Rock Canyon." *True West* (May–June 1963).

Patterson, Alex. *A Field Guide to Rock Art Symbols of the Greater Southwest*. Boulder, Colo.: Johnson Books, 1992.

Parkey, Becky W., and Larry J. Garside. *Geologic and Natural History Tours in the Reno Area*. Reno: Bureau of Mines and Geology (University of Nevada Reno), Special Publication 19, 1995. A similar guide exists for tours in the Las Vegas area.

Schwartz, Seymour I., and Ralph E. Ehrenby. *The Mapping of America*. New York: Abrams, 1960.

Southworth, Michael, and Susan Southworth. *Maps: A Visual Survey and Design Guide*. Boston: Little, Brown, 1982.

Stansbury, Howard. *Exploration of Survey of the Valley of the Great Salt Lake of Utah*. New York: Lippincott, Grambo, 1852; Washington, D.C.: Smithsonian Institution Press, 1988. A vivid, even gripping account of the first systematic survey conducted in the Great Basin, and the first use of triangulation by the Corps of Topographical Engineers in the West, as well as among the first in North America.

Storr, Robert. *Mapping.* New York: Museum of Modern Art, 1994. Catalog of exhibition curated by Storr, and one of the more important ones among numerous shows featuring artists using cartography as source imagery and metaphor.

Thrower, Norman J. W. *Maps and Civilization: Cartography in Culture and Society.* Chicago: University of Chicago Press, 1996. My favorite history of cartography.

Turnbull, David. *Maps Are Territories: Science Is an Atlas.* Victoria, Australia: Deakin University, 1989. A balanced deconstruction of cartographic practice from the viewpoint "down under."

Turner, Richard A. *Inventing Leonardo.* New York: Alfred A. Knopf, 1993. An unusual and engaging study of how Leonardo's life and work have been used to different ends at different times; good material on perspective and landscape art.

Waldie, D. J. *Holy Land: A Suburban Memoir.* New York: W. W. Norton, 1966. Poetic propositions about life on the grid of a 1950s suburb that are almost Wittgensteinian in their formulation; highly recommended.

Winford, John Noble. *The Mapmakers.* New York: Alfred A. Knopf, 1981. A readable and comprehensive history of cartography.

Wood, Dennis. *The Power of Maps.* New York: Guilford Press, 1992. Supremely irritating prose, but interesting speculations on the origin of maps.

"Valley of the Mud Lakes" panorama. In vol. 2 of *Pacific Railroad Survey Report.* 2d sess., 36th Cong. Washington, D.C.: Department of War, 1861.

Alvin McLane submitted a series of reports to the National Park Service evaluating natural areas in northwestern Nevada for eligibility as registered natural landmarks. Of interest to this section are the following: "Fly Creek Pothole" (December 1968); "High Rock Canyon Complex" (May 1969); "Black Rock Desert" (June 1970); and "Soldier Meadows" (June 1970).

& The Sign

Bahn, Paul G., with photographs by Jean Vertut. *Journey through the Ice Age.* Berkeley and Los Angeles: University of California Press, 1997. A revised edition of the 1988 classic, this book is concerned primarily with Paleolithic European cave art; however, in addition to helping place Nevada rock art in a worldwide context, it offers a compact and intelligent review of the history of rock art interpretations, thus offering a powerful cautionary tale to those who think they have "decoded" the meaning of such works.

Bourdon, David. *Designing the Earth: The Human Impulse to Shape Nature.* New York: Harry N. Abrams, 1995. A well-illustrated survey of earthworks in the broadest sense.

Bruce, Rovert. "Gold Rush Carries Environmental Effects." Inter Press Service, March 18, 1977.

Conkey, Margaret W., et al., eds. *Beyond Art: Pleistocene Image and Symbol.* A collection of papers from two symposia on the topic, the volume starts by defining why rock art isn't necessarily art. The most comprehensive, if dense, study available on that aspect of the subject.

Darlington, David. *Area 51: The Dreamland Chronicles.* New York: Henry Holt, 1997. While writing his excellent and informative book *The Mojave* (New York: Henry Holt, 1996), the author also began work on this thorough, disturbing, and funny account of "America's most secret military base."

Hess, Alan. *Viva Las Vegas: After-Hours Architecture.* San Francisco: Chronicle Books, 1993. To date the most useful history of architecture on the Strip.

Koepp, Donna P., ed. *Exploration and Mapping of the American West: Selected Essays.* Chicago: Speculum Orbis Press, 1986. Papers from the Map and Geography Round Table of the American Library Association; in particular, "George M. Wheeler and the Geographical Surveys West of the 100th Meridian, 1869–1879," by Robert W. Karrow Jr.

McLane, Alvin R. *An Annotated Petroglyph and Pictograph Bibliography of Nevada and the Great Basin.* Reno: Desert Research Institute (Quaternary Sciences Center Occasional Paper No. 1), April 1993. Although the number of sources regarding the subject has grown slightly since publication of this bibliography, this is still the only such compilation available and is invaluable.

Spanier, David. *Welcome to the Pleasuredome: Inside Las Vegas.* Reno: University of Nevada Press, 1992. Of particular interest is chapter 4, "Signs and Wonders," which gives a succinct overview of prevailing attitudes regarding the architecture of Las Vegas and the place of signs within it.

Uzes, Francis D. *Chaining the Land: A History of Surveying in California.* Sacramento: Landmark Enterprises, 1977.

Venturi, Robert, Denise Scott Brown, and Steven Izenour. *Learning from Las Vegas.* Cambridge: MIT Press, 1977. The original study that tipped architecture on its ear and identified Las Vegas as a city of signs, this is a primary text in the development of postmodernism.

The current status of both rigorous scientific investigation into and avocational interpretations of rock art are regularly reported in two journals: *American Indian Rock Art,* which as of 1997 was on its twenty-third annual conference edition (American Rock Art Research Center, P. O. Box 65, San Miguel, CA 93451-0065), and *Rock Art Papers,* a publication edited since 1993 by Ken Hedges (San Diego Museum of Man Publications, 1350 El Prado, Balboa Park, San Diego, CA 92101). The articles run from statistical factor analyses of images, to conservation techniques, to more speculative observations concerning potential archeoastronomy.